DEAD MALL RISING

The Story of El Con Mall

El Con Mall c.1981

JON PAUL CALLAHAN

Jon Paul Callahan
Published by Raven's Proffer
3101 N. Central Ave., Ste. 183
P.O. Box 5559
Phoenix, AZ 85012

Printed Worldwide
First Printing 2025
First Edition 2025

ISBN: 979-8-9992003-0-3 (Paperback)
ISBN: 979-8-9992003-1-0 (eBook)

10 9 8 7 6 5 4 3 2 1

Interior Book Design by Walt's Book Design
www.waltsbookdesign.com

Editor: Joya Stevenson
Line Editor: Kevin Miller
Cover Designer: Eoin Ryan
Interior Illustrator: Eoin Ryan

This book is dedicated to Generation X

ACKNOWLEDGEMENTS

They say it takes a village to raise a child, and the same holds for writing a book. I began writing Dead Mall Rising in 2020. Five years and several drafts later, the book is finally a reality. I'll start by thanking my wife, Nicole, who patiently read every chapter and provided valuable feedback. Nicole was my steadfast cheerleader over this long and arduous journey. Through all the highs and lows, she believed in me and stood by my side. I want to thank my kids, too, who, along with Nicole, have been a constant source of support. Their patience and encouragement have been invaluable, and without them, this wouldn't have been possible.

I also want to acknowledge my extended family and friends. They played a significant role in inspiring this book. It was my parents, Jon and Lupita Callahan, who introduced me to El Con Mall. They took my siblings and me shopping there when we were kids. When we were older, they trusted my brother and me enough to spend the day at El Con unsupervised. Our fun-filled trips to the mall with friends form the beating heart of this book. Alex, Rico, Fernando, and Rocky: Thank you for all the great mall memories!

Next, I want to thank Joya Stevenson, my developmental editor. Joya's guidance and direction pulled this book out of me. Throughout this entire process, Joya took the time to check in, answer questions, and offer her support. Joya truly was, as she once facetiously suggested, my writing savior. Joya also introduced me to a line editor, Kevin Miller, who refined the rough edges of my manuscript and polished it to shine. Kevin's attention to detail and professionalism brought this book over the finish line. I also want to thank Eoin Ryan, who designed the book cover, spot illustrations, and several infographics. Eoin's artistry brilliantly captures the mood and tone I wanted for the book.

I want to acknowledge Michelle Gullett of Lee Enterprises. Michelle was instrumental in helping me secure licenses for many of the images. Pictures bring the story to life, and Michelle made the complicated task of acquiring permissions manageable. I owe a debt of gratitude to Jason Damas and Ross Scherdel of Labelscar.com for permitting me to use images of El Con in its dead mall phase. Their blog remains one of the best resources for information on dead malls to this day. The same is true of the Mall Hall of Fame Blogspot (www.mall-hall-of-fame.blogspot.com), a fantastic resource for information about retail history and shopping malls. The curator allowed me to use the site's detailed, custom-made directory maps, which track the mall's evolution over time.

Finally, thanks to Walt W. (@polarbear19325) for formatting this book. Walt worked his magic to ensure the reading experience for all was enjoyable.

Writing this book has given me an appreciation for ephemera, which Merriam-Webster defines as "something of no lasting significance." Much of the material I used to write this book was not available in books or on the Internet. Often, the best information came from newspaper articles, advertising supplements, and random photographs that documented life in Tucson. In short, the information originated from ephemera. Newspapers preserve local history in a way few other mediums can. Tucson owes a debt of gratitude to the history-preserving work of its local journalists and photographers. Absent their contributions, much of the history that makes the Old Pueblo special would no longer exist.

Last but not least, I would like to express my gratitude for my Gen X childhood. Much has changed thanks to the Internet. I was born in the mid-1970s, years before the Internet became a household name. Things were much different back then. Though we lacked modern technological conveniences, life in general was more grounded. In my research, I came across a picture from Reid Park in Tucson, Arizona.

The photo, taken in 1976 by P. K. Weis of the Tucson Citizen, shows a father watching his daughter play on the park swings (see below).

Fleeting moment of joy, P.K. Weis (© Tucson Citizen – USA TODAY NETWORK via Imagn Images)

The caption reads: "In the blink of an eye, he'll see her start school . . . then graduate . . . then marry and have her own toddler. But for this priceless moment, she belongs to no one but him. And for both, there will be few memories as warm and happy as going to the park for a swing." [1]

This photo captures the essence of my Gen X childhood. My home was one mile west of Reid Park, and my parents took me to these same swings when I was a kid. When I became a father, I took my kids to these swings, too. Weis' photo evokes a time when people spent more time outside, engaged with others face-to-face more frequently, and savored life's simple pleasures. The dramatic changes technology has wrought over the last few decades threaten that way of life.

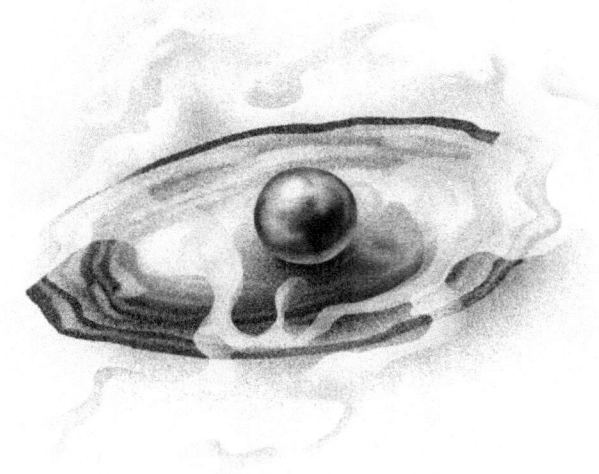

People who grew up in the 1980s were among the last to experience childhood and adolescence in a world with no Internet. Being one myself, I can attest that growing up in the pre-Internet age was a priceless gift. Many derisively refer to the pre-Internet period as a "Dark Age," but I disagree with this negative characterization. If anything, I view it as a precious gem-a rare black pearl. There is wisdom in the analog lifestyles we enjoyed before the digital age. Like treasure hunters searching for a black pearl, we must dive deep, recover this wisdom, and bring it back to the world.

My experiences at the mall, which you can read about in this book, are but one example of the richness of life people experienced before the dawn of the Digital Age. I'm grateful for these experiences and hopeful that more people will adopt an analog lifestyle in the future.

TABLE OF CONTENTS

INTRODUCTION

I enter the building through a deserted corridor filled with natural light. Rows of abandoned stores to the left and right greet me, their interiors dark and empty. As I traverse the polished floors of the concourse, my footsteps echo, and Muzak plays on a loop. Not a soul is in sight. Thriving areca palms in planters throughout the building suggest regular watering. Every surface is clean and dust free. I search for signs of life but find only a mannequin hiding in the shadows of a vacant store. Is this the *Twilight Zone*? What strange world have I wandered into? While this may sound like the setting of a zombie apocalypse film, it's my first experience in a dead mall.

Dead malls—a.k.a. ghost malls, zombie malls, and abandoned malls—are malls that are either on their last legs or already out of business. The technical definition is a shopping mall with low consumer traffic and a high vacancy rate. [2] Dead malls have become increasingly common since 2006. The rise of e-commerce, competition from big-box retailers, and the COVID-19 pandemic have intensified the problem. Due to these factors, scores of partially or completely abandoned shopping malls now blanket the country.

According to a November 2022 article from *The Carolinian*, there are more than 300 abandoned malls in America today. Only 1,000 active malls remain, and a quarter of those are projected to fail in the next two years. [3]

Dead malls have a distinct appeal. Search online and you will find scores of photos of abandoned mall photos from around the world. The images are haunting. Like the rusty Ferris wheel in Pripyat Amusement Park, a survivor of the Chernobyl disaster, dead malls are specters of the recent past. That these malls were teeming with people only recently is difficult to fathom. Their abrupt shift in fortune bewilders the mind. The popularity of this topic is evident in sites like deadmalls.com and labelscar.com, which provide detailed biographies of dead malls throughout America. There's also the r/deadmalls subreddit and a Dead Mall Enthusiasts group on Facebook.

True dead mall fans know the work of videographer Dan Bell, creator of the *Dead Mall* series on YouTube. If dead malls have a patron saint, Dan Bell is it. Since 2015, he has worked to preserve the memory of dying malls through his recorded video tours. "My thought was I wanted to archive malls all across the country that were closing down," Bell said in an interview with ABC News. "I want people to feel like they're walking through the mall, and that's kind of where the whole thing came from." [4] Similar videos are found on Erik Pierson's *Retail Archeology* YouTube channel. Like me, Pierson is a native Arizonan. His first shoot took place at Fiesta Mall in Mesa, Arizona. From there Pierson branched out, documenting numerous shopping malls throughout the Phoenix metropolitan area. "They are going the way of the dinosaur," Pierson says. "It's a slow extinction." [5]

Eventually, Pierson took *Retail Archeology* 113 miles south of Phoenix for an episode in Tucson. On September 28, 2017, he posted a video called *El Con Mall: The Dead Mall That Got Away*. It's described as "a video tour of what is left of El Con Mall." Built in 1960, El Con was Tucson's first mall. It became my second home throughout childhood and adolescence. In addition to being a wonderful place to shop, El Con Mall was a popular community gathering place. By the late 1990s, however, El Con was in decline, achieving dead mall status in the early 2000s. Each year more tenants left, and the mall became a ghost town. As El Con sank lower and lower, community members voiced their frustration. Some, like social worker Robert Kafes, expressed outrage concerning the mall owners' inaction:

> What an unconscionable disgrace.. . . . What attempts have they made to vitalize this spectacular space? There are so many creative, profit-making, community-enhancing possibilities for this property that I scratch my head attempting to understand why its management owners would inflict this slum on their neighbors and our community.. . . . Their inaction offends everyone I know. [6]

Others, like retiree Mary Stanley, begged outright for something to be done: "I have lived in midtown since 1968. El Con was a prosperous and beautiful mall, and I have been so disappointed at what is happening . . . Please bring life back to this mall. We in midtown need it." [7]

Kafes and Stanley's cries were ignored. In April 2011, an article in the *Arizona Daily Star* announced El Con's owners were hiring a demolition crew to tear down the last enclosed portion of the original mall. For most people, the announcement was confirmation of a long-suspected fear. The writing had been on the wall for years, but many Tucsonans remained optimistic that El Con would make a comeback. The demolition announcement quashed that hope for good. "It's a shame the way they let the mall go the way it did," said Tom Fetter, manager of the Poster Warehouse at El Con. "It had a lot of potential." [8] In 2011, the last enclosed section of the mall was demolished, and El Con was converted to a power center.

Pierson's video captures El Con in its post-mall years when the lone remaining store from the original shopping center was JC Penney. The video is mostly a tour of JC Penney, which closed in 2020. Still, *Retail Archeology's* El Con Mall video stirred a deep well of memory. The comment section contains over 250 entries from former mall patrons, each with unique perspectives. Here is a sampling of comments, illustrating how viewers reacted to the video.

> I am a first time shopper at this mall from 1960 or 61. Was there at the grand opening. Biggest shopping thing I had ever seen in those days. Lived in Tucson at the time. Loved it. [9]

I was raised in Tucson, I remember going to Elcon [sic] Mall as a kid. I was really sad seeing it die like it did and seeing most of being torn down. Back in the 80's it was amazing. Have really great memories of going there on the weekends with my family. [10]

El con used to be the BEST. [11]

I remember El Con Mall from my childhood! They had a kick ass arcade and a really cool fountain! [12]

I used to work at El Con! Hot Sam Pretzels next to JCPenney! Lots of memories... I remember walking through the mall long after I had worked there, prior to when it was converted to the open air style. It was so ghostly... the phantom mall music playing in the background. Thanks for creating this channel! Very cool!!! [13]

I grew up next to this mall. It was originally an open-air mall, and I had a morning paper route when I was in high school, and delivered papers to a few of the businesses there. I would then ride my bike through the mall, scavenging ICEE Bear points from discarded cups (which I never did redeem for the beach towel I wanted). They later converted it to an air-conditioned mall, which I remember being jam packed with people during the holidays (I have an old home movie of following a friend through the crowd), and I spent a lot of quarters at the Gold Mine arcade. Last time I was there, the mall was pretty much empty. Now it's pretty much just big box stores, like WalMart [sic], Target, Home Depot, and a few stores nestled in between. [14]

I used to go here all the time in the 70's and 80's. It had a unique character. [15]

> I remember going to this mall a few times a few years ago and thinking "this would be the perfect set for an apocalypse movie or horror movie." [16]

Scan the comment section of any dead mall video on the *Retail Archeology* channel, and you will find similar comments. These videos trigger a range of emotions, including joy, sadness, pride, excitement, and nostalgia. They take us back in time, causing memories buried in the unconscious to reemerge.

I enjoyed reading every comment in Pierson's El Con Mall video, but one comment posted on October 22, 2020, days after the JC Penney store at El Con closed permanently, struck me. The commenter starts by framing the JC Penney closure as "The end for the original El Con Mall I grew up with & loved." He reminisces about El Con restaurants and "countless memories" from the mall, then concludes the post with an astute observation about today's El Con Center. "The surrounding big-box stores, such as Walmart & Home Depot, are fine in their own right, but my guess is that 90% of customers will never know what a glorious mall once stood there," he says. "RIP El Con." [17] I like this comment for two reasons. First, it captures the appreciation I and many others have for El Con Mall. Second, it highlights a problem I authored this book to address: the progressive loss of collective memory about a place that once mattered in Tucson—El Con Mall.

Readers unassociated with El Con may consider putting down this book right now, but wait! Even if you're not familiar with El Con Mall, there's something here for you too. Erik Pierson called El Con the "dead mall that got away," but truthfully, most dead malls match this description. Anyone who has attempted to research a dead mall has struggled to find substantive information. Aside from a handful of pictures and videos, the most useful information comes from comments on blogs, online forums, and social media platforms. Unfortunately, this is the norm with dead malls. Minimal effort was made to document their history because we assumed they would always be around. The mall's structure alone was enough for someone to maintain connection with its past. When malls fail and are torn down, treasured memories disappear too.

Dead Mall Rising is an effort to resurrect El Con Mall through storytelling. This book gives former El Con patrons an opportunity to reminisce about the mall and explore its history. While El Con is the focus, the content should appeal to anyone with an interest in dead malls. You need not live in Tucson or have an El Con connection to partake. This book functions as a case study on one dead mall. While learning El Con's story, you will gain a better understanding of dead malls overall. And since the mall-going experience is universal, everyone will be able to relate with the examples in this book.

Before we proceed, though, I have a confession: I'm not a retail historian, and I don't have degrees in history, sociology, or psychology. What I lack in specific expertise, however, I make up for with fervent curiosity and a desire to tell El Con's story. If this is something you can get behind, join me on a fascinating journey through the history of a dead mall.

Let's talk about the contents of each chapter. Chapter 1 explains what killed El Con Mall, identifying the common factors contributing to the proliferation of dead malls in recent years. Chapter 2 gives El Con's history, from its roots in the El Conquistador Hotel to its golden era in the 1980s. Chapter 3 examines how El Con once functioned as Tucson's unofficial town square. Chapter 4 provides a nostalgic trip back to the 1980s where you'll have the opportunity to experience El Con through the lens of the Gen X youth. Chapter 5 explores the war El Con waged with Park Mall—a nearby competitor—and superstores like Walmart and Home Depot. Chapter 6 covers El Con's big-box controversy. Chapter 7 is a retrospective on El Con's transition from a mall to a retail power center. Finally, Chapter 8 discusses what would need to happen for El Con to become the place to be in Tucson once again.

CHAPTER 1

WHY?

Why?

Should you ever find yourself at 5055 E. Speedway Boulevard in Tucson, Arizona, take a minute to enjoy the mural. The building's exterior features a painting that resembles a scene from the 1956 sci-fi classic, *Earth vs. The Flying Saucers*. It shows flying saucers unleashing laser fire onto Main Street in a small town. The *Earth Bound* mural was created by Ignacio Garcia, a local artist. It's located on the east-facing wall of the building occupied by Fangamer, a company that sells gaming merchandise (see next page).

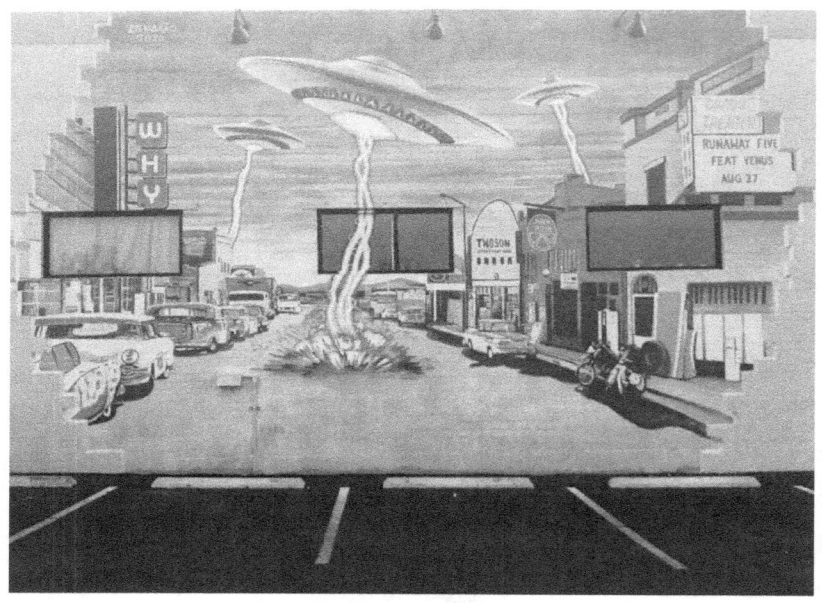

Earth Bound Mural (Courtesy of Ignacio Garcia and Fangamer)

Reid Young is the CEO of Fangamer. When Young was a teenager living in Indiana, he started the website starmen.net for fans of the Nintendo game *Earth Bound*. The game attracted a cult following. As the online community grew, Young began selling T-shirts, posters, and buttons that catered to video game fans. Fangamer was founded in 2007, and the first store launched in 2008. Ten years after the store launch, Fangamer topped $10 million in sales. [18] In 2020, Fangamer moved into the building at 5055 E. Speedway. Ignacio Garcia painted the *Earth Bound* mural as a tribute to the video game that inspired this Tucson-based business. Coincidentally, the second town to appear in the game *Earth Bound* is called "Twoson." Look closely and you can see the word "Twoson" in the mural. [19]

Another iconic mural once graced the wall that *Earth Bound* occupies today. Before Fangamer arrived, the building at 5055 E. Speedway belonged to a real estate developer named Phillip Gaillard. In 2002, Gaillard and his wife relocated to Tucson after living for forty years in Hawaii. They bought the former Carpet Giant building and turned it into Copper Country Antiques, a 32,000-square-foot antique mall. Copper Country opened in November 2004 and quickly earned a reputation for doing things differently. From a sailboat on the roof to Fred the winged buffalo, the store's famous mascot, Copper Country was unconventional. A good example of the store's offbeat approach materialized on September 21, 2007, when Gaillard and others painted *WHY* on the building's east-facing wall (see below).

WHY mural, Copper Country Antiques (Copyright Arizona Daily Star)

The mural generated a lot of local buzz. Six days after Gaillard painted it, the *Arizona Daily Star* newspaper wrote an article about it. When asked why he did it, Gaillard responded, "I had a big building and a desire for people to ask why." [20] The *WHY* mural became a local landmark. Copper Country Antiques closed in 2015. When Fangamer purchased the building, some feared the *WHY* mural would be lost. In April 2019, the owners of Fangamer revealed they were considering keeping the mural or adding to it. Ultimately, Gaillard's painting was replaced with the *Earth Bound* mural. As an homage to its predecessor, however, Ignacio Garcia included a *WHY* sign in the painting of Twoson.

Like the *Earth Bound* mural, entering a dead mall simulates what it would be like to survive an alien attack. It's like the whole town has been abducted, leaving behind only you, empty buildings, and place-inspired memories behind. When a place that was meaningful to you is lost, it's natural to ask "why?" This question surfaces a lot in discussions about dead malls. I'm a Gen Xer. My generation grew up in an era when the mall was king. In the 1980s and 1990s, malls were at the center of all the action in American cities. Malls were vibrant, packed with people, and associated with everything modern and trendy in pop culture.

Many who remember the golden age of malls are shocked by the diminished role that malls play in society today. The one thing they all want to know is, "why?" This is evident in comments people make about dead malls. Sometimes the "why" resides closer to the surface, like this 2006 statement from local educator Norma Guest. El Con was in its dead mall phase when Guest wrote a letter to the editor asking, "Why does El Con Mall remain virtually empty? Whatever happened to the food court that was going to be next to the movie theater? The location of this mall is ideal. Why is it so underutilized? What's going on?" [21]

Other times the "why" is less explicit, but you can hear it bubbling beneath the surface. Such is the case in this 2013 Yelp review of El Con posted by Karen S. At this time, El Con was no longer an enclosed mall. As you read the review, listen for the "why?" implicit in Karen's comment.

> This isn't really a mall anymore. It's a collection of low-end big-boxes with air-conditioned hallways in between. At the bottom is the supervillain Walmart, then your Home Depot and Target on opposite ends where the anchor department stores used to be.
>
> The obligatory movie theater is decent (for a mainstream one) and boosts the mall up to 1-star.
>
> It's tragic, really, this used to be the best mall in Tucson. The closest experience I have to something going this far downhill was when I returned to live in my house in Mid-City New Orleans after Katrina. Watching a neighborhood die is just depressing. What the hell happened to this place? [22]

Whether explicitly or implicitly, the question most dead mall enthusiasts want answered is, "Why did this happen to my mall?" This chapter provides the answer to that question regarding El Con.

El Con didn't become a dead mall overnight. It was a gradual process that unfolded for over two decades. While every mall is different, each has faced similar challenges historically. By identifying the factors that led to El Con's undoing, I will describe the most common reasons malls fail. I'll start by examining the role of anchor stores in a well-functioning mall. Next, I'll discuss three common threats contributing to mall failures in recent years—competition from other malls, big-box retailers, and the rise of ecommerce. Nothing can bring back El Con Mall, but I find a measure of satisfaction in discovering the factors that contributed to its downfall. I'd like to pass this gift on to you, the reader. If you have ever wondered why so many malls are dying, this chapter will provide answers.

Anchors Away

A spiderweb is built strand by strand. Web construction begins when the spider selects an anchor point and lays an anchor thread. The anchor thread is made of strong silk and is usually one thread. Attached to the anchor thread are frame threads, which connect one anchor thread to another for support. The capture spiral is the sticky thread on the web interior that captures prey. [23] Malls are much like spiderwebs. Anchor stores are the foundation on which everything else is built, like anchor threads in a spiderweb. The enclosed arcades connecting one anchor store to another are like frame threads. The smaller retail stores within the arcade are like capture spirals.

A spiderweb is perfectly designed to capture prey, just as malls are perfectly designed to attract shoppers. The primary indicator of a mall's health is the strength of its anchor stores. Anchor stores are the largest tenants in shopping malls. These anchors are usually department stores. Anchors are placed strategically throughout the mall so that shoppers must pass smaller stores to get to them. This increases the likelihood that shoppers will visit the smaller stores. At the height of its popularity, El Con Mall had five anchor stores. Here is a mall directory from 1981, identifying the location of El Con's former anchors, indicated by the letters A, B, C, D, and E.

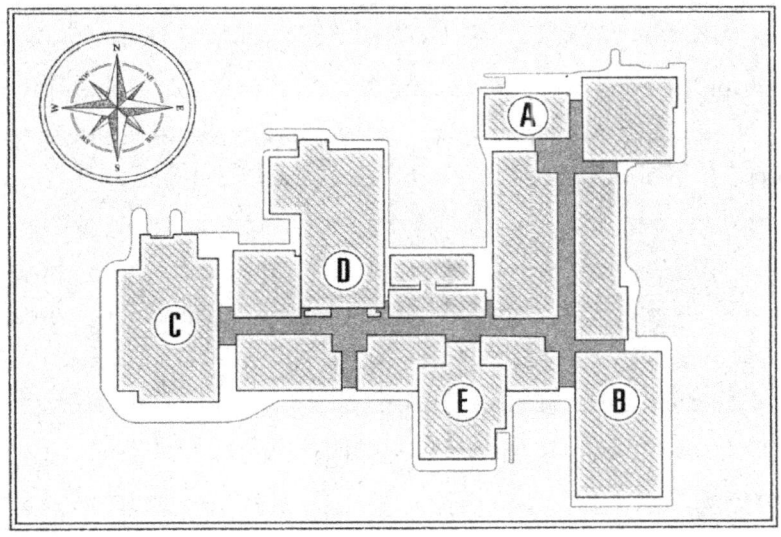

Map of El Con Mall, circa 1981

The unlabeled buildings indicate sections of the mall where smaller stores operated. The dark gray areas identify the interior walkways connecting the anchors and smaller stores. Levy's (Anchor A), El Con's first department store, opened on November 16, 1960. Soon afterward came Montgomery Ward (Anchor B), which opened on February 2, 1961. Levy's outgrew its location and reopened in a new, 226,836-square-foot building (Anchor C) on September 16, 1969. Steinfeld's, El Con's third department store, moved into the building vacated by Levy's on March 29, 1971. JCPenney (Anchor D) opened five months later on August 4, 1971. Goldwater's (Anchor E) joined El Con in 1978, becoming the fifth anchor.

The first signs of trouble for El Con appeared in 1984 with the loss of Steinfeld's department store. The day before Steinfeld's closed, the

Arizona Daily Star ran an article titled, "Final weekend ticks away for Steinfeld's El Con store." Its opening sentence read, "This weekend, the doors at Steinfeld's are to shut for good at El Con, marking the end of an era for what was once one of Tucson's leading department stores." [24] Nobody knew it at the time, but Steinfeld's withdrawal marked the end of an era for El Con as well. It was the first in a series of anchor store departures that ultimately crippled El Con's ability to attract customers. El Con's owner entered discussions with potential replacement tenants for Steinfeld's, but nothing materialized. The building sat vacant for years, leaving a major void in El Con's north wing. Over time, smaller stores in that area of the mall began leaving as well.

One prominent store in El Con's north wing that became a casualty of Steinfeld's departure was Dave Bloom & Sons. This family-run haberdashery sold clothing to the men of Tucson for over fifty years. Dave Bloom & Sons started in downtown Tucson and moved to El Con in 1963. Business was good until Steinfeld's left the mall. In a news article titled "The End of an Era," Ted Bloom discusses the impact the Steinfeld's closure had on their decision to close their store, Dave Bloom & Sons: "It's been rocky the last few years," Ted explains. "Not having an anchor store reduced our foot traffic. This end of the mall has been suffering, and that's a contributing factor." [25]

Many other stores in El Con's north wing ultimately suffered the same fate, including the El Con Menswear store owned by Peter Berens. In an effort to revitalize that section of the mall, Berens pitched El Con Mall management an idea aimed at transforming the north wing of the mall into an "indoor street fair" atmosphere. Berens convinced management to repurpose the vacant Steinfeld's store, gutting the building and turning it into an eclectic retail space that sold crafts and food. The "Pavilion," as it was called, was a food court, farmer's market, and bazaar all in one, occupied by small shops, vendor carts, and kiosks. Though moderately successful in the beginning, the Pavilion ultimately failed.

El Con's transition from a mall to a power center was a process that began quietly in 1998 with the demolition of the Steinfeld's building (Anchor A) in the north wing. In an article announcing big changes coming to El Con, *Arizona Daily Star* columnist Ernie Heltsley noted, "It's sad and a little spooky walking the nearly vacant northeast end of El Con these days." [26] This area of the mall had become a ghost town in the fourteen years following Steinfeld's departure. Heltsley also announced that preparations were underway to demolish the northeast end of El Con and replace it with a twenty-screen theater and another large retailer.

The included graphic illustrates the scope of the change to the footprint of El Con Mall (see below).

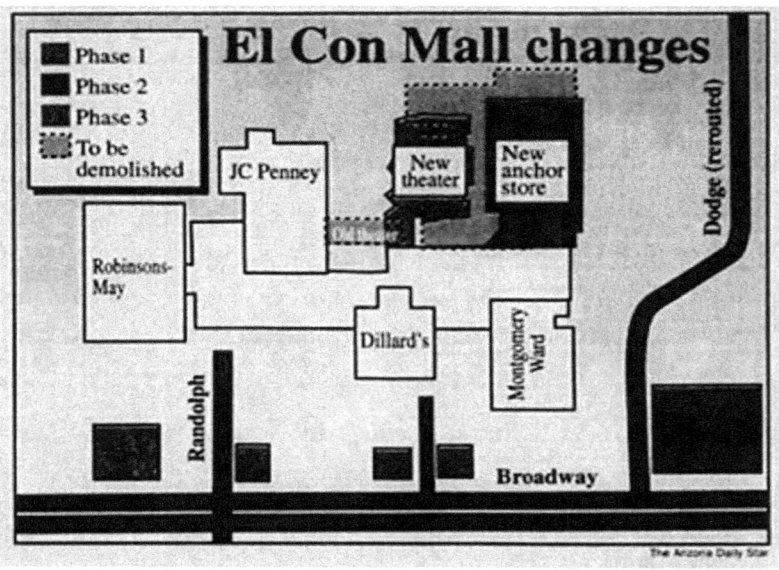

El Con Mall Changes (Copyright Arizona Daily Star)

The new anchor turned out to be a Home Depot store. And with that, the first of many dominoes fell, contributing to the demise of the El Con mall.

El Con's failure as a mall is tied to the loss of its anchor stores. The fate of El Con's north wing following the departure of Steinfeld's soon befell other areas of the mall. As additional anchors left the mall, El Con weakened. With less foot traffic in the mall interior, smaller retailers left for greener pastures, and El Con was slowly transformed into a ghost mall. This phenomenon is not unique to El Con. The health of any mall is directly proportional to the strength of its anchors. The loss of an anchor spells big trouble for all the other stores in a mall. If an anchor vacancy isn't filled quickly, it can set off a chain reaction, resulting in a death spiral.

Having established the effect that vacant anchor stores have on malls, we will now examine three primary culprits contributing to the failure of anchors—competition from other malls, big-box stores, and online retail.

The Other Mall

The Other Mall, a 2006 mockumentary on dead malls, follows corporate manager Derrick Wellman on his quest to pump life back into the aging Middletown Mall. Wellman introduces Middletown as the mall everyone used to go to. "It was the hot spot back in the 80s," he says. "And then came Mall of the Country." Images of a multi-tier mall with jaw-dropping attractions flash on the screen. "They got bigger stores, bigger attractions," Wellman explains. "They're also surprisingly close." The camera zooms out from a map of Middletown to reveal the two malls, side by side, located a few blocks away from each other—Middletown and Mall of the Country.

Though fictitious, *The Other Mall* presents a realistic view of what it's like working at a mall that lives in the shadow of a larger, more popular mall. Middletown Mall is completely outmatched and has no chance of competing with Mall of the Country. Despite Wellman's efforts, it's clear that Middletown Mall's fate is sealed. There will be no comeback. For El Con and countless other dead malls, *The Other Mall* is a great example of art imitating life. In real life, one of the primary reasons malls fail is due to competition from other malls. This is especially true when competitor malls are built in close proximity to pre-existing ones.

El Con Mall opened in 1961 as Tucson's first regional shopping center. It had approximately thirty stores. By 1985, El Con had more than quadrupled in size to 135 stores. Back then, El Con Mall was a magnet for activity in the Tucson community. El Con advertised itself as "the place to be" in Tucson, and it was. But a new breed of rival malls rose to challenge El Con. Tucson's second mall, Park Mall, opened in 1975, located just three miles east of El Con on the same street, Broadway Boulevard. Then in 1982, two additional malls, Tucson Mall and Foothills Mall, opened on Tucson's northwest side. It wasn't long before the new competition began having an effect.

Park Mall gradually overtook El Con's role as the top mall in midtown Tucson. El Con could never compete with Tucson Mall in terms of its number of stores and amenities. Luckily for El Con, though, Tucson Mall was 8.5 miles away in the northwest part of town. Park Mall, however, was just down the street from El Con. For the first twenty years of Park Mall's existence, El Con had the slight upper hand in terms of store offerings and amenities. As a result, both malls were able to coexist despite their rivalry for the same customer base. But Park Mall secured the upper hand in 1996 when it was bought by General Growth Properties, the second-largest mall operator in the United States.

El Con's demise due to the rise of Park Mall was a domino-like process. The first domino to fall in this power exchange occurred on May 25, 1995. On that day Joseph Kivel, part owner and founder of El Con Mall, died at age eighty-five. In addition to a 33 percent ownership stake in El Con, Joseph Kivel owned Park Mall. When Kivel died in 1995, both malls were beginning to show their age. So, in 1996, Kivel's heirs sold Park Mall to General Growth Properties.

Two years later, General Growth Properties began a major three-phase renovation project at Park Mall. El Con was thrown into an arms race of sorts against a competent, well-funded rival just three miles east.

When El Con was in its prime, its department stores brought people to the mall in droves. By 2010, three of El Con's five anchor stores were gone. Steinfeld's and Montgomery Ward were demolished and replaced with big-box stores. Dillard's, formerly Goldwater's, was the last tenant to occupy Anchor E. On January 5, 2000, the *Arizona Daily Star* published an article titled, "Dillard's pulling out of El Con," announcing the department store's decision to leave the mall. Their reason for leaving? The newly renovated Park Mall. "[El Con] Mall officials confirmed this week that Dillard's will terminate its lease May 9 and consolidate at the new, larger 'flagship' store at Park Place (the remodeled Park Mall), several miles farther east on East Broadway." [27]

Anchor E in El Con sat vacant from 2000 to 2010. Then it was replaced with another big-box store, Burlington Coat Factory. Once the Park Mall renovations were completed in 2001, the mall was rebranded as Park Place. The remodeled Park Place immediately attracted significant traffic from El Con Mall. I hate to say it, but I was one of many shoppers who switched allegiance from El Con to Park Place. El Con couldn't compete with Park Place, and plans for El Con's own revitalization were too slow to materialize. After Park Place's new food court opened in 2001, El Con was done for. Like many malls in the country, El Con assumed the role of the "other mall" from that point forward.

Boxed Out

The year 2000 was not kind to El Con. The mall lost two of its four anchors in the span of a year. On December 28, 2000, eleven months after Dillard's said it was leaving the mall, Montgomery Ward announced it was going out of business and closing all its stores nationwide. Montgomery Ward occupied the Anchor B building in the southeast wing of El Con. As with Steinfeld's and Dillard's, no tenants were waiting in line to replace Montgomery Ward. Hence, another core section of the mall was anchorless. The Montgomery Ward building sat vacant for three years until it was demolished in 2003.

My parents' favorite place to shop at El Con was Montgomery Ward. Every trip to El Con with my parents started at "Monkey Wards," as many affectionately called it. Part of Montgomery Ward's appeal was that it had been around for so long. The company was in business for 128 years before calling it quits. Like Sears and JCPenney, Ward's was popular with the older shoppers because they'd gone there most of their lives. Unfortunately, Ward's failed to keep up with current trends. One trend in particular, the emergence of big-box stores in the 1990s, proved fatal for the once great retail giant.

In her book *America at the Mall*, author Lisa Scharoun cites big-box stores as one of the main factors contributing to the decline of shopping malls. "These Big Boxes are becoming ever more prevalent in suburbia, replacing many viable regional malls or turning them into dead spaces," [28] Sharoun explains. With a laser focus on efficiency and low prices, the big-box store has become the destination of choice for cost-conscious shoppers. As they grew more popular, big-box stores attracted business away from shopping malls.

One of the top reasons cited for Montgomery Ward's demise was competition from big-box retailers like Walmart and Target. [29]

Looking back, this was true of my own experience. As much as I enjoyed trips to El Con as a kid, my family spent more time at K-Mart and Target because those stores were more budget-friendly.

Two days after Montgomery Ward announced it was going out of business, the *Arizona Daily Star* newspaper ran an article titled, "Ward's asks buyers to file claims." In it, Ward's management urged customers to file bankruptcy claims for items they paid deposits on but hadn't received. On the same page, directly below the Montgomery Ward article, was another article announcing Target's intention to open a 154,000 square-foot new Greatland store on Tucson's southeast side.

The appearance of these articles on the same newspaper page was ironic for two reasons. First, it captured in stark contrast the diverging fortunes of both companies. The Montgomery Ward article was the retail equivalent of a death sentence. The Target article showcased a company on the rise, opening yet another store in Tucson. A second, less-obvious irony was the fact that Target played a role in Montgomery Ward's demise. Big-box stores were a major competitor for Montgomery Ward, and Target was one of the main offenders. [30] Unable to match aggressive low pricing from big-box stores like Target and lacking a strategy to distinguish itself from competitors, Montgomery Ward had no choice but to close its stores. The El Con Mall location closed for good on March 18, 2001.

Rumors swirled for months about potential tenants for the vacant Montgomery Ward building in El Con Mall. In March 2001, Target Corporation announced that it had purchased two Montgomery

Ward stores in Arizona, and one was the El Con location. Little happened for the next year, and the Anchor B building sat vacant. Then in June 2002, Tucson's mayor and City Council held a public hearing to consider Target's request to demolish the Montgomery Ward building at El Con and build a new store in its place. As described by Tucson City Planner Glenn Moyer, El Con's proposed Target store "would be about 133,000 square feet–some 20,000 square feet smaller than the Target Greatland store planned for Old Spanish Trail on the far Southeast Side."[31] The Target Greatland store on Old Spanish Trail hadn't yet been built, but a new Target store was already being proposed for Midtown Tucson.

The new Target store had a dramatic effect on El Con Mall's footprint (see below).

Infographic (© Tucson Citizen – USA TODAY NETWORK via Imagn Images)

Following Montgomery Ward's demolition, nothing remained of El Con's north-south wing. The new Target was built separate from the east-west wing, the mall's last remaining enclosed section. Like Home Depot, Target was disconnected from the rest of the mall. This meant, in order to access the mall interior, Target shoppers first had to walk back to their vehicles. Most people are unwilling to backtrack after walking to their car. So, rather than spilling out to explore the mall's interior, Target shoppers got what they needed, returned to their cars, and went home.

Big-box stores like Home Depot and Target were a radical departure from the department stores that they replaced. Rather than luring shoppers to the rest of the mall, as anchors are intended to do, they stole the limelight for themselves. Over time, the remaining tenants in El Con's core left for more flourishing locations. Nationwide, big-box stores have had an adverse effect on the health of shopping malls. By weakening mall anchors through their aggressively low pricing, big-box stores have played a role in the rise of dead malls.

Running on Empty

El Con was officially a dead mall by the mid-2000s. All that remained of the original mall was the east-west corridor that ran between Macy's and the area just beyond the vacant Dillard's building. By this time, the mall was virtually empty. In 2007 the *Arizona Daily Star* ran an article about El Con titled, "Hello, Anybody Home?" Columnist Suzanne C. McLean began by characterizing El Con as "a mall in name only." Echoing the disappointment of many Tucsonans, McLean decried the lack of vision and poor results that characterized the El Con revitalization project which began more than a decade earlier. "The Mall is a ghost of its former self, and the topic of revitalization of El Con is a joke in our community,"[32] McLean noted.

In truth, El Con's owners made a number of improvements to the mall between 1995 and 2007. They renovated the parking lots, built a food court, and remodeled the main entrance. To the casual observer, El Con didn't seem to be going anywhere, though. Century 20 Theater, Home Depot, and Target were disconnected from the mall. They attracted business to themselves while the mall's interior was ignored. Here is a directory of the mall from 2007 (see below).

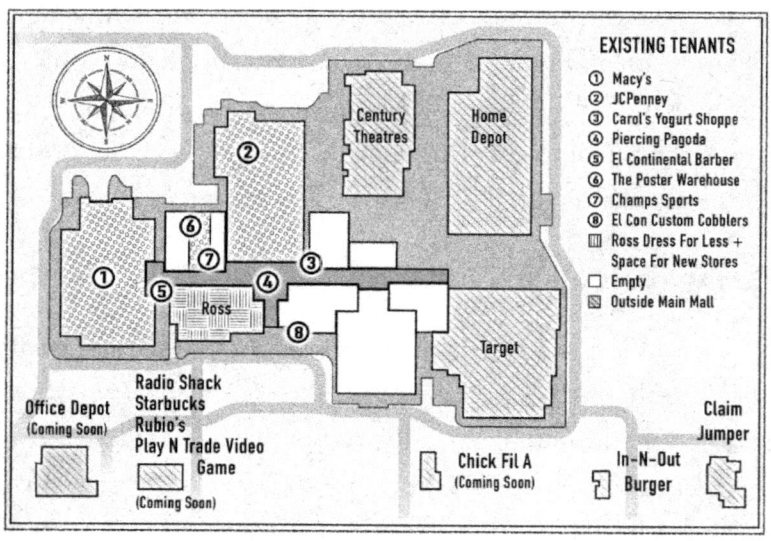

Map of El Con Mall, circa 2007

Note the east-west wing of El Con (the corridor between Macy's and Target). In 1981 this enclosed section of the mall had over sixty-five tenants, anchor stores not included. By 2007, only eight tenants remained. In October 2007, Macy's announced that it was leaving the mall because it was "no longer financially viable to keep the El Con store open." The devastating news came just a few weeks after the grand opening of Ross Dress for Less, a development that many hoped would inject new life into the mall.

With Macy's departure, JCPenney became the lone remaining anchor at El Con Mall. After losing Macy's, El Con's owners essentially gave up on the idea of saving the enclosed mall. Walmart had been floated as a possible tenant since the late 1990s, but residents of El Con's surrounding neighborhoods resisted. With the Macy's vacancy, however, the Walmart option resurfaced with a vengeance. From that point forward, every action El Con's owners took appears to have been aimed at luring in Walmart. In September 2011, demolition began on the mall's last remaining enclosed section. Despite fierce opposition from surrounding neighborhoods, Walmart was ultimately granted permission to build a store location at El Con. On June 20, 2012, demolition of the former Macy's building began. A new Walmart store was built in the footprint of the former Levy's/Macy's building. Walmart opened for business on September 11, 2013.

The last flicker of hope for El Con was extinguished in 2020 when it was announced that JCPenney was going out of business. JCPenney was the only El Con store to survive the de-malling process. The department store chain was hit hard by COVID-19 pandemic restrictions. In May 2020, JCPenney announced it was closing a third of its 846 stores. El Con was one of those stores. Though the pandemic played a role in these closures, JCPenney had been struggling for years due to competition with big-box stores. Online retail also changed the way that people shop. JCPenney struggled to adapt to the changes brought about by e-commerce, and this played a major role in the company's declaring bankruptcy in 2020.

The pandemic may have been the final nail in the coffin, but problems for JCPenney had been mounting for years. In an article for the Associated Press, columnist Josh Galemore states that part of the reason JCPenney filed for bankruptcy was that it "had trouble connecting with shoppers, who are increasingly skipping the mall and shopping online." [33] Many other department and specialty stores face the same problem. In February 2019, online retailers accounted for more sales than brick-and-mortar retailers for the first time in history—a major warning sign for physical retailers. Online shopping poses a threat to shopping malls. In addition to competition from other malls and big-box stores, online shopping has contributed to the spate of dying malls in recent years. As more people choose to shop at home, empty shopping malls are increasingly commonplace.

Conclusion

El Con Mall was demolished in June 2012, but I didn't find out until months later. I was completely caught off guard when I went to the mall one day and discovered it was gone. Wanting to know what happened, I began searching online for information about El Con. That's when I stumbled onto the topic of dead malls. Until then I had no idea that dead malls were a thing. Mark Twain once said, "When someone dies, it is like when your house burns down; it isn't for years that you realize the full extent of your loss." I never thought I'd say this, but this quote applies to malls, too. Never in my wildest dreams did I think I'd write a book about a mall. I knew nothing of El Con's history prior to this book. I never bothered learning about El Con because it was just a place to shop. I never gave it a second thought.

While researching El Con's history, I came across an image (next page) of a Royal typewriter in the abandoned lobby of the El Conquistador Hotel, El Con's namesake (El Con is short for El Conquistador). You will learn about the El Conquistador Hotel in the next chapter. A sheet of blank stationary is loaded in the typewriter, as if someone were preparing to type a letter but vanished before they could start. The image triggered me because it suggested a story cut short, forever untold. After witnessing El Con in its de-malled state, I felt compelled to dig deeper and understand why it happened.

I experienced El Con Mall in its heyday, so I was shocked to see it fail. Like most Tucsonans, I wanted El Con restored to its former glory. We were led to believe El Con's owners wanted this as well, but that was not the case. El Con's owners pulled the plug on the mall and turned the property into a car-friendly complex filled with big-box retailers, fast-food restaurants, and stand-alone stores. To me, it was an injustice. Given its rich history in the community, El Con deserved to go out better than that. Something had to be done to make this right, but what?

Abandoned Typewriter in the lobby of El Conquistador Hotel (Copyright Arizona Daily Star)

The answer came to me while reflecting on the Royal typewriter image: tell the story. For every person who has driven past today's El Con Center and felt a twinge of resentment over what has become of the mall, tell a story that shows they are not alone. For every person who shopped, worked, hung out, walked the mall, and saw movies at El Con, tell a story that provides opportunities to reminisce. For every person who watched El Con slowly deteriorate over the years, wondering why but never getting answers, tell a story that provides closure and, hopefully, inspires them to do something constructive to make things right again.

In the chapters that follow, I tell the story of El Con Mall, from its pre-construction years to opening day to its golden years in the mid-1980s to its decline in the 1990s to its death in 2012. By the end, anyone who has ever wondered what happened to El Con will finally know WHY.

CHAPTER 2

A "PENNEY" SAVED

A "Penney" Saved

El Con Mall was Tucson's first regional shopping center. Its first department store, Levy's, opened in 1960. Three months later a second department store, Montgomery Ward, opened as well. By November 1961, nineteen additional stores opened in the space between the two department stores. El Con's development continued for the next two decades. By 1979, the mall increased to 112 stores, including five department stores. Page thirty-three has a map of El Con Mall from that year. Later in the chapter you'll see that El Con went through different stages of development over its fifty-two-year lifespan. For clarity, the footprint of the mall shown on the next page is the one I have in mind when I refer to El Con Mall throughout this book. This is the mall that I experienced as a child and teenager in the 1980s. This is the El Con Mall where I made so many memories.

At the height of its popularity in the mid-1980s, El Con boasted 135 stores. The good times didn't last forever, though. During the 1990s, El Con began a two-decade period of decline. In 1997, the north section of the mall, formerly anchored by Steinfeld's, was torn down and replaced with a twenty-screen theater. From that point on, a new pattern of development characterized by "subtraction" became the norm at El Con. As more sections of the mall were demolished and replaced with big-box stores, retailers in the mall's interior struggled to attract customers. By 2000, El Con was a ghost mall. Fewer and fewer stores remained in the mall, and foot traffic slowed to a trickle. This pattern continued until 2012, when the last section of the enclosed mall was razed.

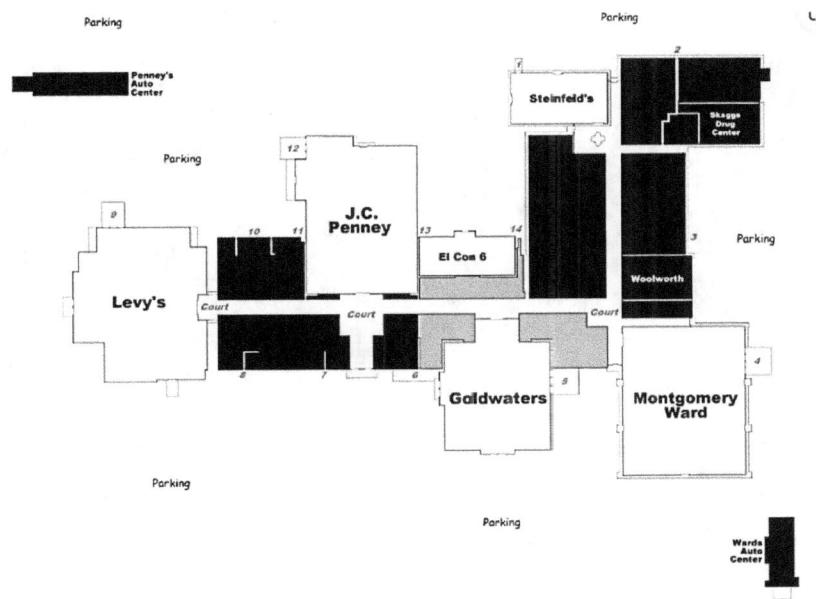

El Con Mall, circa 1979 (Image courtesy of www.mall-hall-of-fame.blogspot.com)

El Con is no longer classified as a mall. It has been re-named El Con Center, reflecting its transformation to a retail power center—an outdoor shopping center typically containing three or more big-box stores, smaller retailers, and restaurants. The next page has a directory of El Con Center circa 2015. As the map shows, El Con Center is a mishmash of big-box stores, restaurants, and a theater unified by arterial roads and a parking lot. To the casual visitor, it is a shopping center stocked with the same assortment of superstores every other city has. To paraphrase benjaminbeede6555 from the *Dead Mall That Got Away* video, most people have no clue that a "glorious mall" once occupied this space.

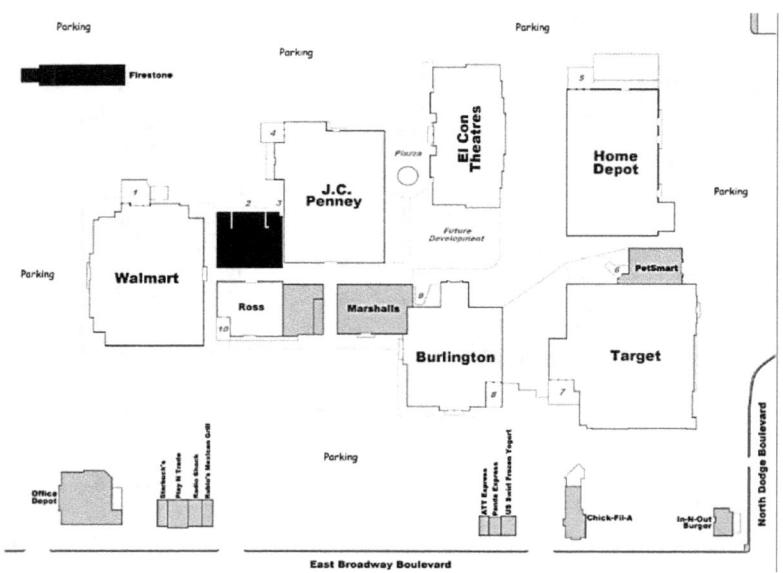

El Con Center, circa 2015 (Image courtesy of www.mall-hall-of-fame.blogspot.com)

Luckily, one relic of El Con's past did survive. Look carefully at it, and you will see glimmers of the "glorious mall" that so many Tucsonans knew and loved. To find this remnant, follow the pedestrian walkway between Ross and Marshalls to an abandoned building adjacent to the theater (see map above). This is the former JCPenney building. Like Montgomery Ward, JCPenney remained a tenant in its original building from the day it opened until it closed. JCPenney outlasted every other El Con anchor store. When Erik Pierson shot his *Retail Archeology* video in 2017, JCPenney was still in business. It closed in 2020, but the building is still standing.

Despite an absence of signage, the building is identifiable as a JCPenney store thanks to the label scar above its former entrance (see next page).

JCPenney: South Main Entrance (Photo by the author)

Label scars are markings left on a wall when a store sign is removed. They are created by a combination of dust and fading behind the letters of a store sign. When a store fails and the sign is taken down, a transfer of the store name remains on the building. A label scar reveals the identity of an abandoned building, allowing it to live on in a way. Similarly, the vacant JCPenney building functions as a memorial for El Con Mall. It's all that remains of El Con's past, when this "glorious mall" was—as advertised—the place to be in Tucson.

Using the JCPenney building as a focal point, in this chapter I will review the history of El Con Mall. I will start with the El Conquistador Hotel, an early contributor to Tucson's growth and the mall's namesake. Next, we will examine the history of downtown Tucson and the detrimental effect El Con had on it as the mall grew in popularity. Finally, we will trace El Con's growth from 1960 through its golden period in the 1980s.

Center Court

We begin our review of El Con history just outside the entrance of JCPenney, an area formerly known as Center Court. El Con's main entrance once led directly into Center Court, making it a major hub of activity in the mall. Center Court fronted a popular JCPenney store, facilitated the movement of shoppers from one area of the mall to another, and hosted a variety of events that lured people to the mall, including the "Back the Cats" rallies for the University of Arizona football team, the annual holiday sale for Tucson Bonsai Society, and the El Con Express miniature train ride for kids. For a thriving mall, creating a striking entrance is key. The entryway must make people feel welcome and create a good first impression. Center Court fulfilled that role for El Con Mall for many years (see image below).

View of Center Court, January 28, 1979 (Copyright Arizona Daily Star)

In the 1920s, forty years before El Con opened, the city of Tucson was looking for its own version of a Center Court. The city found its solution in the El Conquistador Hotel.

The El Conquistador Hotel

Ugh, snowbirds. Few things drive Tucsonans crazier than the annual influx of snowbirds. At the beginning of every October, legions of retirees from the cold northern states descend on the Old Pueblo to enjoy Arizona's mild winter. Locals refer to these visitors as "snowbirds." With blue skies and average winter highs in the low to mid-70s, Tucson has attracted snowbirds for over a century. From the time when snowbirds arrive until they leave in May, life in the city is crowded and complicated. Traffic is heavier, restaurants are fuller, and getting a tee time at the golf course on Saturday is tougher. Life in Tucson does not return to normal until the snowbirds leave at the beginning of summer. Then we get the city all to ourselves again until the autumn chill heralds the snowbirds' return.

As annoying as they can be, Tucson owes its growth to snowbirds. The city has taken steps to entice winter visitors to the city for over a century. Tucson was the most populous city in Arizona until 1920 when Phoenix pulled ahead of it. So, in the 1920s, a group of Tucson investors devised a plan to build a stately hotel that would attract even more winter visitors to Tucson. With the money raised via popular subscription, some 650 Tucsonans banded together and funded the El Conquistador Hotel. Investors gambled that once hotel visitors saw how beautiful Tucson was, they would want to move there.

The El Conquistador Hotel, Early Building Stage

(BN Places-Tucson-Business-Hotels-El Conquistador, Exterior BN, 203,041, Courtesy of the Arizona Historical Society)

The El Conquistador Hotel opened on November 22, 1928. An article in the *Tucson Citizen* newspaper heralded the event with the following headline: "The El Conquistador Hotel Will Open Tonight In Blaze Of Social Splendor." Over 250 guests "representing the wealth, beauty and fashion of city, state and nation" attended the evening dinner and program of events. [34] Columnist Effie Leese Scott described the hotel as "palatial" and "set amid a landscape of unsurpassing beauty." [35] The El Conquistador's first manager, Alexander MacLennan, served as Master of Ceremonies for the event. Mr. MacLennan was a graduate of the hotel management program at Cornell and a respected veteran of the hospitality industry. On December 1, 1928, an article reporting on the hotel's opening night appeared in the *National Hotel Reporter*, a trade newspaper devoted to the hotel industry. Here is a brief excerpt: "The hotel is a beautiful structure, designed and built after the Spanish period and decorated in the spirit of the old Indian craftsmen, and covers a large tract of land just outside of Tucson, with five great mountain chains in plain view of the hotel. The picturesque desert is a feature of the elaborate landscape of the sixty-acre tract." [36] The article ends with an expression of optimism for the hotel's future from El Conquistador's manager.

The El Conquistador Hotel in Tucson, Arizona

(A.E. Magee, PC 177, F. 45, 1597, Courtesy of the Arizona Historical Society)

Based on the guest list and inquiries that the hotel received in its first week, Mr. MacLennan predicted "that El Conquistador will become one of the most popular winter resorts in the country." [37] The hotel investors were right in their assessment that the hotel would lure people to Tucson. When the hotel opened in 1928, Tucson's population was 30,000. By the time the hotel closed in 1968, the city's population had risen to 281,000. This growth was partly the result of tourism and business that the El Conquistador Hotel attracted to Tucson.

Downtown

The JCPenney store at El Con opened in 1971, the fourth anchor store to debut at the mall. It wasn't the first JCPenney store in Tucson, though. That distinction belongs to the former JCPenney store at the corner of Congress and 6th Avenue in downtown Tucson, which opened on May 1, 1920. The day before the event, JCPenney took out a multi-page ad in the *Arizona Daily Star* newspaper. At the time it was one of 297 JCPenney stores in the United States. The first page included a statement explaining why JCPenney made the choice to open a store in Tucson: "First of all—WE ARE HERE TO STAY! Our investigation of conditions in and about Tucson has convinced us that the majority of people will quickly appreciate the advantages offered to them by the service of this store. With new goods always, lowest prices every day and courteous service at all times-this "different" store will fill a long-felt want in this community." [38]

It did indeed fill a need within the Tucson community. With the help of other department stores, local retailers, and restaurants, JCPenney helped make downtown the most popular place in Tucson at the time.

The El Conquistador Hotel was three and a half miles away from downtown Tucson. When the hotel opened in 1928, this was considered the outskirts of town. At that time, downtown was the hub of all commercial, consumer, and social activity in the city. My Uncle, Ralph McCormick, grew up near downtown Tucson during the 1930s and 1940s. He lived one mile south of downtown at a house on 8th Avenue and 19th Street. On the morning of September 18, 2004, I drove with Uncle Ralph to record a family history video at his childhood home on the outskirts of downtown Tucson. I interviewed him in the Barrio Viejo neighborhood where he grew up during World War II. His family used to buy their groceries at Jerry's Lee Ho Market, located at 600 S. Meyer Avenue. It was a four-minute walk from their house. Aside from that grocery store, however, the action was in downtown Tucson.

During the interview, Uncle Ralph revealed that he used to go downtown to "walk the streets" and shine shoes. "During the War [WWII], I'd take my shine box and go polish shoes over there for the soldiers and people. There was a lot of activity then," Uncle Ralph explained. "There was a lot of traffic, a lot of foot traffic because there was no shopping mall. That was it," he said, pointing toward the downtown area. "That's where all the major stores were. And they were, it's within walking distance, it's [downtown] within a mile from here." To earn money, Uncle Ralph made a shoe-shine box out of an old tomato box. "It had a lid on it, and then I took an old belt and nailed it onto it, and I put it on my shoulder and carried it." Uncle Ralph and his friend would walk downtown, plant themselves outside a bar, and wait for customers. They charged twenty-five cents to shine a pair of shoes or boots.

As in most other major cities, Tucson's downtown was the nerve center for much of the city's activity in the 1930s and 1940s. In

Tucson, the era of downtown prosperity extended through the 1950s into the early 1960s. Following World War II, however, a confluence of factors contributed to downtown Tucson's gradual decline. First, the rise in automobile traffic made it increasingly difficult to find parking downtown. The year 1957 was a banner one for businesses in downtown Tucson. On January 4, 1957, the *Tucson Daily Citizen* included a twenty-one-page insert titled "Big Things Are Happening In The Heart Of Downtown Tucson." It contained feature after feature highlighting department store expansions, renovations, and new construction either underway or completed in downtown Tucson. The stories were akin to a collective expression of faith in the future of the downtown area by the Tucson business community. Why else would they make all these investments if they didn't believe downtown would continue to thrive?

Despite all the bluster, the growing parking problem in the downtown area was an issue. The twenty-one-page insert contains five articles devoted to parking. Holden Olsen, chairman of the Parking and Traffic Committee for the Tucson Retail Trade Bureau, summarized the problem as follows: "Every person would like to park, without charge, in front of the place he is going. This is impossible because of the ever-increasing number of automobiles coming downtown, for which parking is desired. Because it is impossible, the parking problem has become one of our nation's greatest challenges." [39]

Some of the solutions proposed included building new parking facilities, roof-top parking at select buildings, a park-and-shop program, and a ride-and-shop program involving the local transit system. Aaron Levy, president of the Tucson Retail Trade Bureau, branded 1957 as a "year of decisions." In what turned out to be a accurate pronouncement, he stated, "We MUST evolve a fundamental plan for parking and traffic.. . . . If we are going to have a downtown for the future, we must provide for parking." [40]

The Suburbs

The second major threat to downtown was Tucson's burgeoning suburbs. A 1929 advertisement by Tucson Realty & Trust Co. illustrates how much of the area surrounding the El Conquistador was undeveloped land when the hotel opened for business in 1928 (see image next page). By the 1950s this was no longer the case. Tucson's suburbs expanded northward and eastward. Newspaper advertisements in the intervening years chronicle how real estate developers aggressively recruited customers to their subdivisions. Here is an 1936 advertisement for a one-day pre-sale of homes in the Broadway Manor subdivision:

> **NATION-WIDE BOOM IS ON—TUCSON IS
> LEADING THE BOOM.** The shortage of homes here is
> unbelievable—the rents are for millionaires only—the
> returns on investments in rental houses are higher than
> anywhere in the U.S., and going higher every day because
> people are flocking here from the "Dust Bowl," from the
> frozen blizzardy east and north, for education, health, rest
> and recreation. We have handled many large subdivisions
> over a period of many years and believe these lots to be the
> best buy as to location for a permanent home, or rental to
> winter visitors, or value for the money, that we have ever
> been able to offer. [41]

Tucson's booming population fueled the growth of the city's suburbs. As this happened, the city center moved farther and farther away from its downtown core. People in these suburban communities required venues for shopping, social events, and entertainment. With the rise in automobile usage and the attendant parking issues, it became increasingly burdensome to make trips downtown. The narrow, congested streets were a nuisance to navigate, and it was difficult to find a parking space. The combination of these factors prompted a need for shopping centers outside the downtown core—a need that soon instigated the construction of Tucson's first regional shopping center, El Con Mall.

1929 Tucson Realty & Trust Co. advertisement (public domain)

Victor Gruen

The issues for downtown Tucson, as the population grew and shifted, were not unique to the Old Pueblo. America's growing dependence on automobiles fueled the growth of suburban communities everywhere. The mass exodus to the suburbs, coupled with parking and traffic issues in urban areas, made trips downtown less appealing. As author Lisa Sharoun explains, "Prior to the great suburban movement of the 1950s, the downtown and main street areas of cities were vibrant centers of civic life.. . . Postwar [WWII] suburbia shattered this fragile co-existence and created a physical boundary, which was to define American behavior for many years to come." [42]

But life in the suburbs wasn't perfect either. The suburbs afforded more space and privacy for people to raise their families, but this new living environment lacked the opportunities for social gatherings and entertainment that people had experienced downtown. For all their newfound freedom, many suburbanites felt isolated and bored. Lisa Sharoun aptly characterized the 1950s suburbs as an environment "devoid of a civic heart." The lack of "a downtown atmosphere or community centers where families could meet and socialize" bred dissatisfaction. As Sharoun concludes, "The shopping mall entered as a welcome addition to this environment." [43]

The shopping mall, as we know it, did not exist in 1950. Shopping centers were on the rise, but the enclosed shopping mall was not invented until 1956. The architect responsible for inventing malls is Victor Gruen. Gruen's life is a characteristically American story of a European immigrant. His family came to America in 1938, following Hitler's annexation of Austria. Victor was born on July 18, 1903, in Vienna. He grew up amid the half-timbered buildings and charming village shops that characterize so many European squares. Gruen graduated from central Vienna's acclaimed *Realgymnasium* in 1917. He went on to study architecture at the Vienna Academy of Fine Arts, learning from famed modernist architects like Peter Behrens and Adolph Loos. [44] Before coming to America, Gruen designed several stores in the First District, the most exclusive shopping center in Vienna.

After emigrating to New York, Gruen found work designing attractive storefronts on Fifth Avenue in New York City. Gruen's design skills attracted a flood of attention. Following a string of successful projects, his meteoric rise in the world of retail architecture began. He landed offers for more significant projects around the country, some involving shopping centers. Drawing inspiration from the Northgate Mall in Seattle and his own designs for Northland Mall in Detroit, Gruen designed the world's first enclosed mall in 1956—Southdale Mall in Edina, Minnesota. Southdale opened on October 8, 1956, to rave reviews. Everyone, from local news teams to *Time* magazine, found something to marvel at. "Beautiful. Just beautiful," said Mrs. John C. Seaburg of St. Paul, Minnesota. [45]

Southdale Mall became the prototype for a new kind of shopping center—the enclosed mall. B. Earl Puckett, board chairman of Allied Stores Corp., had this to say about Gruen's signature creation: "Today we have something different in Southdale, which is destined to be a landmark in the history of shopping center development." [46] Puckett's statement proved accurate, as Gruen's enclosed mall went on to shape the retail landscape in America for the next fifty years. Southdale, says Lisa Sharoun, was "regarded as an ideal community space, superior to the declining, congested Main street areas in the old downtown city centers." [47] Southdale Mall ushered in a new era in retail. Due to its success, it "provoked a proliferation of shopping malls across suburban America and contributed to the decline of many inner cities and Main Street areas across the country." [48]

Joseph Kivel

B. Earl Puckett, the man who said that Southdale would make history, also made another prediction, but this one would be inaccurate. He said the places in America where shopping centers like Southdale would be built would be limited to areas with populations of 100,000 to 500,000, a characteristic that matched only twenty to twenty-five other cities. [49] Instead, malls went on to dominate the retail landscape for the next fifty years. On June 2, 1958, an article in the *Tucson Daily Citizen* announced that construction on a regional shopping center for Tucson would begin in the fall. "The center will be located on East Broadway, adjacent on the east to El Conquistador Hotel. A total of 70 acres of land will be utilized, 40 of which will be developed at the present time.. . . Joint owners in the venture are the Kivel Interests of Tucson and Magna Corp., developers of shopping centers and commercial properties in Utah, Idaho and Montana." [50]

The announcement was the culmination of years of shrewd investing and careful planning on the part of Joseph Kivel, a Tucson real estate developer. Kivel was born in December 1909, in Los Angeles, California. In 1932, he earned a pharmacology degree and opened a pharmacy store in Yuma, Arizona. Joseph moved to Tucson in 1936 to help run the Market Spot grocery store with his brother, Simon Kivel.

The Kivel brothers scrimped and saved to buy up real estate holdings all over Tucson. To illustrate Joseph Kivel's shrewd, frugal nature, consider the following factoid. Although he no longer worked in a pharmacy, Joseph maintained his pharmacology license as late as

1983, when he was already a multi-millionaire. "You never know," Kivel said. "I might have to go back to rolling pills someday." [51] Joseph may have moved on from pharmacology when he left Yuma, but his instincts in the realm of real estate development were just the prescription Tucson needed in the late 1950s. Joe Pesci, a former executive director and manager of El Con Mall, lauded Joe Kivel's abilities in this arena: "Joe's ability to forecast changing trends in real estate is uncanny," Pesci once said. "He has the knack of estimating market conditions years in advance and buying real estate somewhere in that area." [52]

Perhaps nowhere was this more apparent than in Joe Kivel's purchase of the property where El Con Mall was built. After buying and selling properties in Tucson for nearly two decades, Joe and Simon Kivel made their big move. On September 28, 1953, the Kivels spearheaded a deal to purchase the El Conquistador Hotel, along with fellow investors George Amos and Arch Fee. They acquired the hotel from United Hotel Co. of America, a New York-based company. In 1957, Simon Kivel, George Amos, and Arch Fee sold their stakes in the hotel to Magna Investment & Development Corp. of Salt Lake City. One year later, Joseph Kivel's true intention for purchasing the El Conquistador Hotel became clear: so that he could build a shopping center on the property. Joe Kivel had seen shopping centers going up with increasing frequency in Los Angeles and correctly predicted the need for one in Tucson. Once again, his instincts were correct.

Once Magna came on board, it didn't take long for Joseph Kivel to move forward with his plans. As reported in *The Mall Maker of Tucson*, "From the start, the Kivels [Joseph and his wife, Esther] and

Magna knew what they wanted—a regional shopping center on a scale never known before in Southern Arizona." [53] When the Kivel brothers purchased the hotel in 1953, nobody could have guessed that a shopping center was in the works. Yet, the site was picked for a reason. As Joe Kivel explained, "The site was chosen because . . . it is centered both geographically and population wise for greater Tucson." [54] Joe Kivel and Magna planned to incorporate the El Conquistador Hotel into El Con Shopping center someday. In the map below, you can see the hotel just west of the newly built shopping center.

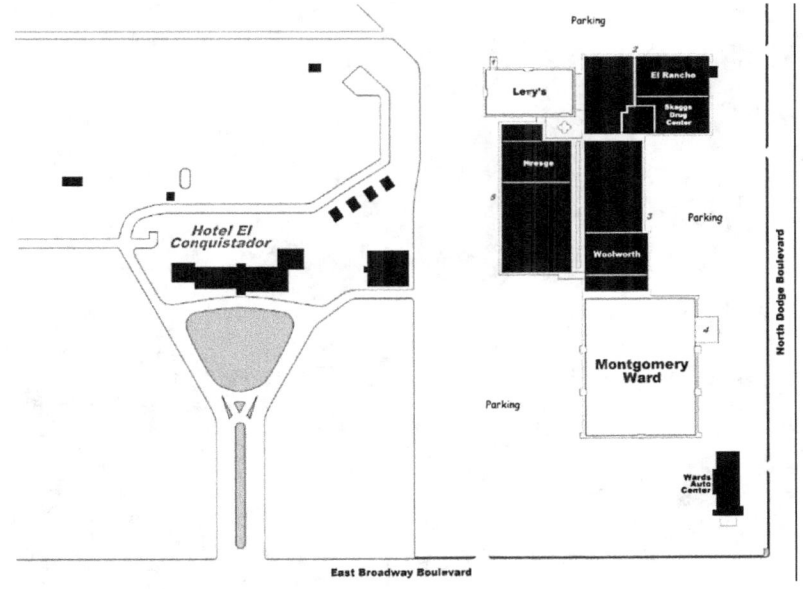

Map of El Con, circa 1961

(Image courtesy of www.mall-hall-of-fame.blogspot.com)

Following two decades of shrewd investing and real estate acquisitions, Joseph Kivel had the capital and business coalition that he needed to bring Tucson its first regional shopping center. In honor of the hotel to which it was adjacent, Kivel named it El Con Shopping Center. On March 10, 1960, a picture of a crane hoisting a massive steel beam on a construction site ran in the *Tucson Citizen* newspaper. While studying a set of blueprints, a foreman motions for the crane operator to move the suspended beam left. "El Con Steel Going Up," the caption reads. The photo captures the beginning of El Con.

First steel beam at El Con (© Tucson Citizen – USA TODAY NETWORK via Imagn Images)

El Con Shopping Center

El Con Shopping Center came to life on November 16, 1960. That was the day that Levy's department store, El Con's first tenant, opened to the public. Levy's occupies a special place in Tucson's retail history. The first Levy's store opened in downtown Tucson in 1931. Over the years, Levy's of Tucson developed a reputation for elegance and unparalleled customer service. Unlike many other cities, Tucson's downtown district was still relatively vibrant by the late 1950s. Automobile traffic and parking were becoming increasingly difficult, though. In January 1959, Leon Levy, acting president of Levy's of Tucson, announced that the company would open a store in El Con Shopping Center. "There will be parking for 3,000 autos at the center adjacent to Levy's," noted Mr. Levy. "There will also be other stores in the center." [55] Montgomery Ward opened three months after Levy's, on February 2, 1961.

The layout of El Con Shopping Center was uncannily similar to Southdale Mall in Minnesota. A store called Dayton's anchored the north end of Southdale Mall, and Donaldson's anchored the south. Similarly, Levy's anchored El Con's north end, and Montgomery Ward anchored the south. A pedestrian walkway with a double row of stores connected the two department stores. El Con was originally, and still was, an open-air mall. There was no central heating or cooling, and the mall was open to the outside at both ends. By August 4, 1961, eight additional stores had opened at the shopping center. Three months later, nine more joined, bringing the total number to nineteen. El Con management had plans for up to twenty-three additional stores in the near future. The mall was off to a fast start, and the shopping center's future looked bright.

El Con embarked on expansion projects in the late 1960s. Levy's had outgrown its original store, so construction on a new store began in May 1968. To the dismay of many, the El Conquistador Hotel was torn down to make room for the new store. The hotel had played an instrumental role in Tucson's growth, but financial difficulties had plagued the hotel from the start. One year after opening, the Great Depression hit. The hotel got off to a rocky start, and the pattern held. The hotel was purchased by the Goodman hotel chain in 1951 and then by Joseph Kivel's investment group in 1953. [56] When he purchased the hotel, Kivel intended to integrate it into the mall. This never happened. "We broke our neck to save the old hotel," Joseph Kivel said. [57] In the end, however, the El Conquistador hotel was torn down to make way for the El Con Mall's westward expansion.

On June 21, 1968, four days before demolition, the hotel hosted a rummage sale. More than 1,300 Tucsonans were present when the sale began at 6:00 a.m. The following day, a public auction took place for kitchen equipment and furniture left over from the hotel rooms and lobby. Roughly 4,000 people attended each day's event. Items for sale included dishes, linens, drapery, lamps, pictures, luggage racks, silverware, and wine glasses. Even a stack of outdated phone directories got snapped up. One gentleman bought a stick for five cents while a woman pulled weeds on the outskirts of the hotel to keep as mementos. Three days after the sale, demolition on the hotel began. "Today, the bulldozers are already beginning to demolish the once proud El Conquistador Hotel," Betty Milburn of the *Tucson Citizen* reported. "But not before many Tucsonians [sic] found some bit of the old place to treasure." [58]

Demolition of the El Conquistador Hotel, 1968 (Arizona Historical Society)

(Places-Tucson-Business-Hotels-Conquistador, F2, 44452, Courtesy of the Arizona Historical Society)

I was born and raised in Tucson. For those who've never been, Tucson is a multicultural city in southern Arizona situated in the desert. The "Old Pueblo," as it's affectionately known, has a small-town feel despite its size. Tucson is home to the University of Arizona, famous for its observatories and Arizona Wildcat basketball teams. For all the foodies out there, Tucson is a bucket list destination. In addition to being named a UNESCO "City of Gastronomy," Tucson is the birthplace of the chimichanga and home to Eegees, a tasty frozen drink available only in Arizona. The Sonoran Desert, where Tucson is located, is the only habitat for Saguaro cactuses, which grow and flourish there. Even in the heart of the city, it's not uncommon to walk out the door and encounter all kinds of desert animals, roaming the neighborhood, including javelina, coyotes, jackrabbits, and road runners.

Tucson has a spectacular skyline, surrounded on all sides by four mountain ranges. In addition to this, jaw-dropping sunrises and sunsets occur there daily—as well as the occasional rainbow during monsoon season. It's a wonderful city, and I'm proud to call myself a Tucsonan. All that said, no place is perfect, and living in Tucson certainly has its drawbacks. The most common complaint you'll hear is that it's too hot. For five months of the year, life in Tucson feels like the inside of an oven, and that's not an exaggeration. Average temperatures exceed 94°F from late May to mid-September. In July, the average high is 100°F. During the summer, outdoor activities are limited to the early morning or after sundown. For adults, this isn't so bad because most of us are working anyway. For kids and teens on summer break, however, that leaves several midday hours with nothing to do but stay inside.

When I was a teen, the solution to the heat was to spend the day at the mall. Tucson had four enclosed malls when I was younger, but the only one on my radar was El Con Mall in the heart of Mid-Tucson. El Con was Tucson's first enclosed mall. As mentioned, when El Con shopping center opened in 1960, it was considered an open-air mall, which meant it was not fully enclosed, nor was it climate controlled. That changed in the 1970s, and it happened in connection with the newly built JCPenney store.

The Beginnings of an Enclosed Mall

The new Levy's, four times the size of its predecessor, opened on September 16, 1969. Steinfeld's, a major department store in downtown Tucson, moved into the former Levy's building at El Con. Following a $500,000 renovation, Steinfeld's opened for business at El Con on March 29, 1971. Four months later, El Con added a fourth department store anchor with JCPenney. The store, located between the new Levy's and Montgomery Ward, held its grand opening on August 4, 1971. El Con's footprint was expanding. In addition to the original north-south corridor, El Con had the beginnings of an east-west corridor (see below).

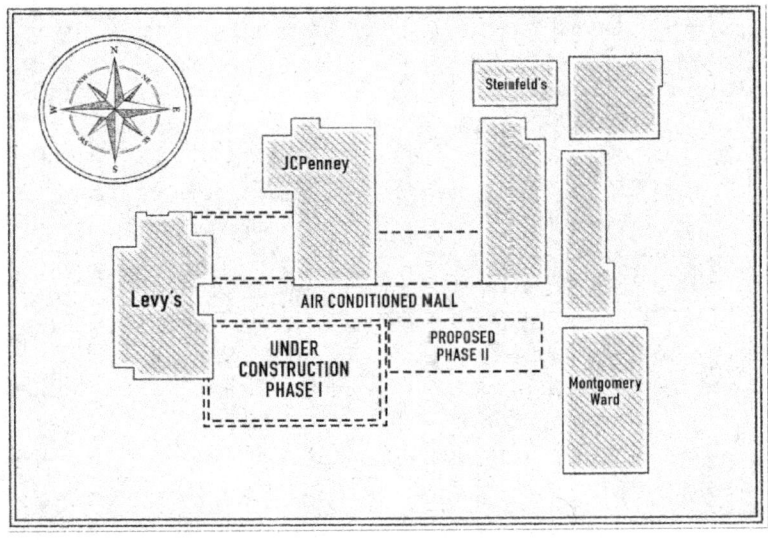

El Con Directory, circa 1971

Directory of El Con Stores 1971

—— • ——

1st National Bank	Kinney Shoes
Baker Shoes	Lee Optical
Captain Orange	Lerner Shops
Cele Peterson's	Levy's
Coffee Dan's	Mills-Touche
College Shop	Mode O'Day
Cox's Bake Shop	Montgomery Ward
Crescent Jewelers	Motherhood Maternity
Daniel's Jewelers	National Shirt Shop
Dave Bloom	Nu Art Photo
David's Shoes	Pipeline
El Con Barber Shop	Russell Stover Candies
El Con Book Store	S.S. Kresge Co.
El Con Cocktail Lounge	Sandy's Fashions
El Con Custom Cobblers	Singer Co.
El Rancho Market	Skaggs
F.W. Woolworth's	Sparkle Cleaners
Gallenkamp Shoes	State Farm Insurance
Grunewald & Adams Jewelers	Steinfeld's
House of Fabrics	Sumiko's
Indian Arts & Crafts	Tie Rack
JCPenney	Wohlfeiler's

The gradual transition of El Con from an open-air shopping center to an enclosed mall began in 1971 as well. That year, the first phase of construction began on an enclosed, air-conditioned section of the mall connecting Levy's to JCPenney. The plan was to connect both sections of the shopping center, north-south and east-west, in an enclosed, climate-controlled environment. In an advertisement for its tenth-anniversary fiesta, El Con announced its vision for the future.

> El Con Shopping Center is entering its 2nd decade of growth in Tucson. The latest expansion phase of the new air conditioned mall, connecting Levy's and the newly opened J.C. Penney store, is just the 1st phase of construction to take place ... A future development for continuing the air conditioned mall to the original El Con Mall has been planned. This phase will tie both shopping complexes at El Con together, as one 900 foot long continuous east to west mall, and the original 750 foot long north-south mall, anchored by Steinfeld's on the north, and Montgomery Ward on the south. [59]

In addition to these exciting developments, the advertisement mentioned that El Con had expanded its parking capacity from 3,000 to over 6,500. Unlike downtown Tucson, parking at El Con was convenient and free.

Goldwater's opened in 1977, joining Steinfeld's, Montgomery Ward, Levy's, and JCPenney as El Con's fifth department store. Throughout the 1970s, smaller stores opened in the mall's enclosed section. Advertisements from this period frequently promoted El Con's "new enclosed mall." The enclosure of the entire mall was a significant milestone in El Con's history. The project took place in phases over nine years, and by 1979 the entire mall was connected and enclosed. As an enclosed mall, shopping conditions at El Con would no longer be impacted by the natural elements. At any time of the year, people could walk into the mall and shop in a safe, dry, climate-controlled environment. By 1979, El Con Mall had become the "largest climate-controlled regional shopping center in the Southwest." An aerial photo taken in 1980 shows the extent of the mall's development—and a parking lot packed with cars (see below).

Aerial photo of El Con

(A.E. Magee, PC 177, F. 45, 1121, Courtesy of the Arizona Historical Society)

After two decades of growth, El Con had 117 tenants, and its standing in the Tucson community was secure.

Twenty-fifth Anniversary

A quarter century after it opened, El Con Mall celebrated its twenty-fifth anniversary in 1985. Although it started in November 1960, the mall celebrated its birthday each year in September with an event called the El Con Fiesta. El Con worked hard to develop strong ties with the Hispanic community in Tucson. The El Con Fiesta, therefore, was timed to coincide with Mexico's National Independence Day. For its silver anniversary, the mall extended the traditionally five-day celebration to eleven days. An advertisement in the *Arizona Daily Star* promoted the event: "During the extended Fiesta, El Con will join with the community in celebrating the historical, educational and cultural heritage of Southern Arizona and its very close relationship with Northern Mexico." [60]

El Con's twenty-fifth anniversary marked a defining moment in the history of the mall. El Con was no longer the only mall in Tucson. Ten years earlier, Park Mall became Tucson's second mall when it opened just three miles east of El Con on Broadway Boulevard. In 1982, Tucson Mall and Foothills Mall opened on Tucson's northwest side. Despite the increasing competition, on its twenty-fifth anniversary El Con remained "the favorite shopping mall and 'community gathering place' for the people of Southern Arizona and Northern Mexico." [61] El Con's silver anniversary was a momentous occasion in the history of the mall. From the placement of its first steel beam in March 1960, El Con had arisen to become Tucson's premier shopping center. El Con was at the height of its popularity, and a major celebration was in order.

Conclusion

The El Conquistador Hotel played a major role in the story of El Con Mall. Not only did the mall get its name from the hotel, but El Con also shared the same property with its namesake. The El Conquistador Hotel is an intrinsic part of Tucson's history too. Every year the hotel attracted visitors from the north to Tucson. As word spread of Tucson's mild winters and its stunning desert landscape, many visitors moved there to live. The hotel contributed to a rise in population, which, in turn, contributed to the growth of Tucson's suburbs. Increased automobile usage caused traffic and parking problems downtown, making shopping inconvenient. So, Tucson's urban center expanded beyond downtown, creating a need for suburban shopping centers. El Con Mall was created to address this need.

The opening of El Con in 1961 accelerated the decline of the downtown area by luring away customers and stores. In the 1940s, 1950s, and 1960s, downtown Tucson was the center of the city, geographically, socially, and commercially. By the mid-1970s, however, people avoided the downtown area unless they worked there. When I was a child, my parents stayed away from downtown Tucson. Back then I perceived downtown as dirty, run-down, and filled with destitute or dubious people. I hated going there. The mall was the place where people of my generation went to shop, socialize, and be entertained. As the first regional shopping center, El Con became the "place to be" in Tucson.

I knew nothing of the history of El Con mall or El Conquistador Hotel until long after both were gone. It was only after researching El Con to write this book that I connected the dots among related matters discussed in this chapter—the hotel, the rise and fall of downtown Tucson, Victor Gruen's work, and the contributions of Joseph Kivel, the man described as "the mall maker of Tucson." In telling this story, I hope I have shed light on some of the people and places that were pivotal to Tucson's early growth. This chapter also provided an explanation for the rise of shopping malls as the dominant retail model in America from the late 1950s until the early 2000s. The history of El Con Mall demonstrates in a microcosm a history of malls that played out in many other cities and throughout the country. Part of this history is still alive today at El Con, all thanks to a "Penney" saved.

CHAPTER 3

WHAT'S ON AT THE FOUNTAIN?

What's on at the Fountain?

Following decades of urban sprawl, many American towns and cities are bereft of vital public gathering spaces. They can be found, however, and many are organized around modern marketplaces. One great example is the Country Club Plaza in Kansas City. The magnificent, Spanish-inspired architecture is convincing enough to make you wonder if you have somehow entered a wormhole and re-emerged in Seville, Spain. The "Plaza," as the locals refer to it, opened in 1922 and was America's first planned suburban shopping district. In addition to stores and restaurants, the Plaza is overflowing with artwork, sculptures, cultural events, and over forty fountains.

With over 200 fountains in the metro area alone, Kansas City has earned its reputation as the "City of Fountains." The most well-known fountain in Country Club Plaza is undoubtedly the J. C. Nichols Memorial fountain, named after the famous real estate developer who planned the Country Club District. The J. C. Nichols Memorial is a round fountain on the south end of Mill Creek Park in the Plaza. It features four majestic horsemen, said to represent four great rivers of the world—the Mississippi, the Volga, the Rhine, and the Seine.

The J. C. Nichols Memorial Fountain is a big reason why the Plaza is more than just a place to shop. Kansas City's fountains originally served a practical purpose. In the late 1800s, the city built fountains to provide drinking water for people and animals. Over time, however, the fountains were used less for utilitarian purposes and more as civic art. Today, Kansas City's 200 plus fountains are an integral part of the city's identity. The J. C. Nichols Memorial Fountain is a key element of the magic that makes Country Club Plaza a hub of communal activity, the place where Kansas City's residents gather for cultural events, entertainment, and social interaction.

Unfortunately, not every city or town in America has a planned shopping district like the Country Club Plaza anchoring its community. My hometown of Tucson doesn't. That's where malls come in. Chances are if you grew up in the suburbs during the 1970s, 1980s, and 1990s, the mall was *the* primary gathering place for your community. The mall was where people went to see other people and be in the mix of things. That was the case in Tucson. If you wanted to experience anything like a town square atmosphere, the mall was the place to do it. While it paled in comparison to something like the Country Club Plaza in Kansas City, El Con Mall was Tucson's unofficial "town square."

Barbed quatrefoil shape

Like Kansas City, one popular element mall developers have traditionally incorporated into their designs is fountains. Whichever mall you visit, there's a good chance it will have a fountain. Fountains are a primary tool that developers use to attract people to malls and make them want to linger. El Con Mall had a fountain in its atrium, an open space in the mall with lots of natural light. Trees, ornamental plants, sculptures, and fountains are items typically seen in an atrium. El Con Fountain was located on the north side of the mall near Levy's. It was shaped like a barbed quatrefoil, an architectural pattern commonly found in Gothic architecture. A quatrefoil is "an ornamental design of four lobes or leaves . . . resembling a flower or four-leaf clover." Formed by taking the outline of four partially overlapping circles of equal diameter, the barbed quatrefoil is pierced by an inscribed square at the points where the circles meet.

If one thing captured the spirit of El Con Mall, it was the fountain. El Con Fountain was dedicated on June 25, 1964. Roughly 400 mall employees attended a breakfast on the morning of the ceremony, and later that evening the fountain was lit for the first time. For the next three decades, this stylish water fountain greeted visitors at the mall's north entrance. El Con Fountain was the backdrop for countless events over the years, including back-to-school fashion shows, auctions, dance performances, concerts, art festivals, puppet shows, and U of A pep rallies. Fountain Court, the area around the fountain, was home to some of El Con's most famous tenants, including Levy's, Steinfeld's, Cele Peterson's, the College Shop, Grunewald & Adams jewelers, Coffee Dan's, Cox's Bakery, and El Rancho Market. Together, the fountain and the stores surrounding it formed the heart of El Con Mall.

This chapter gives a month-by-month sampling of events that took place at one time or another at the fountain. We will examine twelve events, one for each month of the year.

What's on at the Fountain?

'Cat Craze Basketball Pep Rally: January 1984

The University of Arizona joined the Pac-10 Conference in 1978. Sometime in the early 1980s, I recall a poster in my friend's bedroom featuring two athletes walking on a beach. One was wearing a UCLA jersey, the other a USC jersey. The caption at the bottom read: "I mean, besides us, who else is there?" In the background, hovering above the unsuspecting duo, was a giant, pouncing wildcat with dagger-like claws. The image proved prophetic. In 1985, the University of Arizona men's basketball team emerged from anonymity to begin a twenty-five-year streak of NCAA tournament appearances, a feat surpassed only by the University of North Carolina with a twenty-seven-year winning streak. Since then, the Arizona Wildcats have become one of the top ten programs of all time in college basketball.

Wilbur the Wildcat, University of Arizona mascot

*(© 2025 Arizona Board of Regents on behalf of the University of Arizona –
used with permission)*

To build a basketball program with such a track record of success requires an active fan base. A legendary coach like Lute Olson helps, but players want to go where they're appreciated. They want a school with traditions and loyal fans. In the pre-Internet era, before smartphones and social media, fans expressed love for their team by pep rallies. A pep rally is an event where sports fans gather to build excitement for an upcoming game and support their team. On January 28, 1984, Wildcat fans were treated to a pep rally at El Con Mall for the University of Arizona Men's basketball team. Coach Lute Olson, members of the basketball team, the U of A pep band, cheerleaders, pom-pom girls, and Wilbur the Wildcat were all present for the 'Cat Craze pep rally at El Con Fountain. Fans were invited to take their picture with Coach Olson or their favorite player.

In hindsight, the 'Cat Craze pep rally at El Con Mall is a perfect example of life imitating art. The "Who Else" poster depicts a pair of perennial Pac-10 powers, UCLA and USC, reveling in their success. They have no idea that a new power, the Arizona Wildcats, is rising. When the 'Cat Craze pep rally took place at El Con, the Wildcats were unknown in the world of college basketball. Ten months later, on November 23, 1984, the team kicked off its 1984–1985 season with a home game against Houston Baptist. The Wildcats won 63–56, the first of several wins that season that propelled the Wildcats to an NCAA tournament berth. The U of A men's basketball program has never looked back. Though nobody at the pep rally could have guessed, the Wildcats were poised to begin their ascendancy into the ranks of elite college basketball. El Con Fountain had a front-row seat to Wildcat history in the making.

10,000 Frozen Cherry Pies: February 1964

I cannot tell a lie. I didn't know George Washington's birthday was a national holiday. I'm familiar with President's Day, which is the same as Washington's Birthday. George Washington was born on February 22, 1732. Congress established Washington's Birthday as a federal holiday in 1885. The holiday was celebrated on February 22 every year thereafter until the Uniform Monday Holiday Law, passed in 1971, changed it to the third Monday in February. After the switch, the holiday fell between Washington's birthday and Abraham Lincoln's birthday; the latter was born on February 12, 1809. People began referring to the holiday as President's Day in honor of Washington and Lincoln. The two birthday celebrations merged. Over time, the President's Day label usurped the two separately named birthdays of the US presidents (Lincoln and Washington) in the modern vernacular. To this day, though, the official name of the holiday is Washington's Birthday (Lincoln's Birthday also stands).

On February 20, 1964, an advertisement for a Washington's Birthday sale appeared in the *Arizona Daily Star*. It featured a town crier wearing a tricorn hat and a scroll announcing that the annual observance of the holiday at El Con was underway. As part of the celebration, El Con was selling 10,000 frozen cherry pies at a bargain price of twenty-two cents a piece. Four stores participating in the pie sales were located near El Con Fountain.

Every year El Con marked the holiday with a sale and a promotion of some kind involving cherries—cherry pies, cherry tortes, cherry cupcakes, cherry sundaes, and so on. The cherry-themed promotions were nods to the story of George Washington and the cherry tree.

According to legend, young George Washington was given a hatchet for his sixth birthday. Eager to try it out, he chopped down his father's favorite cherry tree. When confronted about the deed, young George famously replied, "I cannot tell a lie, Pa! I did cut it with my hatchet."

Having learned only recently of Washington's Birthday holiday, I must admit I feel cheated. By letting President's Day overshadow Washington's Birthday, Americans lost touch with a valuable tradition. I don't have a single memorable association with President's Day. Had I known about Washington's Birthday, things would have been different. The tradition of eating cherry pie each year on Washington's birthday used to be an act of patriotism that galvanized our nation. Every American could find an enjoyable reason—at least the cherry pie!—to pause and reflect on a hero who embodied our nation's values.

Tom Putnam of the US National Archives once observed, "[George] Washington was our secular role model—and celebrating his birth was part of the glue that united us as Americans." [62] When I think of the many shoppers who walked past El Con Fountain each February, cherry pies in hand, I realize how easy it is to let important traditions slip away. In his inaugural address on January 20, 1989, President George H. W. Bush highlighted the important work being done across the nation by community organizations—referring to them as "a thousand points of light." Through its annual observance of Washington's Birthday, El Con Mall played a small but important role in preserving traditions that kept the light of national pride burning bright. Don't believe I'm telling the truth? Ten thousand frozen cherry pies say otherwise.

El Con's Easter Egg Design Contest: March 1973

After 104 years in business, Art Instruction, Inc. closed in 2018. Headquartered in Minneapolis, Minnesota, Art Instruction, Inc. offered drawing and illustration training for aspiring artists. If the school name doesn't ring a bell, its advertisements likely will. The company's ads featured "talent tests," encouraging prospective students to submit drawings of characters like "Tippy," "Pirate," and "Tiny" for the chance at a scholarship. One famous graduate of Art Instruction, Inc. was Charles Schulz, creator of the Peanuts comic strip. During the Great Depression, Schulz begged his father to cover the tuition so he could attend the school. His father paid the fee, Schulz enrolled, and the rest is history. In addition to creating Peanuts, Schulz later became an instructor at Art Instruction, Inc.

El Con held many contests over its fifty-two-year run, many involving art. In the spring of 1973, for example, the El Con Merchants Association sponsored an event called El Con's Easter Egg Design Contest. Kids from ages five to thirteen were encouraged to enter. After picking up a blank entry form, kids decorated their eggs however they liked. Completed entries were to be turned in at El Con's First National Bank, at the north end of the mall adjacent to Steinfeld's. The bank was part of El Con, a stone's throw from the fountain. From the over 1,000 submitted entries, twenty-eight winners were chosen in three categories—Most Beautiful, Most Unique, and Funniest. A total of $410 in prizes was awarded to the winners. Perhaps more importantly, twenty-eight kids came away from the contest feeling proud of their artwork.

You never know what impact a small win may have on someone's life. When Charles Schulz submitted his talent test to Art Instruction, Inc., he was just another aspiring artist. The boost Schulz experienced after "winning" and gaining acceptance to the school fueled his desire to become a better artist. Once he landed his teaching job there, he met a fellow instructor by the name of Charlie Brown. So, the world has Art Instruction, Inc. to thank for Charlie Brown and the Peanuts gang. There's no telling what effect El Con's contests had on people's lives. I'd like to think that somewhere today, a winner of the Easter Egg Design Contest is using her or his artistic talent to do good in the world.

New Books for Old Sale: April 1985

If you find yourself walking a nature trail on Block Island, Rhode Island, keep your eyes peeled for hidden treasure. Scattered around the island in random locations are hundreds of glass orbs. They are replicas of glass floats, used by Norwegian and Japanese fishermen to buoy their fishing nets. Rhode Island glass artist Eben Horton creates 550 stamped and numbered glass floats every year and hides them on Block Island. Anyone lucky enough to find an orb gets to keep it and register it on a list published by the Block Island Tourism Council. People come from far and wide in search of the elusive orbs. Through this interactive public art project, Horton has transformed Block Island into a sought-after destination for treasure hunters.

Block Island Glass Float (Image courtesy of Eben Horton)

Take a ferry from Block Island to Narragansett, then drive ninety minutes on I-95 N, and you will arrive at Brandeis University in Waltham, Massachusetts. Named after Supreme Court Justice Louis D. Brandeis, Brandeis is a private research university and liberal arts college. When Brandeis opened in 1948, it consisted of a horse stable converted into a library. Eight determined women organized a network of volunteers to support library operations, founding the Brandeis University National Women's Committee (BUNWC). Ten years later, the Boston and North Shore, Illinois, BUNWC chapters invented a hit fundraiser for the library—the New Books for Old used book sale. Over time, the sale evolved into a nationwide fundraiser.

Here's how it worked. Each year, BUNWC chapters around the country collected, organized, and priced donated books for the upcoming book sale in their town. Local volunteers also staffed and managed the sale. The proceeds were donated to Brandeis University, enabling the library to purchase new books, hence the name "New Books for Old." Tucson got its first BUNWC chapter on October 28, 1952. The first New Books for Old sale at El Con took place from October 14 to 17, 1963. Each year thereafter, El Con hosted the popular multi-day book sale at various locations in the mall. By 1980, the Tucson New Books for Old sale was one of the biggest in the country. In April 1985, the twenty-second annual New Books for Old sale happened at El Con Fountain. It netted more than $15,000 for the Brandeis library.

Book sales are like treasure hunts. Sometimes you search the tables for something interesting to take home and find nothing. Every now and then, you come across a gem that changes your life. Robert G. Ingersoll once said, "There are treasures in books that all the money in the world cannot buy but the poorest laborer can have for nothing." Not everyone has the time or money to travel to Block Island for a real treasure hunt, but that doesn't matter. Thelma Frankel, former president of the Tucson BUNWC chapter, once identified an easy, inexpensive way to travel to faraway places: "Read!" she said. In hosting the annual New Books for Old sale, El Con brought treasures into the lives of Tucsonans for over thirty years by connecting them with books.

Mother's Day: May

Every year on the second Sunday in May, Americans celebrate Mother's Day, honoring the most selfless individuals who give everything to make our lives better. I have wonderful memories from childhood, largely thanks to my mom. My days at home followed an established routine. It began with cartoon watching in the morning, followed by game shows like *The Price is Right* and *Press Your Luck*. Beginning around 10:30 a.m., the soap operas started, marking the start of Mom's TV time. Even the commercials at that time of day were different. One commercial was for Calgon's bath oil beads. Each Calgon commercial featured a woman confronting common life stressors—traffic, an angry boss, a crying baby, a barking dog. Overwhelmed, the woman shouted, "Calgon take me away!" Moments later the woman was seen enjoying a luxurious bath with a look of serenity on her face.

I didn't understand that commercial back then, but I do now. A mother's work is never done. My mom stayed home with four kids all day. She never got a break from us. Even when Mom went shopping, we went along too. It takes a special patience to navigate grocery store trips with kids. The constant whining, pestering, and mischief making are enough to break even the strongest person. As a treat, Mom occasionally went shopping for clothes with her sister, Terry. My cousins, my siblings, and I went along with them. While Mom and Aunt Terry looked for clothes, us kids played hide-and-seek under the circular clothing racks until Mom and Aunt Terry had had enough. Then they'd relent and allow us to go to the store's toy section.

Shopping with kids isn't easy. It's no secret why the most requested Mother's Day gift for moms with young kids is time alone. El Con Fountain was once an oasis of peace for mothers who were shopping with their kids. By offering a diversion for kids, the fountain gave mothers the moment of grace they needed to collect themselves.

~ 76 ~

Moments before they were ready to go home, the tranquil splash of the fountain waters revived each mother's spirit. Moments later they find themselves reaching into their purse, then handing their kids pennies to throw into the fountain while making a wish. The mothers may have been on the ropes, ready to throw in the towel, but now that they had their second wind, they summoned the will to buy their kids an ice cream cone.

El Con Fountain was made for mothers. The fountain embodied the one thing moms wanted on Mother's Day—rest, not to mention a chance to make memories with their kids and the grace to keep moving forward. So, here's to El Con Fountain and all the "Take me away" moments it provided to mothers over the years.

Two Boys throwing pennies in El Con Fountain

(© Tucson Citizen – USA TODAY NETWORK via Imagn Images)

Sumiko's: June

June is the hottest month of the year in Tucson. By then the snowbirds have all left town, fleeing to cooler climes in the north. With average daytime temperatures of 102°F, you might think it's crazy for anyone to stick around Tucson over the summer. We're not cuckoo, though. The intense heat and summer adventures are all part of life in the Old Pueblo. Birds in these parts have adapted to the extreme temperatures of the season too. The roadrunner, a member of the cuckoo family, remains in Tucson year around. Over time, this fascinating bird has developed a number of adaptations to compensate for the high heat. Roadrunners decrease their activity by 50 percent in the midday when desert temperatures peak. Instead, they find a shady place to rest and save hunting for the early morning or afternoon hours. Finding ways to minimize activity during the hottest hours of the day is crucial to the roadrunner's survival.

Like roadrunners, one strategy for managing the summer months in Tucson involves indoor activities at midday. For many years, the four malls provided the perfect habitat for this survival mechanism. Rather than staying stuck at home or braving the outdoors, people hung out in the air-conditioned mall. With its splashing waters and mist, the El Con Fountain provided an oasis-like atmosphere that lured visitors from all over the mall. The stores in El Con's east wing undoubtedly benefited from the fountain during the summer months. One such store was Sumiko's, an oriental import and gift shop that specialized in Japanese goods. In addition to selling household items, native crafts, foods, soft goods, ironware, and hand-carved pieces, Sumiko's had a tea room used for tea ceremonies. [63]

Sumiko's was steps away from El Con Fountain. Its advertisements used the tagline "by the tinkling fountain." The store's crest featured the Japanese character "Kotobuki," which, when combined with two other characters, spells "Sumiko." Alone, the Kotobuki character translates to "lucky and long life." In November 1965, Sumiko's owners stated the store's goals in a newspaper ad: "To introduce and make available to Tucsonans, and visitors alike, representative items, both Traditional and Contemporary of Oriental Culture, primarily Japan; 'Shibui' in taste (Japanese-English dictionaries define 'Shibui' as simple, unaffected, tasty or elegant) . . . and in a price range to fit all desires and aspirations." [64] The ad identified the store's policy as well: "To provide an attractive, quiet store where shopping is a relaxing and pleasant experience and, to make available a selection of personal, household and gift items, fairly priced, to satisfy the most discriminating customer." [65]

I never had the opportunity to shop at Sumiko's, but it was the kind of store to which people gravitated on a hot summer day. First, Sumiko's was near the fountain. Second, Sumiko's had novelties from Japan and Asia that weren't available anywhere else. Third, Sumiko's owners demonstrated a level of thoughtfulness and respect for their customers that is rare in the retail world. Sumiko's carried a collection of wood-carved animals called "Tiny Treasures," with over forty varieties to choose from. In 1968, a newcomer to the collection arrived in the store: the southwest roadrunner.

Like the other Tiny Treasures collectibles, the Roadrunner was made from Cryptomeria wood. Cryptomeria, otherwise known as Japanese cedar, is Japan's official tree. Native American and Mexican folklore has long characterized the roadrunner as a symbol of luck. Tucson was lucky to have the El Con Fountain, a cool oasis, and stores like Sumiko's in which to hide out from the oppressive heat. Like a shrub that shades the roadrunner from the midday sun, El Con Mall was a refuge for Tucsonans during the scorching summer months.

Night Owl Sale: July 1968

Magic hour. To photographers, it's the time just before sunrise and after sunset when low-angled sunlight produces warm hues of gold, pink, and blue. Magic hour is a special window of time when the absence of bright light makes it difficult to overexpose or underexpose a photo. Pre-dawn and late-night sales are magic hours in the retail world as well. El Con Mall was no stranger to such events, as evidenced by its popular Night Owl Sale held each January and July. Advertised as "the great two-hour shopping spree all Tucson waits for," El Con invited shoppers to take advantage of store deals from 9:00 to 11:00 p.m. "Don't be caught napping," the ad read. "Join the happy crowd at El Con Shopping Center."

Before- and after-hours sales are unique shopping experiences, but have you ever wondered what it's like to work them? While everyone else is relaxing at home, store employees are hard at work, preparing for the evening event. I have never been employed at a mall, but I know what it's like to work retail late into the night. Before we were engaged, my wife, Nicole, worked at a home-specialty store called Table Talk. The store sold kitchenware, cookware, furniture, art, and specialty food items. Each year Table Talk completed an annual inventory at the close of business on a designated day. All employees took part in the process, which went on well into the evening.

I participated in two of these inventory events with Nicole. It was tedious work, but it was fun too. We finished close to midnight, and I'd leave the store feeling good about what we had accomplished. To be part of a team working toward a common goal was satisfying. I've always felt sorry for people who have to work on Black Friday, but many such employees report feelings of fulfillment similar to those I experienced doing inventory at Table Talk. For some it's the camaraderie of being in the trenches with their coworkers. "The best thing about working on Black Friday was having most of my coworkers with me," an Old Navy sales associate named Kristen says. [66] For others, it's the excitement of the work atmosphere itself. "My store makes it really fun," says Allison, a clothing store employee. "I've always loved all my coworkers and the work atmosphere we have created over the years.. . . Sometimes it doesn't even feel like work!" [67]

El Con Mall hosted one of its Night Owl Sales on July 21, 1967. Four stores down from Sumiko's, near El Con Fountain, was NuArt Photo, a camera store. For the sale, NuArt Photo offered an Optima 1-A 35 mm camera for the bargain price of $49.95. We don't know who worked that night or what challenges they encountered, but it's likely they didn't leave the store until sometime after 11:00 p.m. By then the mall would have emptied out, and the fountain, with nobody around, would have looked sublime. After two hours of chaos, the shift to that moment of calm would have made for a magic-hour moment at El Con. Having already locked the store, the worker from NuArt Photo would have rushed back, fetched his camera, and snapped a picture of the fountain with its glimmering lights before heading home for a good night's rest.

Back-to-School Fall Fashion Show: August

August is National Back to School Month. After a summer of fun and relaxation, the start of August signals that it's time to return to school. For kids, the first step to facing the music is the annual ritual of shopping for school supplies. El Con Mall hosted a back-to-school fashion show every year at the fountain. Students of every age, from primary level to college, could discover what was in style and catch a look at all the new outfits. The fountain was the perfect place to host the event, surrounded as it was by fashion heavyweights like Cele Peterson's, the College Shop, Levy's, and Steinfeld's.

I didn't know a single kid who enjoyed shopping for school clothes. Having endured it, however, why not swallow the frog and get the obligatory new school haircut too? In conjunction with the back-to-school fashion show, every August El Con hosted the MDA Cutathon. For the bargain price of $6.00, students could get a professional haircut from a stylist and member of the Tucson Cosmetologists Association. Proceeds went to the Muscular Dystrophy Association.

With the school clothing and haircut boxes checked, kids could move on to the more exciting part of the outing—school supplies. The selection started with the little things like Elmer's glue, scissors, a Pink Pearl eraser, pencils, pens, and a new box of Crayola crayons. If you were lucky, you also got a set of Mr. Sketch scented markers. I loved the dark green color, which smelled like apples. Next came the backpack, binder, folders, and spiral notebooks. These items required more discernment because they would be used daily for the next year. Do I go with the Thundercats folders or Voltron? Those were difficult choices. The toughest decision of all, though, was the lunch box. It was like your avatar for that school year. The style expressed something about you to all the other kids. You didn't want to be the kid showing up to school with a Bee Gees lunch box. The choice of lunch box was serious business.

No matter your lunch box tastes, El Con had you covered with its annual back-to-school sale. After the last item on the checklist was checked off, there were plenty of places in the mall for indulging one last summer hurrah. Perhaps Mom would spring for the Ringmaster's Special lunch at Big Top Deli. The mall-based delicatessen franchise was within a stone's throw of El Con Fountain. After lunch, you'd convince Mom to take you to Toy World, a few shops south of Big Top Deli, for an end-of-summer treat. After paying for the toy, Mom would decide that she'd treat everyone to an Orange Julius smoothie. This was totally unexpected, making it all the more enjoyable. As you walked past the fountain on your way to the parking lot, you'd have all your supplies with you and feel a bit more enthusiastic about the approaching first day of school. Confidence never goes out of style.

Sesame Street: September 1974

"Can You Tell Me How to Get to Sesame Street?" This is the title of the iconic theme song from *Sesame Street*. It's also a question kids have asked since the show premiered in 1969, and for good reason. Set in a fictional New York City neighborhood, Sesame Street is a welcoming place to which even the most disadvantaged kids in America can relate. John Stone was the show's executive producer, writer, and director. In 1968, Stone was approached by Joan Ganz, president of the Children's Television Workshop, to produce a new series that would "teach educational skills to preschoolers through sophisticated use of the television medium." [68] Stone agreed and spent the next year interviewing kids, parents, teachers, and daycare center workers to identify the needs of preschoolers, especially those from disadvantaged areas.

Stone's challenge was partly to create a setting all kids would identify with. He found his inspiration after watching an Urban Coalition commercial that had the tagline, "Send your kid to a ghetto this summer." The commercial featured images of a typical Harlem neighborhood: kids were running in the street, jumping rope, and sitting on a brownstone stoop. The scene was Stone's lightbulb moment. "All of a sudden it was so obvious," Stone said. "To a four-year-old who never gets out, that's where it happens, in the street where his big brother plays with the other kids." [69] *Sesame Street* utilized a rotation of real actors and puppets to teach kids letters, numbers, and the meaning of words. The result was a show that has kept children glued to the TV set for over fifty years.

One way to pry children away from the TV set is to bring *Sesame Street* to them. In the fall of 1974, El Con Mall did just that. From September 18 to October 3 that year, the *Sesame Street* show came to town. From 10:00 a.m. to 9:00 p.m., visitors could meet Big Bird, Ernie, Bert, Grover, Oscar, Cookie Monster, and eight other *Sesame Street* friends. The event was produced by Creegan Productions Company, an outfit renowned for its traveling animated puppet displays. "Our big thing is creating traffic builders in shopping centers, banks, department stores and the like," [70] George Creegan, the company's president, said. In 1974, Creegan Productions Company secured a license to produce animated figures of *Sesame*

Street characters for a traveling show. The event took place at El Con Fountain.

The characters from *Sesame Street* may be the stars, but the unsung hero of the show is the set itself. John Stone described the set as "a rundown neighborhood that people take pride in." [71] Among the more famous set locations on Sesame Street is Hooper's Store, a general store where the show's characters congregate frequently. In addition to offering diner-style food and a wide range of dry goods, the store operated an old-fashioned soda fountain. These amenities were part of what made the store a popular hangout. As David Borgenicht explains in *Sesame Street Unpaved*, "Hooper's Store is what all good communities and neighborhoods require–a gathering place. Hooper's Store is to *Sesame Street* what Cheers was to *Cheers*. . . . A place where Muppets and humans alike could go to get whatever they needed, whether that be a Figgy Fizz soda or a chocolate-egg cream (Hooper's specialty)." [72]

To that statement, I add one more fitting comparison: El Con Fountain was to Tucson what Hooper's Store is to *Sesame Street*. It was fitting, then, that the fountain was chosen as the site for the *Sesame Street* show when it came to Tucson. For sixteen days in the fall of 1974, Tucsonans had a clear answer to the question of how to get to Sesame Street: "Head to El Con Mall."

Cox's Bakery: October

As I write this chapter, the first hints of autumn are everywhere. There's a chill in the morning air and a softness in the afternoon sunlight. Every fall my wife and I look forward to Starbucks' pumpkin spice lattes. Since its introduction in fall 2003, this delicious drink has become so popular that it has earned its own acronym—PSL. In 2003, a group at Starbucks' Liquid Lab convened to create a seasonal fall drink on par with its winter offerings. Following months of experimentation, they created a drink made of steamed milk, espresso, a proprietary pumpkin spice sauce, and whipped cream topping. The PSL became an instant hit. Now, millions of people mark the PSL's release date as the unofficial start of the fall season.

In a 2021 *Insider* article, Hillary Hoffower cites a Johns Hopkins University study identifying the PSL'S comforting smell as the main reason for its success.

> Jason Fischer, a JHU professor of psychological and brain sciences and one of the researchers behind the study, told Insider that nostalgia for pumpkin spice is stronger than other flavor and aroma combinations because of the 'whimsical feelings of familiarity' that it summons up. It's a 'feeling that has been built up over the years as pumpkin spice products emerge to mark the change of the season,' he said. [73]

Before Starbucks, people marked the seasons with comforting smells emanating from a different kind of store—the bakery. Cox's Bakeries, a chain of twenty-two bakeries from the northern plains states, came to Tucson in 1959. George Cox, the chain's owner, was a hardworking man from Manitoba, Canada. He moved to North Dakota at age sixteen and obtained US citizenship. After saving $560 working as a gas station attendant, he opened his first bakery in North

Dakota. Cox and his family moved to Tucson in 1958. When asked what prompted the decision, he replied, "Well, it's obvious isn't it? I've been living here during the winters for the last five years—always thought this was a fine area for our bakeries." [74]

Tucson's first Cox's Bakery opened in November 1959 at Monterrey Village Shopping Center on Speedway and Wilmot. Four years later, on September 26, 1964, Cox opened his fifth Tucson branch in El Con Mall. The El Con branch featured Arizona's first "FUL-VU," baking oven, which allowed customers to watch the baking process from beginning to end. By baking on site at each of his locations, George Cox was able to eliminate distribution costs and sell his bread at a low price. Using high-quality ingredients and eliminating spoilage deterrents and softeners, Cox's Bakeries were set up to move large volumes of product daily. The chain's motto was, "Our bread is made to eat, not to keep."

Cox's Bakeries' El Con branch was located near the fountain. Every day the bakery brought large volumes of people to the north end of the mall with standard offerings like white, whole-wheat, rye, cracked-wheat, and pumpernickel breads. The bakery also sold cakes, cupcakes, cookies, doughnuts, and hot-cross buns. Cox's Bakery also offered a number of seasonal items to make the holidays memorable. For example, in October 1976 Cox's advertised an assortment of Halloween-themed cupcakes, cookies, and doughnuts. The bakery offered similar promotions during Easter and Christmas.

Like Starbucks' pumpkin spice latte, Cox's Bakery at El Con Mall provided Tucsonans with an enjoyable way to memorialize the holidays and other important life events with its delicious offerings.

It's not difficult to imagine people making a special visit to the bakery each October to buy Cox's Jack O' Lantern cake or some other baked treat as a way to enjoy the season. American food journalist M. F. K Fisher once said, "The smell of good bread baking, like the sound of lightly flowing water, is indescribable in its evocation of innocence and delight." [75] At Cox's Bakery near the fountain in El Con Mall, both of those pleasures could be experienced at the same time. What a bargain!

Mini-Concert: November 1981

The wedding of Prince Charles and Lady Diana took place on July 29, 1981. Like many women, my mom tuned in for the royal wedding and related tea-spilling sessions in the media that followed. Sometimes I got sucked into watching because there was nothing better to do. In hindsight, the event provided one of my earliest brushes with class consciousness. I knew I was witnessing a world that I would never be part of, and I found it off-putting even at my young age.

Around that time, PBS aired a show called *Masterpiece Theater* on weekends. The show's intro was a classical song called "Fanfare-Rondeau." I had heard the song many times before, and it conjured images of royalty in my young mind—a jeweled crown, a scepter, a royal mantle, and a throne. Subconsciously, I began associating this song with the alien world that I encountered during the royal wedding. For this reason, I have avoided listening to classical music for most of my life.

On November 6, 1981, the Arts Trio of America kicked off the popular El Con mini-concert season at the fountain. There is nothing extraordinary to report about this concert aside from the fact that it was one of hundreds of free concerts that occurred at El Con Fountain over the years. From 1979 to 1980, Arizona Mini-Concert events took place downtown. In 1981, the concert series moved to El Con, "following the exodus of business, money, and people" leaving downtown for the suburbs. [76] A joint venture of the El Con Merchants Association and the Arizona Mini-Concert Committee, El Con's Mini-Concert performances took place every other Saturday at noon. They featured musicians of every sort, including brass quintets, barber shop quartets, bluegrass bands, bagpipe players, mariachis, harpists, cellists, pianists, and opera singers, among others. All the performances were free, and they took place at the fountain.

Pianist Ron Vogel gave El Con's inaugural mini-concert performance on January 13, 1981. In attendance was Lawrence W. Cheek, music critic for the *Tucson Citizen*. He described the scene as follows:

> The pianist wore a brown velvet coat. The fountain pool was surrounded by resplendent poinsettias, and its water was the color of Liv Ullman's eyes. The misty, delicate tracery of Chopin's Berceuse floated like a wisp over the lightly rippling water. Across the pool, one young woman munched a Magoo burger, and another sucked on a Slush Puppie. Thus did culture meet Suburbia yesterday. [77]

Perhaps, like me, you detect a hint of snobbery in Cheek's characterization of the event. Unfortunately, it's a symptom of the stuffiness and self-importance that drives people away from concert hall performances. Afterwards, Vogel was asked how it felt to play a serious recital in a shopping mall. "Fine," he replied. "The atmosphere is bright and shiny—better than a stuffy concert hall." [78]

Ron Vogel's brown velvet coat is the perfect symbol of El Con's mini-concert series. The brown color suggests earthiness and humility while the velvet imparts an air of nobility and refinement. Through El Con's unassuming mini-concerts, Tucsonans were provided an opportunity to enjoy free musical performances worthy of a king. On November 15, 2022, a string quintet from the Tucson Symphony Orchestra came to play at the school where I teach. Among the handful of pieces they performed was Mouret's "Fanfare-Rondeau." As I listened, I drifted back to my childhood watching *Masterpiece Theater* on TV. It was the first time I had heard the song played live by an orchestra, and it lacked even a hint of stuffiness. I felt joy welling up inside me, as many must have experienced when attending El Con's mini-concerts at the bubbling fountain.

Ron Vogel's recital at the fountain

(© Tucson Citizen – USA TODAY NETWORK via Imagn Images)

Holiday Sharing Center: December

In December, the demand for memory-making opportunities skyrockets. El Con Mall was a great place for making holiday memories. Each year, the mall's festive environment combined with the energy from bustling crowds fueled Tucson's Christmas spirit. The typical holiday scene at El Con included mall-wide Christmas music, a twenty-foot Christmas tree, holiday decorations, fashion shows, artwork displays, concerts, and performing arts shows. The most popular event, however, was pictures with Santa Claus. Assuming your kids didn't burst into tears the moment you placed them on Santa's lap, these photos were potential family treasures. In 1980, my siblings and I took a picture with Santa at El Con. Santa sat on a bergère chair with a silver frame and burgundy upholstery. After waiting in line, we crowded around Santa and took a picture that became an instant family classic.

Speaking of classics, as a kid I looked forward to the *Rudolph the Red-Nosed Reindeer* TV special every December. This stop-motion animated feature by Rankin/Bass premiered in 1964 and has aired every Christmas since, making it the longest continuously running Christmas TV special in America. [79] Like a toddler taking pictures with Santa, I was terrified of the abominable snow monster in the TV special. The real monster, however, was Santa. Rudolph is a misfit reindeer with a red nose. Rudolph's father, Donner, forces Rudolph to hide his nose by wearing a false one. When Rudolph's secret is exposed during sleigh team tryouts, Rudolph is mocked by his peers. Santa arrives in time to witness Rudolph being humiliated, but instead of coming to Rudolph's rescue, Santa shames him as well. Not a good look for Father Christmas.

Although Rudolph is the protagonist, the story's real hero is a character named King Moonracer, a winged lion who rules the Island of Misfit Toys. As explained by its official sentry, Charlie-in-the-Box, the Island of Misfit toys is a place where abandoned toys are given a second chance. "Every night he [King Moonracer] searches the entire Earth," Charlie explains. "When he finds a misfit toy, one that no little girl or boy loves, he brings it here to live on this island till someone wants it." Unlike Santa, who only accepts Rudolph when it's clear that Rudolph's luminescent nose can save Christmas, King Moonracer values the misfit toys in their broken state. Whereas Santa behaves like a bully and uses others for his selfish ends, King Moonracer demonstrates the characteristics of a true servant leader. He puts the needs of others before his own.

El Con's pictures with Santa event often took place at the fountain. A few feet from the fountain was the College Shop, one of El Con's first tenants. The College Shop closed in 1986 and the vacant store was used for El Con's Holiday Sharing Center. This popular non-profit coordinated gifts of food boxes and toys to thousands of local families during the holidays. The Holiday Sharing Center collected donations of money, canned goods, clothing, household items, and toys to distribute to families in need. The Center relied on the generosity of its donors, from local businesses to kids offering change from their piggy banks. Its success also depended on the tireless work of hundreds of volunteers, like the Martins. This couple volunteered for four years in a row, "an experience they said continually brings home the true meaning of the holidays." [80]

The Holiday Sharing Center is something El Con can be proud of. Each year, in the shadow of Santa's chair by the fountain, the Center went about the business of helping local families during the holidays. "In the season of celebration and bounty, one of the greatest sources of satisfaction can be sharing our bounty with others," the *Arizona Daily Star's* Colette Bancroft wrote. "One of the easiest ways to do so is through the Holiday Sharing Center … in El Con Mall." [81] Each December, an army of volunteers and donors contributed their time, money, and effort to the Center. Following the example of King Moonracer, they sought no acknowledgement for the good they accomplished. Their reward was in giving to others, which is the true meaning of Christmas.

Conclusion

Each year on Thanksgiving night, Country Club Plaza in Kansas City features a lighting ceremony for the annual Plaza Lights event. More than eighty miles of Christmas lights are strung about the buildings of the shopping center. For over ninety years, Plaza Lights has kicked off the Christmas season. The popular event draws tens of thousands of people to the Plaza to see the colorful lights, shop, eat, and to be a part of the festivities. Kansas City's residents can go anywhere to shop or see Christmas lights, but they choose the Plaza because it's a central gathering place for their community. Popular events like Plaza Lights illustrate the important role that shopping centers still play in community building.

Before El Con opened in 1960, Tucson had become a city without a center. The rise in automobile usage made parking downtown difficult, discouraging people from visiting. Combined with a nationwide exodus to the suburbs, this contributed to the decline of downtown Tucson. Urban sprawl resulted in people moving away from the city center. As the downtown's influence waned, people became isolated because the suburbs lacked places for community members to congregate. When El Con Shopping Center opened in 1960, it provided the central gathering place that Tucsonans were looking for. This is precisely what Victor Gruen, "father of the shopping mall," envisioned for his shopping centers.

When Gruen formulated his vision for shopping centers, he sought to replicate the thriving community he experienced as a boy in Vienna. To achieve this, Gruen had to find a way to make malls more than just places to shop. Malls had to be places to sample bread, see a movie, hang out, enjoy coffee with a friend, do your banking, buy a Thanksgiving turkey, and so on. Stores play an important role in luring people to the mall, but getting people to stick around is another matter. For a mall to fulfill its role as an informal town square, it must provide opportunities for people to linger. Enter fountains. Fountains were an element of Viennese life that Gruen built into his mall designs. People enjoy being immersed in beauty, and fountains create the kind of atmosphere that attracts people and encourages lingering.

The J. C. Nichols Memorial Fountain is one reason why Country Club Plaza in Kansas City has become more than a shopping center. Similarly, El Con fountain played a role in making El Con Mall the community gathering place for Southern Arizona. The fountain quickly became the go-to spot for community events at the mall. When El Con Mall was in its prime, you would be hard pressed to find a week where something wasn't happening at the fountain. By the tinkling water, crowds gathered to rest, socialize, people watch, enjoy a performance, or simply take in the surroundings. Some of my earliest memories of the mall involve moments at El Con Fountain. As a young boy, I recall visiting that light-filled space with my parents and brother to throw pennies into the water, according to the time-honored tradition.

El Con Fountain, July 1974 (Copyright Arizona Daily Star)

Nothing embodied the town square nature of El Con Mall better than the fountain. Like the J. C. Nichols Memorial Fountain, El Con Fountain had a lot to do with the mall becoming the place to be in Tucson. The fountain wasn't extravagant, but its graceful outline gave the mall an element of understated refinement. I find it appropriate that El Con Fountain was built in the shape of a barbed quatrefoil, a common architectural feature in cathedrals throughout the world. The four lobes of the quatrefoil radiate from a common center. As the symbolic heart of the mall, the fountain was at the center of all the activities and events that made El Con the central gathering place in Tucson. The delightful splashing of its water embodied the pulse of vitality that El Con Mall brought to the city. Though events were not restricted to this area, the fountain's vital energy spilled over to the rest of the mall, making El Con a place where many Tucsonans came to spend the day.

Sadly, El Con Fountain was removed sometime in the mid 1980s to make room for a food court. The area the fountain once occupied was renamed "Fountain Court" in its honor. Fittingly, El Con continued staging events at Fountain Court until the northeast wing of the mall was demolished in 1998 to make room for a new Century 20 theater. When the fountain was torn down, El Con Mall lost an important part of its history. More importantly, Tucsonans lost a key part of what made El Con the central gathering place in Tucson. When the fountain went away, much of the magic that made El Con such a special place disappeared with it.

CHAPTER 4

GHOST DIRECTORY

Ghost Directory

"Remember this?" Ever receive texts that start with those two words? I get them often from my brother, Alex. They're often followed by pictures or videos of toys, commercials, cartoons, TV shows, or movies that we experienced as kids in the 1980s. Alex and I are proud members of Generation X, the demographic born between 1965 and 1980. As of 2023, this entire generational cohort has entered middle age, with the youngest Gen Xers being at least forty-two years old. Turning forty is a significant milestone, and it's common for people that age to experience nostalgia for their youth. One way to relive the good old days is by reminiscing about things you did when you were younger.

Another way is to revisit special places, and for Gen Xers, few places were more beloved than the mall.

The mall played a significant role in many Gen Xers' childhood and adolescent years. After our parents dropped us off, Alex and I used to spend the whole day at the mall with our friends. We'd play video games, watch movies, shop, eat, and skateboard. For Alex and me, the mall was more than just a place to shop; it was our hangout. With a few bucks we could entertain ourselves for hours. In *America at the Mall*, author Lisa Scharoun states, "The mall is a place where, unfettered from the overt control of adults, teens can work out their identity and place in society." [82] A crucial part of adolescence is the process of uncovering scattered clues about who we are—our strengths, weaknesses, interests, desires, talents, values, beliefs, and goals. For many Gen Xers, much of this identity-clarifying process happened at the mall.

Shopping, however, remains the primary reason people go to malls, and for that you need stores—lots and lots of them. On average, regional malls occupy 590,000 square feet of space and host between forty to eighty stores. At the height of its popularity in the 1980s, El Con Mall boasted 130 stores spread out over 1.4 million square feet of space. That was during the golden age when over 1,000 new malls a year were being built. Due to their size, malls use directories to help shoppers find their way around. A directory is like a map, showing the name and location of every store. Without directories, shoppers get confused and lost.

When I began researching this book, one of the first things I looked for was an old directory of El Con Mall. I searched everywhere, but the only thing I could find was an incomplete directory from the 1990s. It did me little good because it lacked a key to identify the store names. This was a problem because over time I'd forgotten the names of many stores. After nearly a year of searching, I found a 1981-era directory of the mall in the *Tucson Citizen* newspaper. It contained a diagram of El Con and the names and locations of all 119 stores. Locating this directory was like finding buried treasure. As I perused the list of store names, a flood of memories came rushing back. (see list next page).

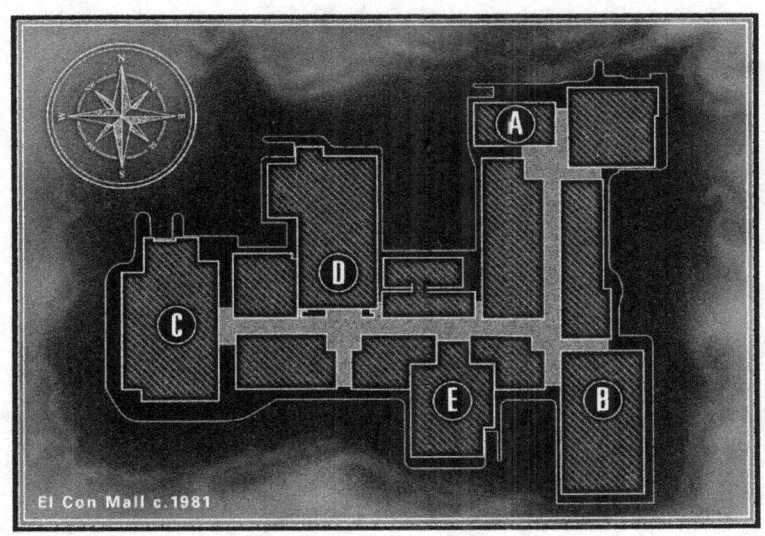

El Con Mall c.1981

Directory of El Con Stores

Athlete's Foot
Baker's Shoes
Bel Aire
Big Dipper
Big Top Deli
Body & Soul
Brown Bag, The
Card America
Carousel Snack Bar
Cele Peterson's
Chess King
Coach House Gifts
College Shop
Cookie Connection
Hot Doggies
Cooper's Western Wear
County Seat
Craftworks
Dalton, B. Books
Daniel's Jewelers
Dave Bloom & Sons
Eagledancer
El Con Barber
El Con Book Store
El Con Cocktail
El Con Custom Cobbler
El Con Merchants Association
El Con Six Theatres
Farrell's Ice Cream Parlour
Fashion Conspiracy
First Federal Savings
First Interstate bank #1
First Interstate bank #2

Florsheim Shoes
Food Giant
Foxmoor Casuals
Frederic W. Rubel Jewelers
Gallenkamp Shoes
Game Keeper, The
Gap, The
General Nutrition
Gilbert's Fashions
Goldmine
Goldwaters
Great Expectations
Grunewald & Adams
Hardy Shoes
Helzberg Diamonds
Herbert Hall, J.
Hi-Health
Hot Sams Pretzels
House of Fabrics/Singer
Indian Arts & Crafts
Inspiration
Jeans West
Kinney Shoes
Lederman Piano & Organ
Lee Optical
Lerner Shops
Levy's
Life Uniform
Limited, The
Lynn's Hallmark
Merle Norman Cosmetics
Merry Go Round
Michael's Buster Brown
Mills Touche
Montgomery Ward
Morrows Nut House
Motherhood Maternity
Musicland
National Shirt Shop
Naturalizer Shoes
Nu Art Photo
Orange Julius

Oshman's Sporting Goods
Pearl Vision
Penny, J.C.
Person to Person
Phone Center Store
Pisa Pizza
Radio Shack
Rainey's Luggage
Record Bar
Red Eye
Regal Shows
Russell Stover Candy
Salad Kitchen
Schroeder's Organs & Pianos
Size 5.7.9 Shops
Skaggs Drug Center
Sparkle Cleaners
Spencer Gifts
Stamina
Steinfeld's
Stride Rite
Swiss Colony
Tequila Mockingbird
Things Remembered
Thom McAns
Tinder Box
Topps & Trowsers
Toy World
T-Shirts Plus
United Jewelers
V.I.P. Coachroom
Waldenbooks
Walters & Sons Goldsmiths
Wicks'N'Sticks
Wild Pair
Wohlfeilers
Woods Hallmark
Woolworth's, F.W.
World Imports
Yodel Yogurt
Zales Jewelers
Zarfas Luggage & Gifts

In this chapter, you will experience El Con Mall in the 1980s through the eyes of Generation X. You will visit fourteen stores at the mall between 1980 and 1990. By the end of this chapter, you will see that Generation X left its mark on the mall in more ways than one.

Montgomery Ward

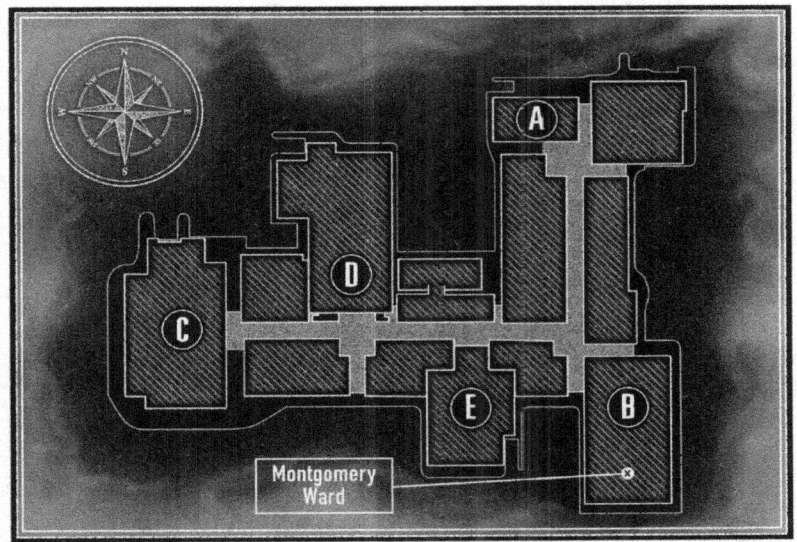

Montgomery Ward held its grand opening in El Con on February 2, 1961. On the morning of the event, a mob of shoppers converged on El Con, causing a traffic jam. The *Citizen* newspaper reported an estimated 20,000 cars inched through the section of Broadway between Country Club and Alvernon. Police Captain Thomas Rickel described the traffic jam as "the biggest I've seen at a store opening." [83] El Con parking lot, which had a 3,000-vehicle capacity, was packed all morning, forcing shoppers to park up to a half-mile away. The crowds continued all day, and 40,000 shoppers attended the store opening by day's end. Montgomery Ward executives said it was the biggest turnout of all the new stores in its western region.

At 154,122 square feet, Montgomery Ward was El Con's largest store when it opened. It offered various services, including a ten-car automotive service shop, an optometry shop, a snack bar, and a customer accommodation center. The *Star* newspaper described the building's modern look:

> The all-new look at Ward's is apparent from the exterior of the building which features "sunburst" stone panels accented with an attractive geometrically designed porcelain enamel façade, to the interior of the new store which is as modern as any found in the country. More than 25 harmonious pastel color tones decorate the walls and décor treatment of the store's 42 individual departments. [84]

Two years prior, the chairman of the board, John A. Barr, announced a national multi-million-dollar expansion and renovation program for the company. The El Con location was the fortieth store that opened under this expansion program. E. E. Pederson, the regional general manager, identified the Tucson location as "one of the key projects" in the program. "We have tried to create a store which everyone will find to be a convenient and comfortable place to shop, and one that will be an asset to the community," [85] Pederson said.

When I started shopping at Montgomery Ward with my parents in the early 1980s, the store was twenty years old. My parents usually shopped at discount stores like K-mart, Woolco, and Target. They only shopped at El Con department stores for big purchases when a windfall allowed for expensive home-improvement purchases such as new furniture for the living room, updated decor for our bedrooms, or a new stereo system. My parents liked JCPenney and Montgomery Ward but preferred the latter for big purchases. Montgomery Ward had an old-fashioned charm that appealed to their generation.

My favorite Montgomery Ward purchase was a large color TV. My family had two small TV sets when I was a kid, one color and the other black and white. Each set had two channel knobs, one for VHF and another for UHF. I never figured out how to use the UHF knob, but the VHF knob accessed the TV channels. The knob made clicking sounds when we changed stations. The TV also had a focus dial, which we turned to enhance picture quality. If we turned the VHF knob to a blank channel, the screen filled with static snow, and the speakers hissed.

The color TV set was the main one my family used. I watched several great shows on this TV set during my pre-school years, including *Captain Kangaroo, The Electric Company, Mister Rogers' Neighborhood, Sigmund and the Sea Monsters, Land of the Lost, Little House on the Prairie,* and *Battlestar Galactica.* When I started school, my viewing habits changed. Shows I watched during this time were *The Greatest American Hero, Knight Rider, Voyagers!, The A-Team,* and *Wizards and Warriors.* My favorite, however, was *The Incredible Hulk.*

Years before the Marvel Cinematic Universe achieved international fame, superhero movies and TV shows existed. By 1980, Superman, Batman, and Spiderman each had TV shows and films, but none were as good as *The Incredible Hulk* TV series. Perfect casting, great acting, and a compelling story made it must-see TV when it debuted in 1978. In the show, Bill Bixby plays a scientist named Dr. Bruce Banner. Intense exposure to gamma radiation changed Banner's body chemistry. Thereafter, every time Banner got angry, he transformed into a green monster named the Incredible Hulk, played by former bodybuilder Lou Ferrigno.

Like most viewers, each episode I eagerly anticipated Dr. Banner's transformation into the Hulk. The special effects used to create the Hulk haven't aged well, but they were effective for that time. Without computer-generated imagery, the show's creators had to rely on rubber prosthetics, green paint, and a wig to make the Hulk. The true strength of this show was the compelling storyline. The writers did the impossible: They made a serious show about a grunting superhero that appealed to young and mature audience members alike.

When *The Incredible Hulk* TV series ended in 1982, our antiquated color TV set was on its last legs. The antennae had broken, so we used metal coat hangers as replacements to extend the TV's life. It worked, but the time had come to buy a new set. Cable TV usage was on the rise, as was the use of home gaming systems made by Atari, Intellivision, and ColecoVision. We needed a modern TV to get cable and an Atari gaming system, so my family went to Montgomery Ward at El Con to look for one. As a kid, big family purchases meant long waits in the store while my parents negotiated with a sales associate. This particular negotiation wasn't an issue because the appliance department at Montgomery Ward had TV demos where I could sit and watch shows.

My parents bought a twenty-five-inch color TV console, opening the door to all sorts of new entertainment possibilities: cable TV, Atari video games, VHS video movie rentals, Nintendo, and so on. Later that year, we watched the MTV premiere of Michael Jackson's "Thriller" video on our new TV. HBO had a standard movie intro in the 1980s that began with a fly-over of a typical suburb and ended with the chrome HBO logo in outer space. Thanks to this TV, we watched that iconic intro many times, experiencing the anticipation it generated for all the HBO movies that followed. I watched two of my favorite 1980s TV series, *Miami Vice* and *Robotech,* on that TV. I also played Nintendo (NES) games on that TV and experienced the satisfaction of beating the Mother Brain (*Metroid*), Ganon (*The Legend of Zelda*), Iron Mike (*Mike Tyson's Punch-Out!!*), Dracula (*Castlevania*), and Medusa (*Kid Icarus*).

So many wonderful memories are connected to that Montgomery Ward TV purchase. I wasn't alive when the El Con's Montgomery Ward store opened in 1962, but I can imagine how people felt. Thousands of shoppers drove to the new department store on opening day, filled with anticipation. Perhaps, like me, shopping for a TV with my parents in 1982, they left the store that day with something that enriched their lives.

The El Con 6 Theater

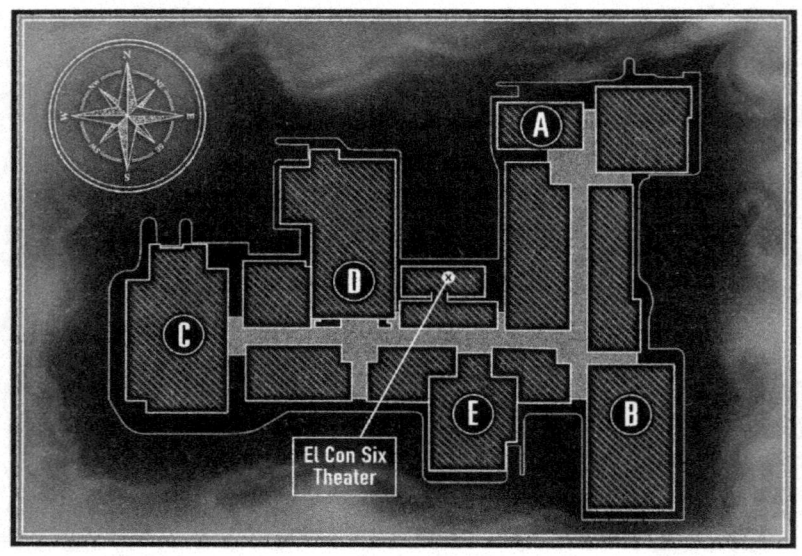

Like many malls, El Con had an onsite movie theater, the El Con 6. On September 27, 1978, the *Tucson Citizen* newspaper announced that TM Theaters, a local company, bought the six-screen theater complex being built at El Con Mall. "We are delighted to have the El Con theaters as we consider this the most desirable location in the city," [86] said Jeffrey Weiner, part-owner of TM Theaters. Competition for the coveted mall location was fierce. TM Theaters, a home-grown operation that owned thirteen additional screens in Tucson at the time, was thrilled to acquire it. "Theaters have been trying to get into El Con for 10 years," Weiner said. "The number one and number two chains in the United States competed for the right to build in El Con. Naturally we are very pleased to get the location." [87]

El Con 6, the first six-screen theater in Tucson, held its grand opening on August 15, 1979. Located between Steinfeld's and JCPenney, El Con 6 was a stand-alone building with no entrances to the mall. The 20,000-square-foot complex had a 1,500-person seating capacity, including two theaters with 350 seats, two with 250 seats, and two with 150 seats. [88] One of the larger theaters had high-resolution, 70 mm projectors and Dolby stereo sound. Another had the standard 35 mm projectors and Dolby sound. The front entrance had large glass panels, exposing the main lobby on the other side. The concession stand was divided into three self-contained sections to manage heavy traffic. Above the concession area was a fifty-six-foot-long mural painted by David Fitzsimmons that featured caricatures of movie stars. [89]

One of my earliest El Con 6 memories includes my parents and brother. A palpable energy pervades the theater. The lights dim, and all goes silent. The screen is black, and after a pregnant pause, the opening line of the story materializes in static blue text:

"A long time ago in a galaxy far, far away . . ."

Seconds later, a blare of horns, trumpets, and trombones erupts from the speakers. The film title, *Star Wars*, appears in bold yellow, accompanied by the London Symphony Orchestra score. A text crawl reveals essential backstory elements of the film, then recedes into the far reaches of outer space. The *Star Wars* main title song and the text crawl combine to create the perfect opening sequence for one of the best film trilogies in history. Alex and I share a seat as we take all this in for the first time, our eyes as big as saucers, glued to the screen. We are so small that our feet don't touch the ground. I was only four and a half, but the wonder of that moment has remained with me ever since.

Malls are the ideal location for movie theaters. Mall theaters beat stand-alone theaters because everything you need for a fun movie night—food, drinks, entertainment, and people—is available in one location. The best movie nights begin with a meal out, and El Con had plenty of dining options. In 1981, moviegoers seeking a meal at the mall had many options to choose from. Here are a few:

- Big Top Deli-Submarine
- The Brown Bag (gourmet sandwiches on homemade bread)
- Hot Doggies
- Orange Julius (smoothies, hamburgers, hot dogs, fries)
- Pisa Pizza
- Hot Sam's Pretzels
- Carousel Snack Bar
- Cookie Connection

Farrell's Ice Cream Parlour and the Territorial Room were options for people wanting a nicer sit-down meal. Tequila Mockingbird and El Con Cocktail Lounge were great places to get a drink. After the movie, people could drop by the Brown Bag for Indian Fry Bread or Yodel Yogurt for a sundae or a cone.

In addition to dining venues, malls have lots of stores—a boon for mall-based theaters because movie studios commonly license merchandise to market blockbuster films. An article on the Factual America website explains how film-related merchandise contributes to a movie's success.

One crucial avenue for boosting a film's success lies in its merchandising and tie-in products. From action figures to branded clothing, these items not only generate significant revenue but also keep the audience engaged well beyond the movie theater. Effective merchandising intertwines with film narratives, creating deeper emotional connections with audiences. [90]

Film-related merchandise increases an audience member's anticipation for a movie and also affirms their connection to it long after the show ends. The stores at El Con Mall carried every kind of movie-related merchandise. El Con 6 Theater benefitted from this arrangement because many mall stores carried products that doubled as advertisements for current films.

Some of the most memorable films of the 1980s created and sustained hype through the sale of movie-related merchandise, including T-shirts, posters, toys, action figures, and soundtracks. Having a movie theater and stores selling tie-in products in the same location was convenient. Millions of kids wanted E.T. dolls after seeing the Steven Spielberg movie. As the official E.T. fan club headquarters in Tucson, Levy's sold an acrylic fiber E.T. doll for $15. Two years after *E.T.* came *Gremlins,* a horror movie marketed as a family film. Every kid wanted a *Gremlins* T-shirt at the start of the 1984 school year, and JCPenney sold them for $4.50. *Ghostbusters* is famous for its catchy theme song by Ray Parker Jr. The "Ghostbusters" song, which topped billboard charts for three consecutive weeks, was available at Musicland and the Record Bar on cassette or vinyl. In 1986, *Top Gun* launched bomber jacket sales into the stratosphere. Foley's and Dillard's sold bomber jackets for just over $200.

El Con hosted promotional events for films too. The Tucson Boys Chorus sponsored a dinner benefit on June 17, 1980. Tickets cost $250, buying dinner for two at the Spaghetti Company restaurant and admission to an advanced showing of *The Empire Strikes Back*. The promotion also included a Darth Vader appearance at Levy's department store in El Con Mall on June 7. The lineup to see the iconic villain stretched across the entire second floor.

Darth Vader promotion appearance at Levy's Department Store, June 7, 1980

(© Tucson Citizen – USA TODAY NETWORK via Imagn Images)

"The 7-foot-tall Lord of the Empire walked slowly down the line of several hundred admirers who had gathered to meet him," wrote Dan Huff of the *Tucson Citizen*. "The archvillain mounted the platform next to the store's kiddie shoe department, which happened to be selling Darth Vader tennis shoes. Across the aisle was the infant's clothing area, where Darth Vader T-shirts were available for tots." [91] The event was a huge success. "This is a much bigger crowd than Santa Claus could ever hope to draw on a given day," [92] a Levy's employee said.

For me, seeing a movie at El Con 6 without my parents was something of a tween/teen rite of passage. Back then, seeing a movie indoors was not a given, as it is today. When I was little, my family went to the Tucson Five drive-in theater because indoor theaters were more expensive. A drive-in is an outdoor theater where you park and watch a movie from the comfort of your vehicle. The film is projected onto a large screen. Most drive-ins have a concession stand and a playground for kids. My family only went to walk-in theaters for special occasions, like blockbuster movies. So, even when I was older, I regarded going to indoor theaters like El Con 6 as a privilege.

I also associate El Con 6 with independence. Going to the movies without my parents was a big deal for an eleven-year-old. Alex and I regularly met friends at the mall to watch a movie. On those occasions, we arrived at the mall two hours before the movie to hang out. By that age, toys no longer appealed to us much, but we scouted the Kay-Bee Toy Store for Nintendo (NES) games. We played video games at Goldmine Arcade and spent our remaining time browsing Champ's Sporting Goods, Musicland, Athletic X-Press, and stores that carried clothing brands we liked, including Gotcha, Billabong, Jimmy Z, Stussy, and Vans.

This pre-movie routine made movies at El Con Six more memorable. Spending time at the mall increased our anticipation for the film, generating excitement that carried over to the movie itself. Half an hour before the film started, we bought candy at Woolworths. Our favorites included Nerds, Lemon Heads, Alexander the Grape, Cherry Clan, Now and Later, Pop Rocks, Sour Patch Kids, Swedish Fish, and Red Vines. With the money we saved sneaking candy into the theater, we had enough left to buy popcorn and soda at the concession stand. Before heading to the theater, we ate lunch at one of the mall restaurants, usually Orange Julius or Round Table Pizza. After the movie, we used the mall pay phones to call our parents for a ride.

By modern standards, El Con 6 was a small theater. It had personality, though. Just past the main entrance was the lobby, which smelled like buttered popcorn and felt like a cozy living room. The decor inside the theaters utilized calming shades of brown and blue. Nothing beat settling into our seats with a bucket of popcorn, a large drink, and our favorite candy. As the empty seats filled, anticipation for the film grew. Slide shows featuring movie trivia questions helped to pass the time. Then came movie trailers with exciting sneak peeks of coming attractions. When the lights finally dimmed for the feature presentation, we were in the right frame of mind to get the most out of the movie experience. This theater was a big piece of the magic that made El Con Mall special.

Toy World

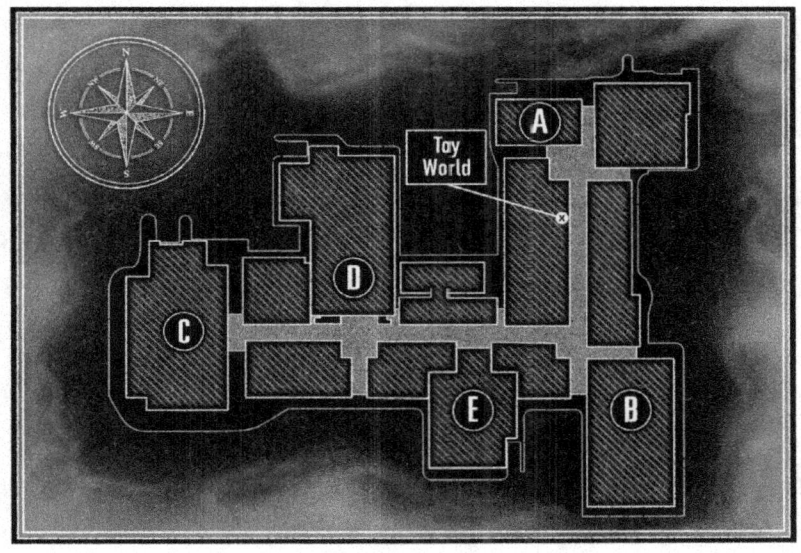

Few things at the mall brought a bigger smile to kids' faces than toy stores. Stand-alone toy stores like Toys "R" Us, Child World, PlayWorld, and Lionel Kiddie City were popular in the 1980s. Mall-based toy stores included K & K Toys, Circus World, and Kay-Bee Toys. El Con Mall had two toy stores at different points in its history. The first was Toy World, a store chain owned by the Santa Monica-based Wickes Companies. Toy World opened at El Con in 1979 near the fountain in the mall's north end. Some of my happiest childhood memories at the mall happened in that store.

My family rarely shopped at Toy World because specialty toy stores were more expensive than discount retailers. A price survey conducted by the Tucson Consumer Council in December 1981 illustrates the pricing disparity. After comparing the prices at over forty Tucson stores, Toy World's prices were above average for seventeen of the twenty-four toys sampled. The number of overpriced toys at Kmart and Woolco was five and three, respectively. [93] Since my parents' money went further at discount stores, Alex and I got most of our toys from Kmart, Woolco, Yellow Front, and LaBelle's. Dad and Mom treated the family to dinner at Bob's Big Boy, The Double L, or Gordo's restaurant every payday. Afterward, we shopped at discount stores, but once in a blue moon, we went to El Con instead. Alex and I scored unplanned trips to Toy World thanks to those rare payday excursions to the mall.

Our parents usually went to Montgomery Ward, located in the mall's south wing. Toy World was in a section of the mall that we rarely visited on the far north end near Steinfeld's. When Toy World opened in 1979, construction crews had just finished a $6 million renovation of the mall's north-south wing. The walk from Montgomery Ward to Toy World showcased those renovations. El Cons' new floors, white-and-gold terrazzo tiles with brown accents, shimmered under a polished finish. Oak-faced columns spanned the center of the concourse, each supporting two lamp post fixtures with globe-shaped diffusers. The glow of those lamps created a warm, cozy ambiance. As people neared Toy World, the El Con Fountain came into view, accompanied by the sound of splashing water. White lights inside the fountain gave the water a bright, ethereal glow. It was magical.

Toy World at El Con (Copyright Arizona Daily Star)

My Toy World memories illustrate why online toy shopping will never match the shopping experience in a brick-and-mortar toy store. The mall atmosphere, the people, and the sights and sounds inside the toy store are part of the excitement. When you buy something online, it's just you and the computer screen. There's nothing substantive for memory to root itself in. After more than twenty years of online shopping, there's only one purchase I would describe as memorable because it involved outbidding another shopper at the last second on eBay.

The Toy World store at El Con was a feast for the senses. Stepping into the store, a symphony of mechanical and electronic sounds greeted shoppers. The space was alive with sound—the turning gears of wind-up toys, revving noises from friction spark guns, the robotic utterances of a Speak & Spell, and the beeping sounds of a programmable Big Trak vehicle. And it wasn't just the sounds that captivated me. The jaw-dropping spectacle of aisles packed with every toy imaginable made it challenging to focus. Minutes after entering, when I'd had sufficient time to take everything in and compose myself, there was much to see and delight in, like box art. The box art for toys in the 1980s was exceptional, with lines like Star Wars, G.I. Joe, Transformers, Advanced Dungeons & Dragons, M.A.S.K., and Visionaries setting a high bar. However, my vote for best box art goes to Masters of the Universe.

The Masters of the Universe (MOTU) toy line became an instant hit after its 1982 debut. At a height of 5.5 inches, MOTU action figures were taller than typical action figures at the time. Star Wars and G.I. Joe action figures were only 3.75 inches tall. In addition to height, each MOTU character had the physique of a world-class bodybuilder. MOTU figures were ripped from head to toe, making other figures look scrawny by comparison. MOTU figures had cool accessories, too. Take Skeletor, a blue-skinned, skull-headed humanoid who was He-Man's arch-rival. The Skeletor action figure included a removable breastplate, a protective skirt, a Havoc Staff, and a Power Sword. Few toys at the time had this many accessories, making MOTU action figures unique.

Aside from its action figures, the MOTU toy line's box art was exceptional. MOTU falls into the sword and sorcery genre, which was hugely popular in the early 1980s, thanks to movies like *Excalibur, Conan the Barbarian, The Beastmaster, Krull,* and *Clash of the Titans.* Renowned artist Frank Frazetta brilliantly captured the essence of this subgenre in his artwork. The box art for MOTU vehicles, creatures, and playsets deftly mirrors Frazetta's fantasy aesthetic. Artist Rudy Obrero illustrated many of MOTU's most iconic box art scenes, including the artwork for Castle Grayskull, Wind Raider, Battle Ram, Battle Cat, Screech, and Zoar.

As a child, I gazed in awe at the box art in the MOTU section of Toy World. Obrero's artwork had a way of pulling people in. His illustrations played a key role in establishing the world that the MOTU characters inhabited. The action in each box art scene suggests a larger story operating in the background. It intrigues the viewer, making people want to learn more about this world and its characters. MOTU box art demonstrates why stores like Toy World were so intoxicating to kids. Like MOTU, each toy line offered colorful and exciting things to look at. Even if I left the store empty-handed, it was fun to go inside, look around, and immerse myself in a sensory wonderland. The excitement of imaginative play inspired by these toys was palpable, sparking creativity and joy during every visit.

Toy World wasn't exclusively for kids either. Toy stores attracted consumers of all ages in the early 1980s thanks to home video game systems like the Atari 2600. In 1972, five years before the Atari 2600's debut, Magnavox introduced the world's first commercial home video game console: the Odyssey. Atari released its first game console, Home Pong, in 1975. [94] It had one game, the video game equivalent of table tennis. The Fairchild Camera and Instrument Corporation released the Fairchild VES in 1976. It was the first home video game system to use ROM cartridges and a microprocessor. [95] The following year, Atari introduced its VCS console with the same features.

Being alive to experience the birth of home gaming was an unforgettable part of my 1980s childhood. Home gaming systems have dramatically improved since the debut of the Atari 2600 in 1977. Modern games offer graphics with cinematic quality, a far cry from the blocky graphics of second-generation consoles. Atari games may seem primitive today, but they opened pathways to a new entertainment world. Consider this example from my childhood.

The original *Superman* movie starring Christopher Reeve premiered on December 15, 1978. Like many boys, after seeing the film I wanted to be Superman. I did this by tying a towel around my neck and running around the backyard with outstretched arms. In 1979, Atari released a *Superman* game cartridge. In the game, players control Superman as he flies across New York, searching for pieces of a bridge that Lex Luthor destroyed. The ability to direct a character's movements on the TV screen with technology and player creativity had been unimaginable one year earlier. Atari created novel ways for people to express their imagination with each game cartridge.

Whenever I went to Toy World, I loved browsing game cartridges in the Atari section. Atari's eye-catching box art communicated the essence of the games through images. I liked Activision's box art the best. It was simple and colorful, and every game incorporated Activision's iconic rainbow stripes into its artwork. Activision designer Garry Kitchen created *Keystone Kapers* in 1983. The game takes place in a department store called Southwick's. The player's job is to prevent a store burglary by helping Officer Kelly arrest Harry Hooligan. Using the store's security system, escalators, and elevators, players guide Kelly through the store in pursuit of the crook.

Reading the instruction handbook, it's clear that careful attention went into the game's design. A creative opening monologue by Officer Kelly identifies the problem and what the player must do. Later in the handbook, "Those Dashing Men In Blue" explain how cops got their name from the copper badges police officers wore in the late nineteenth century. There was no practical need to include these historical details in an instruction handbook. The fact Activision did this reveals a high level of craftsmanship. Any player who scored 35,000 points or more could send a photo of their qualifying score to Activision. Players who did so received an official Billy Club patch, featuring Officer Kelly and Activision's signature rainbow stripes. Great memories.

Toy World toys inspired many nostalgic pastimes, beginning with toy collecting. My brother and I collected Star Wars toys. Our first Star Wars action figure was Greedo, the alien bounty hunter Han Solo shoots in the Mos Eisley Cantina. To help us tell them apart, Mom painted our initials on the underside of each figure's foot with red nail polish. From then on, Alex collected the good guys, and I collected the bad guys. It set a pattern for every toy we collected thereafter, including MOTU, Transformers, GoBots, M.A.S.K., G.I. Joe, and so on.

Alex and I had a few Star Wars spaceships—the Millenium Falcon, an X-Wing fighter, a Y-Wing fighter, a snowspeeder, a TIE fighter, a twin-pod cloud car, Slave I, and a Speeder bike. But most of our collection consisted of inexpensive action figures. Visits to Toy World allowed us to see the more expensive spaceships we didn't have, such as the Death Star space station, the radio-controlled Jawa sandcrawler, Darth Vader's TIE Fighter, the scout walker, the rebel transport, the B-wing fighter, the imperial shuttle, and the crown jewel of every dark side fan's collection, an AT-AT. It was also an opportunity to see the entire line of action figures and vehicles displayed together, which was an impressive sight.

Another nostalgic pastime indirectly connected to Toy World was cartoon-watching. Many after-school cartoons had toy lines, which wasn't an accident. Toy companies in the 1980s often used cartoons to market their products to kids. Cartoons also provided another way for Gen Xers to connect with their toys. At different points in our childhood, Alex and I watched *He-Man and the Masters of the Universe, Transformers, GI Joe, Thundercats, Silverhawks, M.A.S.K., Voltron, Tranzor Z,* and my favorite, *Robotech.* We had toys or merchandise (i.e., coloring books) from all these cartoons except *Tranzor Z,* the US equivalent of Japan's *Great Mazinga,* of the Shogun Warrior toy line. Cartoons provided backstories for characters and the worlds they inhabited, strengthening our loyalty to various toy lines.

The final Toy World-inspired pastime was imaginative play. Of all the toy lines in the 1980s, G.I. Joe had the best action figures and vehicles. G.I. Joe commercials were also the best at conveying how kids played with toys. After the opening animation, commercials would cut to a scene with real kids using G.I. Joe toys to simulate a battle with the enemy, Cobra. The play area was staged with props to create a realistic battleground. For example, kids would play in the sand when driving a tank in the desert or a backyard pond if the vehicle was a hovercraft. As they fought, kids spoke in the character of whichever action figure they were playing with. Destro's voice and manner of speaking are different from Cobra Commander's. Those commercials spurred us to use our imagination.

Sometimes rather than playing with toys, we used them to inspire the characters in our imaginative games. When I was a kid, it was typical for boys to engage in war play. Alex and I frequently played war at our house with friends. We divided into teams and set up bases, one in the front yard and the other in the back. The goal was to shoot or capture our enemies and take over their base. We used standard household tools for guns. Dad's Estwing hammer was a Uzi submachine gun, the gravel rake balanced between the ridges of our board fence was an M60, and dirt clods were grenades.

America was obsessed with ninjas in the 1980s. Ninja movies, toys, and weapons were extremely popular. During the ninja craze, we traded our machine guns for throwing stars made of paper, foam nunchucks from the Tanque Verde Swap Meet, and katana swords made from sawed-off broomsticks. We used white or black T-shirts, depending on what team we were on, to make our ninja masks. For inspiration, Alex and I based our ninja personas on two characters from the G.I. Joe toy line: archrivals Snake Eyes and Storm Shadow. Snake Eyes is a member of G.I. Joe while Storm Shadow sides with the enemy, Cobra.

This rival pair broke the number-one convention of every toy line: the bad guys are always cooler than the good guys. Whichever toy line we collected, Alex got the good guys, and I got the bad guys. My figures were superior to Alex's regarding their coolness factor in all but one case: the G.I. Joe toy line. Garbed in an all-black combat suit and face mask, Snake Eyes became an instant fan favorite. In addition to his mysterious appearance, Snake Eyes never speaks, never shows his face, and has a pet wolf named Timber. It doesn't get any cooler than that. Storm Shadow was a remarkable character too. But in this one instance, I begrudgingly concede that Alex's character was cooler than mine.

Like the fleeting childhood years, all good things come to an end. In April 1982, the owner of Toy World, Wickes Companies, filed for protection under Chapter 11. The following year, Kay-Bee Toys purchased Toy World as part of the Wickes Companies' reorganization plan to pay off $1.6 billion of debt. Kay-Bee Toys moved into the former Toy World store at El Con. For the short time it lasted, though, Toy World was a wonderland for children in El Con Mall.

T-Shirts Plus, Woolworths, and Spencer Gifts

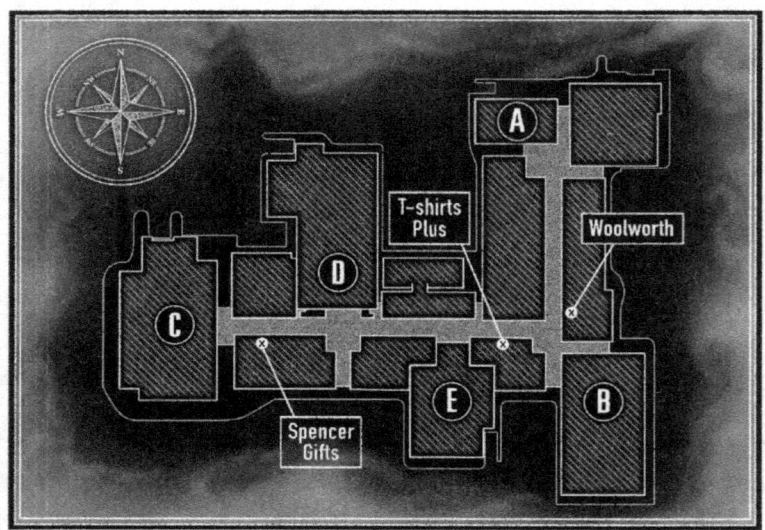

Three's Company debuted in the 1970s, the decade of my birth, and it still holds a special place in my heart. The show's premiere aired on Tucson's KGUN-9 TV station at 8:30 p.m. on March 15, 1977. Paul Henniger included it as one of his three top choices in the *Tucson Daily Citizen's* television log. He described the show this way:

> And yet another comedy series from the network which keeps coming up with winners in this field. Two young women are looking for a roommate to share expenses, and the roomie doesn't necessarily have to be female. In tonight's debut, they find their perfect candidate in their bathtub following a party—a young man who also just happens to be studying the culinary arts and promises he won't chase the girls. [96]

I grew up watching this show with my parents. *Three's Company* is a sitcom about three roommates—Janet Wood (Joyce DeWitt), Chrissy Snow (Suzanne Somers), and Jack Tripper (John Ritter)—who live together in an apartment in Santa Monica, California. Memorable secondary characters include Larry Dallas (Richard Kline), Stanley and Helen Roper (Norman Fell and Audra Lindley), and Mr. Furley (Don Knotts). Though characters came and went over the show's eight seasons, one constant was Apartment 201, where the three roommates lived.

Apartment 201 is the show's primary setting and a time capsule of the 1970s. Consider these elements of the apartment interior—earthy color tones of yellow, orange, brown, and beige; arched wooden front door; wicker furniture, indoor plants, and macrame wall hangings; patterned sofa and floor-to-ceiling curtains; framed *Life* picture of a female with butterfly wings; landline telephone, wallpaper, and linoleum kitchen floors. Apartment 201's decor perfectly captures the vibe of my 1970s childhood.

Like Apartment 201 and the 1970s, certain shirts take me back to the 1980s. When I see these shirts, I remember my childhood and adolescence. This section examines three iconic 1980s shirts and the El Con stores that sold them.

T-Shirts Plus

Custom shirts were all the rage when T-Shirts Plus, a nationwide franchise specializing in custom shirt design, opened a store in El Con Mall in March 1979. Ken Scofield, the store's owner, was impressed by the success of a similar store at Park Mall, T-Shirts Etcetera, which opened two and a half years earlier. Four months after T-Shirts Plus opened, the store was doing so well that Scofield planned to open nine more in the state. [97] In July 1979, the *Tucson Citizen* featured an article touting the popularity of custom shirts. "Now, three out of every 10 Americans own printed T-shirts," *Citizen* writer Marilyn Evans said. "Fashionable bosoms these days advertise bars and restaurants, Little League, bowling teams, beer companies, organizations with similar sexual preferences and macho motorcycle clubs." [98]

Custom T-shirts were everywhere in the early 1980s. In May 1981, Dr Pepper partnered with JCPenney for "National Be A Pepper Month." That month, the JCPenney store at El Con sold various Dr Pepper merchandise, including T-shirts with the company's iconic "I'm a Pepper" slogan, a popular catchphrase from a Dr Pepper advertising campaign. In addition, Dr Pepper bottles with gold caps had T-shirts, mugs, and iron-on prize giveaways. If the words "I'm a Pepper Iron-On Transfer" appeared under the cap, people could redeem it for an iron-on transfer at the JCPenney layaway department. Then they could iron the transfer onto a blank shirt at home to make an "I'm a Pepper" shirt.

The T-Shirts Plus store in El Con sold hundreds of vinyl iron-on transfers. People could purchase a transfer and make the shirt themselves or pay to have T-shirts Plus do it. Alex and I had three T-shirts made from vinyl iron-on transfers featuring the movies *Superman* and *The Empire Strikes Back* and the *Pac-Man* video game. There was an indescribable magic to those shirts. Glossy and loaded with color, the transfers often featured metallic glitter, which made the shirts sparkle. When new, the transfers were as smooth as a soft leather glove. After several washes, the vinyl cracked, and the colors faded. When we put one on for the first time, though, these shirts were pure 1980s perfection.

Woolworths

Another memorable 1980s shirt was the polo with the embroidered logo. Prep fashion, short for "preppy," was popular in the 1980s. It embodied the exclusivity of the Ivy League schools where it originated. The style was characterized by clean-cut, classic clothing, often featuring pastel colors and minimalist patterns. In addition to Ralph Lauren, who created the classic polo shirt, the Izod Lacoste clothing brand was synonymous with preppy fashion.

The most popular item from Izod Lacoste's line was a polo-style shirt with an embroidered crocodile logo. Many people called them "alligator" shirts, but the logo was a crocodile. Izod Lacoste polos came in various colors, each featuring the iconic 1.25-inch stitched crocodile. There was more driving this brand's popularity than quality; it was the social prestige of wearing a status brand. All the cool kids wore alligator shirts, but not every family could afford them. Sadly, teens and kids who didn't have alligator shirts were left out.

(© Tucson Citizen – USA TODAY NETWORK via Imagn Images)

Being the odd child out at school is no fun. In the "Mini Page Advice Column" of the June 24, 1983, *Tucson Citizen* newspaper, a child wrote, "I am unhappy because I do not have any designer jeans. I do not even have any shirts with alligators, polo ponies or designer names on them." [99] Dr. James Egan, director of the Department of Psychiatry at the Children's Hospital National Medical Center, said this in reply:

> That new designer outfit might make you happier for a short time. Since the thrill lasts for such a short time, how many would it take to really make you happy? Could you ever really have enough? I doubt it. Dress to be yourself and do not depend on someone else's label to make you happy.

It is who you are and not the label you are wearing that is important. [100]

Since not everyone could afford Ralph Lauren or Izod Lacoste polo shirts, a market of lower-priced competitors emerged. Even department stores got in on the action. JCPenney introduced the Fox clothing line, featuring a fox logo on its polos. Sears had a fire-breathing dragon logo called the "Braggin' Dragon." Other popular polos included Le Tigre, Hunters Run, and Ralph Lauren, featuring stitched logos of a tiger, a horse and rider, and a polo horseman, respectively. But my favorite animal-emblemed polo came from Woolworths.

Woolworths, one of El Con's original tenants, opened on August 24, 1961. Before becoming a nationwide variety store chain, Woolworths began as the "Great 5c Store." Frank Winfield Woolworths opened the Great 5c Store in Utica, New York, on February 22, 1879. The price of every item in the store was five cents. Business was good at first, but the store closed within four months. Frank Woolworth opened a second Great 5c Store with his brother in Lancaster, Pennsylvania, on June 21, 1879. This location succeeded, and the renowned five-and-dime chain known as Woolworths was born.

Like other retailers in the 1980s, Woolworth had an animal-emblemed polo shirt line, the "frog shirt." Its logo featured a frog with a crown, reminiscent of the frog prince. In addition to Woolworths, The F. W. Woolworth Company owned Woolco, a full-line discount department store. The frog shirt was a Woolworth and Woolco exclusive. My parents bought me a navy blue Frog Shirt in 1982. They shopped at the Woolco on 22nd and Alvernon, so my frog shirt most likely came from there, not the Woolworths store in

El Con. Still, the frog shirt cost the same at both stores—$12 regular price or $9 on sale. Here's what other polo shirt brands cost that year:

- Ralph Lauren Polo Shirt: $31 at Levy's
- Izod Lacoste alligator shirt: $24 at Steinfeld's
- Le Tigre shirt: $20 at Levy's
- The Fox shirt: $18 at JCPenney
- Braggin' Dragon: $15.99 at Sears (Park Mall)

In 1982, a $24 Izod Lacoste shirt was the equivalent of $79.01 in 2025, a hefty sum to spend on shirts we wore to school. For some families, such expenses weren't a big deal. For my family, such prices weren't feasible. Discount stores like Woolworths and Woolco offered cool, low-price alternatives. Whether people rocked the alligator, tiger, Fox, dragon, or frog, the animal-emblemed polo shirts were a quintessential example of 1980s style.

Spencer Gifts

On January 20, 1982, Ozzy Osbourne, former lead singer of the heavy metal band Black Sabbath, hosted a live concert in Des Moines, Iowa. That night, seventeen-year-old Mark Neal brought a dead bat to the show in a bag and hurled it onto the stage. Thinking it was fake, Osborne picked up the bat and bit off its head. The moment he bit down, Osbourne realized, to his horror, that the bat was real. Osbourn went to the hospital immediately after the concert, receiving tetanus and rabies shots. [101]

This incident is one of the most infamous events in rock 'n' roll history. According to Osbourne's spokesman, the medical report read, "Patient bit head off bat." [102] On January 20, 2024, forty-two years after it happened, Osbourne posted this on Instagram: "Today marks the 42nd Anniversary since I bit a head off a fucking bat!" The Ozzy Osbourne Official Store sold a twelve-inch plush bat toy with a detachable head to commemorate the occasion.

Such offbeat items remind me of the typical fare sold in Spencer Gifts stores. Spencer Gifts began as a mail-order catalog business in 1947. Their first retail store opened in 1963 at the Cherry Hill Mall in New Jersey. As the self-labeled "paradise of paraphernalia," Spencer Gifts carried items no other store had. The national chain developed a reputation for its specialty gifts, such as Steve Merritt's viral 1983 gag gift, Damitol. This candy placebo came in a pill bottle with a label that read: "Damitol acts safely and quickly to provide temporary relief from the effects of unemployment, unhappy love affairs, and depression due to long economic recoveries. Also ideal for minor irritations due to cars that won't run, politicians, grumpy store clerks and people who refuse to leave a message on your answering machine." [103]

Damitol is an example of the novelty items Spencer Gifts became known for. In addition to gag gifts, Spencer Gifts sold merchandise like jewelry, bar accessories, posters, candles, black lights, adult games and puzzles, buttons, and T-shirts. Here is a sampling of Spencer Gifts sale items from 1983:

- Gusto Mugs: $2.99
- 1983 calendars: $2.25–$6.35
- Bamboo Curtains: $7.99
- E.T., Pac-Man, Smurf, Garfield, and Unicorn Balloons: $1.99
- Pre-printed T-shirts: $2.97

Band T-shirts were popular with Gen X teens, and Spencer Gifts in El Con Mall was the place to get them. Cindy Cox, staff writer for the *Lancaster New Era* newspaper in Lancaster, PA, penned a Christmas gift-buying guide in December 1983. In it she wrote,

> 'Tis the season for buying gifts for teens. As the number of shopping days dwindles, more and more parents will be faced with the bewildering task. What's the best gift? A Smurf T-shirt? Or maybe a Ziggy bulletin board? How about a Christie Brinkley poster? Take heed, anxious moms and dads. Area merchants and those in the know have helped us to compile a guide for trendy holiday gift items for teens. [104]

Cox makes recommendations in several categories, including collectibles, books, music, and games. In the clothing category, Cox's first recommendation is band T-shirts. "Rock 'n roll seems to be one of the leading influences for the fashionable 14-to 18-year-old these days," Cox says. "When teens go casual, a very popular item is a T-shirt emblazoned with the picture and name of their favorite group (or their favorite group's latest album)." [105] According to sales clerks at Spencer Gifts, the most popular band shirts in 1983 were Def Leppard, The Police, and Black Sabbath. Spencer Gifts sold them all for $8.99.

My three female cousins were in high school when I was still in grade school. I remember all three wearing shirts from bands like Duran Duran, OMD, Wham!, Hall & Oates, and Bruce Springsteen. My friends wore shirts from rock bands like Def Leppard, AC/DC,

Motley Crue, Metallica, Iron Maiden, and Guns N' Roses. Other commonly worn band shirts of the decade include:

- Michael Jackson, Thriller
- Prince, Purple Rain
- Madonna, True Blue
- Beastie Boys, License to Ill
- N.W.A., Straight Outta Compton
- Frankie Goes to Hollywood, Frankie Says Relax
- The Ramones logo
- The Misfits skull logo
- Run DMC

The success of MTV popularized these bands. Like music, teens used band T-shirts as a means of self-expression. In 1985, Hard Rock Cafe shirts were trending as well. By the late 1930s, people couldn't go anywhere without seeing a Hard Rock Cafe T-shirt.

Vinyl transfer iron-ons, animal-embroidered polos, and band T-shirts were memorable aspects of life in the 1980s. They were popular at different times, and each offered a unique insight into pop culture. In a 1989 article in the *Flint Journal* newspaper, Sue Briggs says, "Unique to other articles of clothing, T-shirts bear testimony to current pop culture, fads and ideals." [106] I agree with this statement and add that T-shirts also say something about the person wearing them. In the article, Briggs quotes twenty-year-old Kathy Morris of Flint, Michigan, who said, "I may not be emotional about every T-shirt I wear, but I have to at least relate to the idea behind it." [107]

Through shirts, Gen Xers found a way to express elements of our collective and personal identities.

The Game Keeper

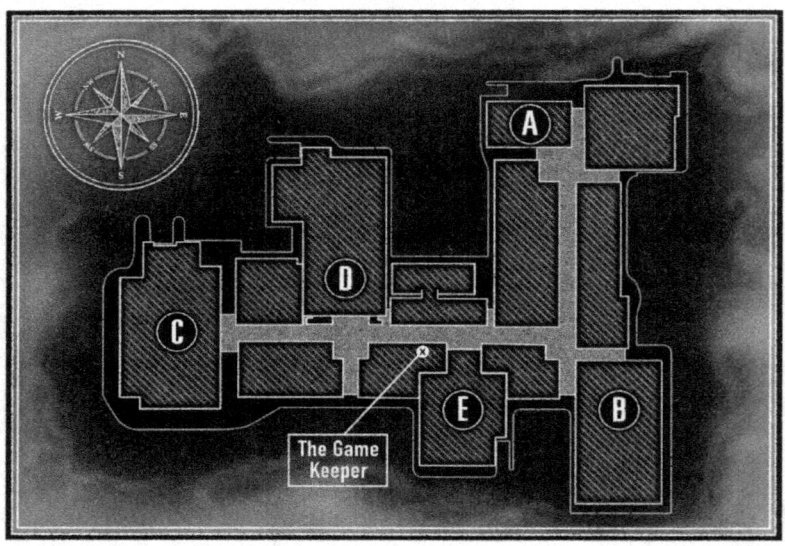

The Game Keeper

In 1974, Hungarian professor Erno Rubik invented a puzzle unlike any the world had seen—a three-D cube with faces that rotate horizontally and vertically. In the cube's unaltered state, each face contains nine identically-colored squares. One side is blue, another red, another green, and so on. Players create the puzzle by rotating the cube faces, which scrambles the squares into random color combinations. Players must return the cube to its original state to solve the puzzle. Sounds easy, but 94 percent of people who attempt this puzzle fail. If you haven't guessed, I'm talking about Rubik's Cube, the 1980 gaming phenomenon that remains the top-selling puzzle game of all time.

In October 1981, The Game Keeper store at El Con Mall averaged over one hundred Rubik's Cubes sales a month. "It's by far the most popular puzzle I carry," said Bob Buteau, the store manager. "It's also the most difficult puzzle we carry." [108] For many, solving the Rubik's Cube became an obsession. Some played for so long that they developed "cuber's thumb," a condition characterized by joint swelling between the fingers and wrist. Others sought clues in books like *The Simple Solution to Rubik's Cube* by James G. Nourse and *Mastering Rubik's Cube* by Don Taylor. Both appeared on the *New York Times* best-seller list. When all else failed, many of us resorted to peeling off and re-attaching the stickers.

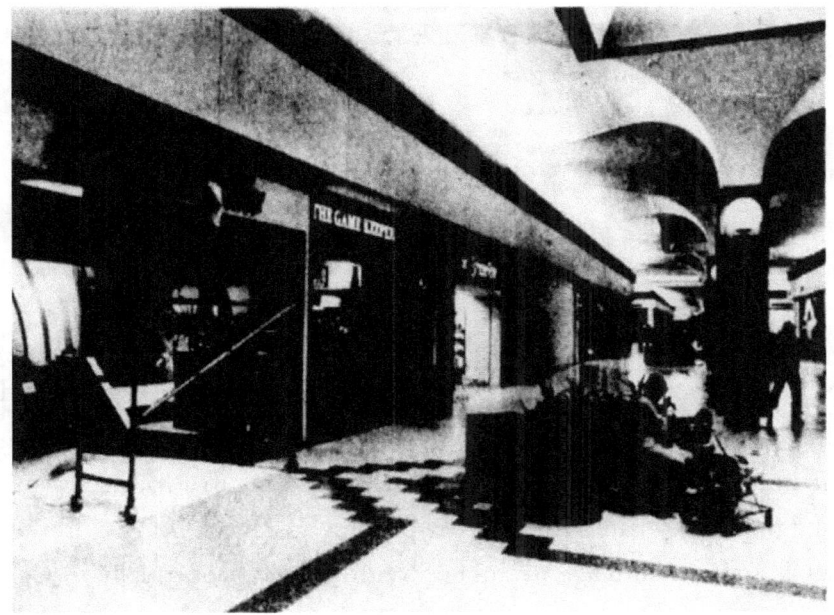

The Game Keeper at El Con (Copyright Arizona Daily Star)

The Game Keeper at El Con was a game enthusiast's wonderland. Whatever game people were looking for, this store was sure to have it. The Game Keeper was a national chain based in Santa Barbara, California. Promoting itself as "the store for people who like to play," it carried a wide selection of board games, strategy games, puzzles, gamebooks, game tables, and game room accessories. The Game Keeper opened for business in El Con on January 28, 1979. It was one of seventeen new tenants to join El Con following a $6 million renovation that brought the entire mall under one roof.

In addition to older games like chess, checkers, cribbage, backgammon, and Mahjong, Game Keeper had all the classics Generation X grew up playing. Here is a list of Gen X games that were popular before 1980:

1900 to 1940s Games		1950s & 60s Games		1970s Games	
Uncle Wiggily	1916	Yahtzee	1956	Ghost Castle	1970
Sorry!	1934	Risk	1957	Water Works	1972
Monopoly	1935	Stratego	1958	Perfection	1973
Canasta	1939	The Game of Life	1960	Connect Four	1974
Chutes & Ladders	1943	Hi-Ho! Cherry-O	1960	Payday	1974
Candy Land	1948	Aggravation	1962	Fat Chance	1978
Scrabble	1948	Mouse Trap	1963	Simon	1978
Clue	1949	Frustration	1965	Hungry Hungry Hippos	1978
		Operation	1965	Rummikub	1978
		Twister	1966	Guess Who?	1979
		Battleship	1967	Pente	1979
				Bonkers!	1978

Playing board games and card games with the family is a cherished pastime. If you had siblings growing up, you have likely experienced the thrill of family game night. You know the exhilaration of beating an older brother and the disappointment of losing to a younger sister. The first board game I remember playing was checkers. My brother has a fifteen-month age advantage over me, which was usually enough to beat me in checkers every time. Finding a game everyone could play, win, and enjoy regardless of age was challenging, but that's what my family found in the card game Uno.

Uno was a game night favorite in my house. I fondly remember playing it with family and friends at the kitchen table. Not only is Uno easy to learn, it's loads of fun, and everyone has a chance to win, regardless of age. Merle Robbins, Uno's inventor, also enjoyed playing card games with his family. After several arguments over the rules for Crazy 8s, Merle wrote instructions on some cards. For example, he wrote "reverse" on the king card, indicating that the order of turns switches when a participant plays a king card. Merle, a barber, realized he had created a new game and began selling it from his shop.

The winner of Uno is the first player to get rid of all their cards. Each card has a color (red, blue, yellow, green) and either a number (0-9) or action (Draw 2, Draw 4, Reverse, Skip). The exception is wild cards, which players can use to change the color played. When something other than a wild card gets played, the next player must put down a card of the same color, number, or action. If the player doesn't have it, they can play a wild card or pick up cards from the deck until an eligible card surfaces. When a player is down to their final card, they must remember to shout, "Uno!" If they forget, they must pick up two cards.

Uno's popularity spread by word of mouth. Advertisements in the 1970s described Uno as "America's newest card game craze." By 1980, practically everybody was playing Uno. "People hear about it [Uno] via some kind of grapevine, a neighbor, relative or whatever, and it seems once they play, they're hooked," [109] said Bob Tezac, president of International Gamed Inc. Fifty years later, *Uno* remains one of the most popular card games. To this day, nothing beats the thrill of throwing down your last card after calling out "Uno!" Well, nothing except handing your sibling a Draw 4 card.

Licensed TV shows, movies, and arcade games inspired many 1980s board games. Trivia games were also in demand thanks to Trivial Pursuit, arguably the most iconic game of the decade. Introduced in 1981, Trivial Pursuit became so popular that game stores couldn't keep it in stock. Detective games were a hot commodity in the second half of the decade. That year, *Gaming Magazine's* top seven best sellers were all detective games. Finally, several games introduced in this decade incorporated technology into traditional gameplay. Given the popularity of VHS players at the time, many games included VHS tapes as an element of play. Here's a list of memorable games introduced in the 80s:

1980s Games			
Axis & Allies	1981	Pictionary	1985
Bargain Hunter	1981	Pig Pong	1986
Enchanted Forest	1981	Jenga	1986
Trivial Pursuit	1981	Outburst	1986
Monster Mansion	1981	Win, Lose or Draw	1987
Grabbin Dragons	1982	Shark Attack!	1988
Domination	1982	Chicken Out	1988
Scavenger Hunt	1983	Mall Madness	1988
Crossbows and Catapults	1983	Scattergories	1988
Balderdash	1984	Taboo	1989

Dark Tower was my favorite of all the games introduced in the 1980s. It's set in a medieval world, combining a traditional game board with an electronic tower unit. The tower in the center of the game board functions like an electronic referee, dictating the outcome of each player's move. The goal is to lay siege to the dark tower, defeat the brigands, and retrieve the ancient magic scepter, freeing the land from the tyrant king's reign. Before this can happen, players must find three magic keys—brass, silver, and gold—in foreign kingdoms. Once all three keys are collected, players mount their attack on the tower.

Dark Tower carried a hefty price tag at an average retail price of $50. For comparison, when Dark Tower debuted in 1981, Milton Bradley's The Game of Life retailed for $7.99. The cool factor for this game was off the charts, though, and the high price added to its mystique. Everything about this game exuded mystery, especially the imposing black tower with its sound effects and flashing lights. Even Dark Tower's box was intimidating, measuring 19.75 inches long, 12.5 inches wide, and 7 inches deep. As if all this weren't enough, Dark Tower's official spokesman was Orson Welles, who filmed the commercial advertisement for the game. Dark Tower was ahead of its time in every way.

Finally, The Game Keeper was also a go-to store for role-playing games (RPG). Throughout history, militaries have used wargames to prepare for real threats and develop strategies to attack their enemies. Outside the military, there's an equally longstanding tradition of recreational wargaming. At first, recreational wargames mainly focused on actual military forces engaged in real historical battles. That changed in the 1970s, thanks to a surge of interest in science fiction and fantasy literature. Due to the explosion in popularity of books like J. R. R. Tolkien's Lord of the Rings, a new genre of wargames based around fantasy characters burst onto the scene. Leading the charge was Dungeons & Dragons.

Dungeons & Dragons (D&D) is a role-playing game set in a fantasy world. Rulebooks explain the basic elements of the game, aiding the planning and execution of a D&D session. The game's success hinges on the skills of the dungeon master, the moderator who maps out the world (often a dungeon or at least including a dungeon) that players navigate. Players build their characters, selecting from a predefined list of classes (e.g., ranger, thief, hero), backgrounds (e.g., acolyte), and species (e.g., elf). Elements such as ability, hit points, and armor class ratings are also calculated, further defining the character. After creating a character, players use it to participate in a session. D&D does not require a gameboard. All that's needed are the rulebooks, a seven-dice set, and a paper and pencil.

Gary Gygax and Dave Arneson created Dungeons & Dragons in 1974. Gygax moved to Lake Geneva, WI, at age eight. When he was a child, his father read fantasy books to him, cementing a lifelong interest in the genre. In the 1960s, Gygax discovered recreational wargames and became hooked. He quit his job as an insurance underwriter and became a shoe repairman to free up time to create fantasy-themed games. Gygax met Dave Arneson while playing wargames, and the pair teamed up to develop Dungeons & Dragons. Then Gygax co-founded Tactical Studies Rules (TSR) with Don Kaye, a childhood friend. TSR was the first company to publish Dungeons & Dragons games, which exploded in popularity, creating a new genre of recreational wargaming. [110]

In 2024, D&D celebrated its fiftieth anniversary. An estimated 50 million people have played Dungeons & Dragons since its launch in 1974. In today's world, where technology is part of everything, it's astonishing that a game that relies heavily on imagination remains relevant. Gygax took his passion for fantasy books and turned it into a game that has enriched the lives of millions, a game that brings people together, strengthens social skills, and gets people to think on their feet and use their imagination. Dungeons & Dragons is the quintessential Gen X game, and despite early setbacks, it has cemented its place in popular culture.

The Game Keeper at El Con supplied Tucson with the best games around. For Generation X individuals like me, these games were a crucial part of our cherished childhood memories.

JCPenney

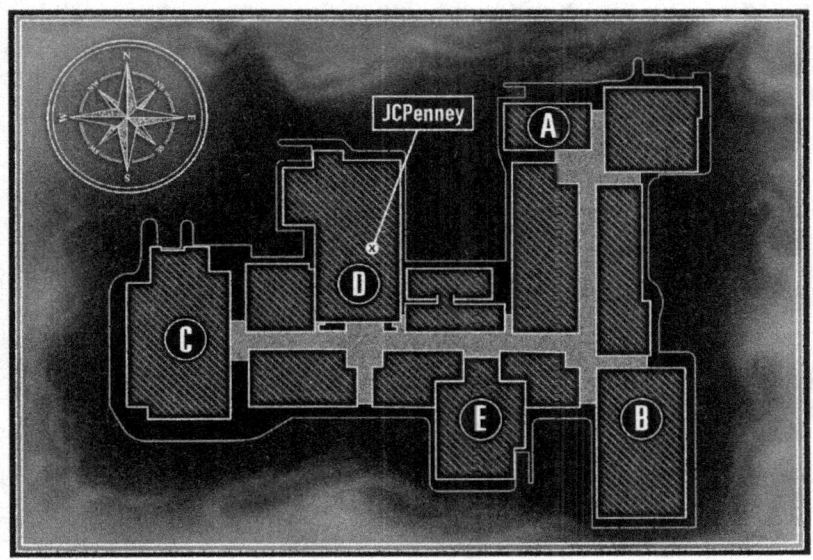

My brother Alex and I spent significant time with our cousins, Ray and Mike, throughout childhood. Whenever Aunt Terry visited, she ran errands with my mom and took us kids along. Ray, Mike, Alex, and I piled into the bed of Aunt Terry's Ford Courier pick-up truck and sat with our backs against the cab. After a few minutes on the road, the truck bed overheated and burned our rear ends. It hurt, but that was nothing compared to the ordeal we faced when Mom and Aunt Terry went shopping for clothes. The worst was when they went to women's clothing stores, like Fashion Gal at 4724 E. Broadway. Such stores had nothing of interest for young boys like us.

We trailed our moms around the store for what felt like an eternity as they browsed one clothing rack after another. They spoke a foreign language, repeating words and phrases we didn't understand like spaghetti strap, off-the-shoulder, cute top, blouse, culotte, huarache, and jellies. We had no clue what they were talking about. They bought strange, egg-shaped items called L'eggs. They came in containers with cardboard bottoms and plastic tops. I later discovered these were pantyhose, leggings made from nylon.

Nylon is known for the same quality that makes department stores desirable—versatility. Nylon is an adaptable material with applications in many industries, including automotive, electronics, medical, music, clothing, construction, and sports, to name a few. [111] The department store is often the most popular spot in a mall for this very reason. They offer something for everyone. Stores like Fashion Gal are great for women of a certain age. For everyone else, they are useless. This dynamic does not apply to department stores. Collins Dictionary defines a department store as "A large retail store for the sale of many kinds of goods arranged in departments." [112] Because it offers so many products, chances are everyone can find something of interest in a department store. This section contains memorable experiences from three stages of my life at the JCPenney department store in El Con Mall. In keeping with the versatility theme, each example involves a different application of nylon.

The first item comes from a time in my life when I had little interest in shopping. It is one of my first jackets—a nylon taffeta quilted parka from JCPenney. It came with a zip-off hood, reflector tape stripes on the sleeves, and acrylic pile lining. It was orange with a navy-blue interior. I must have been three or four years old when I wore it. It came along for one of my first trips to Yosemite National Park. My family went camping with relatives at Tuolumne Meadows in the Sierra Nevada high country. Snow blanketed the rocks by the riverbank, and fog hovered above the frigid Tuolumne River. I was gazing at the slow-moving water when—splash! I went headfirst into the river. Dad jumped in and pulled me out. I made a mess of the situation because all my warm clothes, including that nylon jacket, got soaked. I had to stay inside the tent in my pajamas until everything dried.

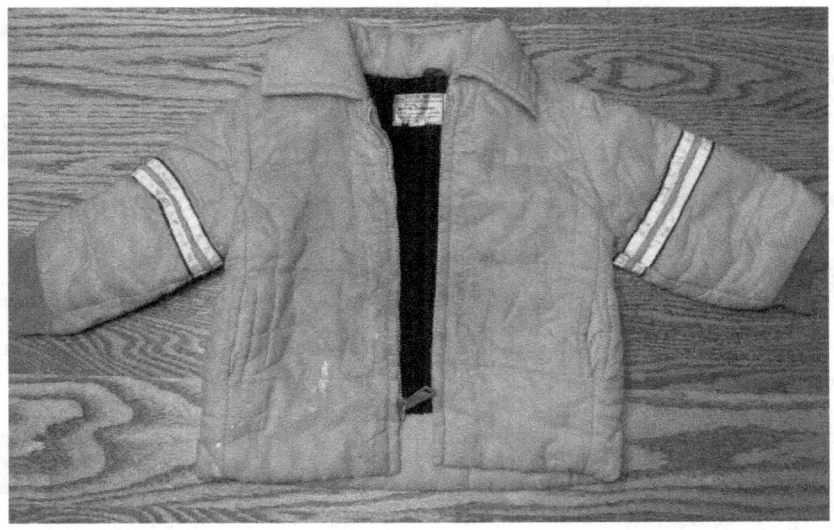

My old jacket (Photo by the author)

The second JCPenney item is from 1984, when breakdancing was popular. I was nine years old. For the first time, toys and video games weren't the only things I wanted to shop for. My brother and I shopped in the clothing department for parachute pants. Nylon parachute pants were popular with breakers because they allowed ease of movement and looked stylish. Alex and I each had a pair of black parachute pants. Kids wore them with muscle shirts and high tops. We also shopped in the electronics department to look at ghetto blasters. Breaking and ghetto blasters go hand in hand. The portable stereo with twin cassette decks, or boom box, was essential breaking equipment. Combined with a cardboard or linoleum sheet, that was everything we needed to practice breaking. I can still hear the swish sound of my parachute pants as I dropped to the cardboard and did a backspin to the beat of "Jam On It," bumping on the ghetto blaster.

Fast-forward to my adult years. By then the mall was in a downward spiral, so visits to El Con were few and far between. Occasionally, I'd go to JCPenney during a big sale to buy crew-neck T-shirts, belts, and jeans, but that was it. The only hook that brought me to the mall regularly was the nylon lighting umbrella at the JCPenney Portrait Studio. Once a year, my wife and I would take our kids there for Christmas pictures. The photographers did a great job getting the kids to focus and smile for the camera. Thanks to the JCPenney Portrait Studio, I have wonderful family pictures and a shared El Con Mall memory with my wife and children. Apart from these annual pictures, my kids had no connection to El Con because it became a dead mall long before they were born.

The Gold Mine Arcade

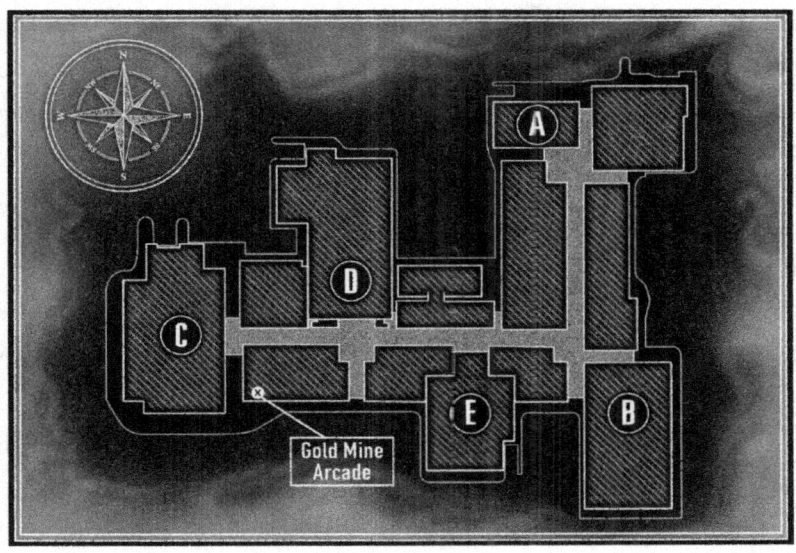

Gold Mine
Arcade

It's love at first sight. I stand awestruck before a monitor with crisp black-and-white graphics. The control panel has five buttons, one for the laser and four others to pilot the spaceship. Sounds erupt from the game's speakers, booming explosions when the spaceship's lasers pulverize their target and blaring sirens when enemy spacecraft appear. The artwork on the side of the cabinet mirrors the action on the screen. It shows a laser-blasting spaceship maneuvering through a meteor field. A single word in bold yellow draws my eye to the backlit marquee: "Asteroids."

I have just described my first encounter with an arcade game, which occurred in the concession area of the Tucson 5 drive-in theater. Arcade games and Generation X go together like butter and popcorn. The eldest members of Generation X were six years old when

Computer Space, the first commercial arcade game, debuted in 1971. In it, players pilot a rocket ship in battle with two UFOs. Next, Atari introduced *Pong* in 1972. An electronic table tennis game, *Pong* was the first arcade game to achieve broad commercial success. Then came *Gun Fight* (1975), a game that pits two cowboys against each other in an Old West shootout. *Gun Fight* was the first commercial arcade game to use a microprocessor, resulting in better graphics.

These early contributors brought arcade games into the mainstream, but *Space Invaders* (1978) was the first to become a global phenomenon. In this groundbreaking game, players use a scrolling laser cannon to defend Earth from an alien attack. *Space Invaders* was wildly popular, particularly in Japan, where rumors surfaced that the government minted more coins to feed the nation's gaming addiction. *Space Invaders* initiated the golden age of arcade games from 1978 to 1986. A succession of blockbuster games followed, including *Asteroids* (1979), *Galaxian* (1979), *Berzerk* (1980), *Defender* (1980), *Pac-Man* (1980), *Missile Command* (1980), *Rally-X* (1980), *Centipede* (1981), and *Donkey Kong* (1981). [113]

Arcade games were everywhere in the early 1980s. You could find them in the lobbies of restaurants, movie theaters, convenience stores, laundromats, bars, bowling alleys, pizza joints, roller skating rinks, supermarkets, and video arcades. Malls were perfect arcade locations thanks to guaranteed traffic and a broad customer base. Popular mall-based arcades included Tilt, Aladdin's Castle, Time-Out, Space Port, and Station Break. El Con had the Gold Mine Arcade, a lesser-known chain operating in regional malls. Gold Mine arcades often incorporated a mineshaft theme as part of their design, with rock-faced entrances and wooden beams.

Some of my favorite mall memories in the 1980s happened at the Gold Mine Arcade, and I'm willing to bet many Gen Xers feel the same about their local arcade. What made arcades a fundamental element of the Gen X experience? A big part of the allure was the arcade ambiance. There was a special kind of magic in dimly lit arcades. People's senses were overwhelmed with visual and auditory stimuli within seconds of entering, and much of it came from the arcade cabinets. With their colorful designs, enchanting sounds, and glowing lights, arcade cabinets functioned like storefront windows. Aspects of a game's backstory emerged in the cabinet's side art, bezel, control panel, and marquee.

Consider Atari's *Centipede* cabinet. The side art for this cabinet, showing an alien centipede weaving through starburst-patterned explosions and mushrooms, is in a class all its own. With its vibrant colors and compelling action, this iconic image epitomizes the thrills and excitement that made arcades irresistible. The game's control panel has more starburst patterns and mushrooms while the bezel features cameo illustrations of three additional enemies—the spider, the scorpion, and the flea. The marquee at the top of the cabinet is the showpiece. It displays the game's name, artwork, and the Atari logo in a pleasing purple, orange, green, and yellow color scheme. The backlit marquee, combined with flashing colors from the monitor, makes it feel like Christmas in a dimly lit arcade.

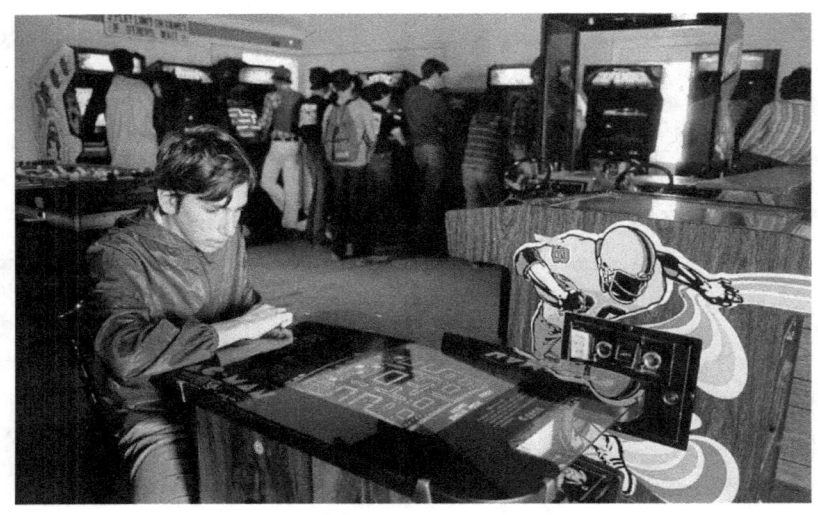

Arcade ambiance (Copyright Arizona Daily Star)

Sounds contributed to the arcade ambiance too. The 1980 Pima County Fair included an arcade tent with fifty video games. When asked why *Space Invaders* was so popular, Kem Johnson, the arcade supervisor, said, "The noise is the thing." Al Scanlan, another arcade supervisor, agreed. "The noise is about 80 percent of the game. They want to hear that noise." [114] Johnson and Scanlan's point, that sound plays a significant role in a game's popularity, also applies to arcades. Every pinball machine and video game produced unique sounds. Combined with rock and pop music playing on speakers overhead, these sounds created a stimulating soundscape that Gen Xers couldn't get enough of.

Generation X also loved arcades for the entertainment value of video games. Simply put, video games were fun to play. Everyone has favorites, but some games, like *Pac-Man,* achieved universal fame. *Pac-Man* debuted in 1980 and quickly became the most successful video game in history. The game features a yellow circular character (Pac-Man) on a mission to eat all the dots in a maze without getting eaten by four ghosts. Prior to *Pac-Man*, most arcade games catered to adult males. Toru Iwatani, *Pac-Man's* creator, designed the game to appeal to everyone by making the characters non-threatening. Judging by *Pac-Man's* popularity, it worked.

Journalist Ellen Goodman wrote a syndicated column for the Washington Post Writers Group about her *Pac-Man* obsession. "I met him in the Detroit airport," Goodman says. "I was between planes with time on my hands. He was available, enticing. So what if I'd been warned about him. I figured it would be different for me, for us. Then, before I knew it, I was hooked on the guy. Pac-Man was his name." [115] Goodman describes her love-hate relationship with *Pac-Man*. Despite her resistance, "He took me for every quarter I owned," Goodman concedes. What made Pac-Man so alluring? "I was seduced by the challenge, the high energy of the chase, the intrigue of the maze," [116] Goodman says. Millions of *Pac-Man* fans could relate.

Pac-Man or *Pole Position*? Whatever your preference, arcade games were great entertainment. I had so much fun with some games that I remember when and where I first played them. Here's a list of some of my favorite games and the memories I associate with them:

- Dig Dug: Classmate's birthday party at Skate Country roller rink
- Vanguard: mini-arcade at St. Ambrose pool
- Centipede, Galaga, Galaxian, Pac-Man, and Star Wars: Peter Piper Pizza restaurant at 4202 E. 22nd St.

- Frogger: a pizza joint in Boulder, Colorado
- Zaxxon: Gift store in Rocky Mountain National Park
- ALCON, Ghosts 'n' Goblins, Indiana Jones and the Temple of Doom, and Paperboy: the Circle K at 745 S. Tucson Blvd.
- Defender: Malibu Grand Prix at 4002 E. 22nd St.
- Joust: Zachary's Pizza on Sixth Street near the U of A football stadium
- Tron: the Food Giant grocery store on 22nd and Country Club
- Cyberball, Dragon's Lair, Gauntlet, Guerilla War, Punch-Out!!, and Rampage: The Gold Mine Arcade

My favorite Goldmine Arcade game was *Gauntlet*, a fantasy-themed "hack-and-slash" game. Players choose one of four characters:

- Thor, the Warrior
- Thyra, the Valkyrie
- Questor, the Elf
- Merlin, the Wizard

My favorite characters to play were Questor and Merlin. Questor was fast and could shoot enemies from a distance, and Merlin had the most potent magic. To succeed in *Gauntlet,* players must work as a team, using each character's strengths to advance to the next level. At times, a player's character is up front, leading the attack. Later, their character falls back and lets a teammate do the heavy lifting. Players share food and magic or suffer the consequences as team members die, leaving them alone to fight the enemy.

One thing I love about *Gauntlet* is the narrator, who speaks at random points in the game. The narrator offers warnings about each player's health (e.g., "Wizard needs food badly" or "Elf is about to die") and admonishes players when they make mistakes (e.g., "Remember, don't shoot food"). My friend Rico had a terrible habit of shooting food. Every time a player was close to death, Rico accidentally shot the food, preventing an ailing team member from using it to increase their health. Seconds later, the narrator called Rico out for his mistake: "Someone shot the food." The admonishment incited a cascade of complaints from the group, and we razzed Rico mercilessly.

Finally, the arcade was a hot spot for social interaction. One primary reason people went to arcades was for competition. For hardcore gamers, arcades provided opportunities to showcase their skills, achieve high scores, and secure bragging rights. *Space Invaders* was the first arcade game to record high scores. Henceforth, most games had a high-score table where top players registered their initials. High scores became the standard all players measured themselves against.

In October 1981, Charles Bowden of the *Tucson Citizen* interviewed Evan Goldberg, a twelve-year-old video game hotshot. Evan spent fifteen hours a week honing his gaming skills at local arcades, paying for games with the thirty to fourteen tokens he won weekly in contests. Bowden describes Evan as "a known player in his neighborhood around Craycroft and Broadway. Video machines list the top scores. Usually Evan or his competition, 14-year-old Scott Thomas, hold first place. They are veritable tigers at Defender and Centipede." [117] Playing *Star Castle* for over an hour, Evan's prowess attracted a crowd of observers. Competition and the recognition of being a top scorer were hooks that commonly lured people to arcades.

Gen Xers also hung out with friends and interacted with peers at arcades. People of all ages patronized arcades, but they were especially popular meeting places for Gen X teens. Nothing beat the excitement of walking through the Gold Mine arcade's doors. Before spending a quarter, the colorful lights and sounds emanating from arcade cabinets and pinball machines pull our focus in every direction. There was excitement in the air, a feeling of limitless possibility. We alternated between playing games and watching our friends play, immersing ourselves in the unique world each game offered. When it was over, we left with the memory of good times with friends.

The ability to attract younger crowds was, ironically, one of the factors that led to the undoing of arcades. Many viewed arcades as magnets for juvenile delinquency and crime. They also argued video games desensitized kids to violence. But for the vast majority of Gen Xers, me included, the arcade was a place to relax and have fun. With five dollars or less, I could spend hours at the Goldmine with my brother and our friends. It was the perfect hangout for the kids of my generation. In 2024, I took my family to the Ground Kontrol Arcade in Portland, OR, which was fantastic. I'm thankful for the opportunity because, for the first time, my kids got to experience a genuine arcade, the kind Alex and I had at Gold Mine.

Ghost Directory: Food Court

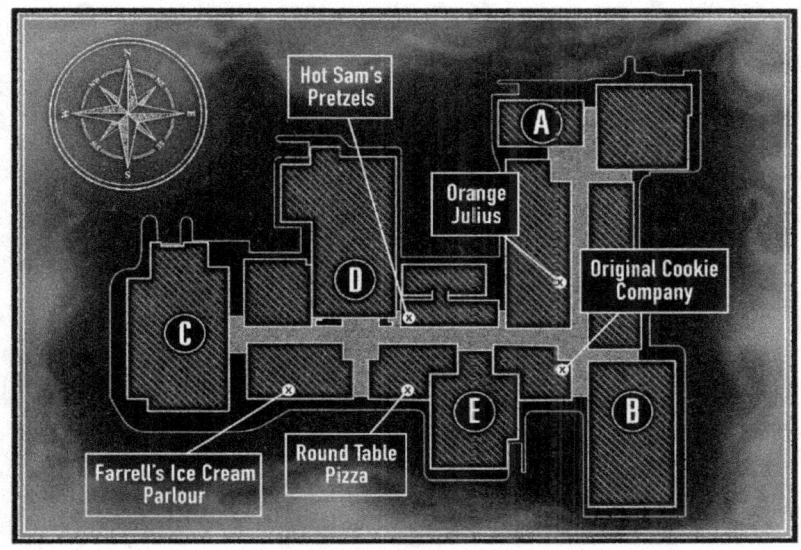

It's a typical Tucson weekday in 1983. The final bell of the day rings at St. Ambrose School, classroom doors open, and a mob of kids make their way to the parking lot. My brother and I are among them, and we're walking with purpose. The afternoon cartoon lineup is about to begin. If we make it home fast enough, we can catch *Super Friends* at 3:00 on channel 11, a solid lead-up to our favorite cartoon, *Scooby-Doo, Where Are You!*, which starts at 3:30.

Two things come to mind when I think of *Scooby-Doo* today—mysteries and food. The main characters are a group of teens, including Fred, Daphne, Velma, Shaggy, and their Great Dane, Scooby-Doo. The show follows the group as they travel around in their van, solving mysteries. Shaggy and Scooby spend most of their time looking for something to eat and always manage to find it, including everything from five-decker sandwiches to fourteen-stack pancakes. Based on the volume and frequency of their eating, Shaggy and Scooby would need superhero-level metabolisms to maintain their trim figures. I will always be a fan of *Scooby-Doo,* but the show didn't exactly promote healthy eating habits.

TV commercials in the 1980s were even worse. At each commercial break, kids were bombarded with ads for sugar-loaded food and snacks of every kind. Remember Hostess commercials, like the one where Fruit Pie the Magician appears at Franklin School to ask kids what they like most about Hostess fruit pies? "I like cherry best," one kid says, cherry pie in hand. "And apple," he adds, grabbing an apple pie with the other hand. "And . . ." He holds up another pie and is about to add lemon to the list when Fruit Pie the Magician interjects. "And that says it all!" he says as if even he is embarrassed by the child's overzealous display. "Hostess Fruit Pies, Twinkies Cakes, and Cupcakes. Fresh snacks, heh heh, with a snack in the middle!"

Hostess promoted its Cupcakes, Fruit Pies, and Twinkies with the slogan, "Fresh snacks with a snack in the middle." The phrase "in the middle" is a good way to describe Generation X's predicament thanks to government deregulation policies in the 1980s. Restrictions on marketing and advertising to children were virtually nonexistent at the time. Using every means available, companies went after kids to secure their business. This was the reason for product mascots like Fruit Pie the Magician, a member of what *Baltimore Sun* columnist Kevin E. Dayhoff describes as "the holy trinity of spokespersons for Hostess." [118] The other two were Captain Cupcake and Twinkie the Kid. Like Hostess, other companies created mascots to market their products to kids. As a result, Gen X kids were perpetually caught between an army of marketers and their parents, whom Gen X kids relied on to buy the products pitched at them.

Many instances of this come to mind with respect to fast-food marketers, McDonald's being the prime example. Has there ever been a better fast-food marketing tool for kids than the Happy Meal? As a child, getting a Happy Meal at McDonald's was the ultimate coup. In addition to a hamburger, fries, and soda, kids got a toy. One of the best Happy Meal toys I got was a rubberized space creature named Dard. It smelled like a pencil eraser. For this promotion, we got a *Space Raiders* alien or spaceship in our Happy Meal. My cousin Mikey lucked out and got a cool spaceship named Krygo 5. My brother, my cousin Ray, and I tried to convince Mikey to trade prizes with us, but he refused. Mikey had the best toy, and he knew it. It was all part of the Happy Meal's allure. We never knew which toy we'd get, which made it more exciting.

The problem with Happy Meals was we had to convince our parents to buy them, which was never a sure bet in my family because it was cheaper to just order the food. This dynamic applied to all food-related matters in my house. Back in the day, decisions about where, when, and what the family would eat were largely determined by my parents. For example, my siblings and I often accompanied Mom on her grocery runs to Lucky Market. I was the kid who always asked to try something new. I remember pleading with Mom to let us buy *Gremlins* cereal when the movie came out in 1984. It didn't work. We left the store that day with a box of Cheerios or Raisin Bran, the standard breakfast fare in our house. Every so often, though, Mom approved something we didn't normally buy, but that was the exception, not the rule. For many Gen Xers like me, it wasn't until we were old enough to go to the mall alone that we experienced the freedom of picking whatever we wanted to eat.

El Con never had a dedicated food court. Various food establishments were scattered around the mall, including sit-down restaurants, bars, fast-food chains, and places to buy snacks and desserts. One long-time resident at the mall was Farrell's Restaurant & Ice Cream Parlour. Farrell's was an 1890s-themed restaurant known for singing servers and prodigious ice cream servings. Costumed in late Victorian-era uniforms, the servers wore skimmer hats, red vests, bowties, and white long-sleeve shirts with old-fashioned sleeve garters. Farrell's was a popular place for kids' birthday parties. With menu options like the Hot Fudge Volcano, which featured thirty scoops of vanilla ice cream covered in chocolate, it's easy to see why. Farrell's banana split, called the Pig's Trough, was also something to behold. The dish was served in a wooden trough lined with metal. In addition to bananas, the Pig's Trough contained "six scoops of ice cream and all the topping and muck that our fountain people could sweep off the floor." [119] Anyone who finished eating it received a badge stating, "I made a pig of myself at Farrell's."

As good as Farrell's was, it wasn't the sort of place where kids and teens went to eat. It was more of a family restaurant, the kind people went to on birthdays or special occasions. I only remember going there once for a schoolmate's birthday party. I spent most of my time and money at the smaller food vendors in the mall. Two of the more common eateries I frequented at El Con were the Original Cookie Company and Hot Sam's Pretzels. If I wanted to save money for shopping or entertainment, I ate at one of those two places. If I wanted a more substantial meal, I chipped in to get pizza with my friends at Round Table Pizza. The map at the start of this section shows the locations of these food vendors and restaurants.

My favorite place to eat at the mall was Orange Julius. If you were a regular mall goer at any point in the 1980s, chances are you are familiar with Orange Julius. For the unacquainted, an Orange Julius is a creamy drink made with fresh-squeezed orange juice, crushed ice, simple syrup, and a proprietary powder blend. [120] It was available in several flavors, including the original orange, strawberry, peach, banana, pineapple, piña colada, tropical cream supreme, and raspberry cream supreme. Orange Julius also offered hamburgers, cheeseburgers, and six hot dog varieties—Chicago Relish, Southern, New York Kraut, California Chili, Wisconsin Cheese Dog, and the Reuben.

The success of Orange Julius owed to its proprietary powder blend. "It's the powder that makes Orange Julius so smooth and creamy," said Alma Shepherd, manager of the OJ store at Hanes Mall in Winston-Salem NC. "Without it, the ingredients won't blend." [121] In 1926, Julius Freed opened an orange juice stand in Los Angeles, CA. Freed's real estate broker, Willard "Bill" Hamlin, found the drink's acidity upset his stomach. So, Hamlin, an amateur chemist, created an additive made of "pure food products" to improve the drink and suggested it to Freed. [122] The addition of the powder prompted an immediate uptick in sales, and the franchise took off from there. In the early days, customers placing an order with Freed would say, "Give me an orange, Julius," [123] and that's how the franchise got its name.

To a twelve-year-old boy who grew up having to ask my parents for everything, stepping up to the counter at Orange Julius and placing an order was a change every bit as refreshing as the drink itself. Part of becoming an adult is learning to make your own choices and acting on them. Spending the day at the mall unsupervised was one of the first steps that many Generation X kids took on the road to adulthood.

Fitting Rooms

Anyone who has shopped for clothes online knows the value of a fitting room. How many clothing items have you purchased online, only to have them delivered and find they don't fit or flatter you? The inability to try things makes product assessment difficult. An article of clothing might look great online, but then you get it and discover you don't like the texture, it doesn't look right on you, and so on. For these reasons, many people prefer brick-and-mortar stores over online shopping.

The mall was where Gen X teens shopped, hung out, and, whether or not they knew it, learned about themselves. Like a fitting room, the mall allowed teens to try on things that shaped their personalities. The mall was a safe space for Gen X teens to sample what they liked, who to spend time with, where to go for fun, and how to project their self-image to the world. Teens conducted these identity-shaping fittings every time they bought clothes, watched movies, sampled music, or ate at the food court. With so many stores under one roof, the mall was the perfect place to try new things. This section delves into four "fitting-room" experiences at the mall.

B. Dalton Books

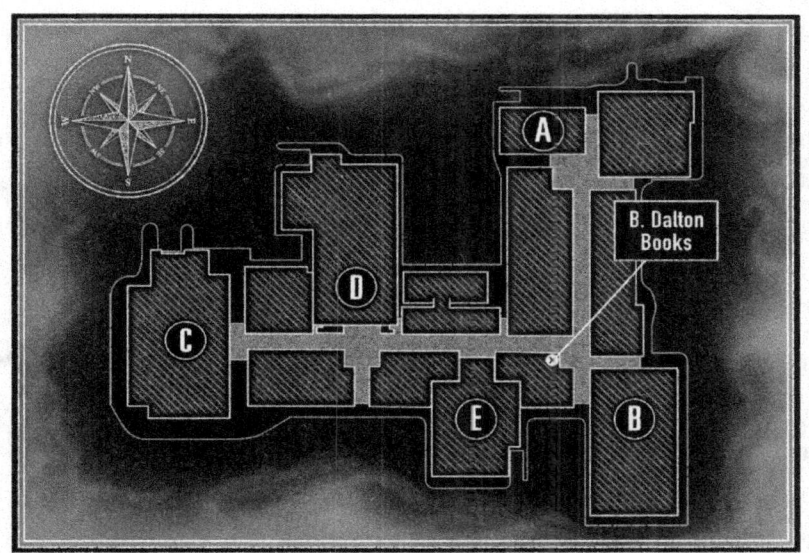

In 1987, the first *Where's Waldo?* books appeared in bookstores everywhere. These books feature intricate illustrations and incredibly detailed scenes to challenge visual attention. Each scene has a theme, and somewhere in the confusion of cartoon imagery on each page is a spectacled fellow with a red-and-white striped sweater and matching beanie. Your job is to find him. Waldo's appearance never changes, but he's always hard to spot.

Where's Waldo? books were a cultural phenomenon in the 1980s and 1990s for good reason. Whether or not you're a fan, it is impossible to resist looking for Waldo once you open the book. The visual complexity of the scene challenges your innate desire to find hidden objects, compelling you to look for Waldo. Anyone who has tried a *Where's Waldo?* puzzle knows the thrill of finding Waldo in the chaotic scene. When you finally locate Waldo in his trademark red-and-white-striped sweater and beanie, it's like finding a fifty-dollar bill on the ground.

Where's Waldo? books were a popular item in mall bookstores during the 1980s. El Con had three bookstores, beginning with the El Con Book Store, which opened in the early 1960s near Steinfeld's (Anchor A). In 1983, Sheldon and Linda Hubbell purchased the business and renamed it Linda's El Con Book Store. Unlike most mall bookstores, which are chains, El Con Book Store was independent. Linda's El Con Book Store closed sometime after June 1985. In the early 1980s, El Con Book Store shared the mall with two well-known bookstore chains, Waldenbooks and B. Dalton Bookseller. Waldenbooks opened in 1973 near Levy's (Anchor C). B. Dalton opened in 1979 near Montgomery Ward (Anchor B).

Bookstores were not just another store in the mall but a beloved destination. Like a *Where's Waldo?* scene, every bookstore contained something for people to discover. But bookstores offered more than books; they were cozy spaces for people to relax, have fun, and socialize. The bookstore ambiance was not unlike a coffee house. Crossing the store threshold, the scent of new books, the bookstore equivalent of roasted coffee beans, greeted shoppers. Classical music played overhead, a melodic barrier separating the calm within from the commotion outside. People's mood lightened as they approached the stacks and surrendered to the secret power of every bookstore—serendipity.

Online retail has undoubtedly made book shopping convenient, allowing consumers to purchase virtually any book from the comfort of their living room. However, the unique charm of bookstores lies in the potential for serendipitous discovery. No algorithm can replicate the joy of stumbling upon unexpected treasures as you wander the bookstore aisles. Some of my best bookstore finds happened accidentally—for example, *The Far Side* comedy series by Gary Larson. I didn't buy comic books when I was a kid. I never read comic strips, either. As a teenager, however, I stumbled upon Larson's *The Far Side* books at El Con's B. Dalton bookstore and became an instant fan.

I got my first *The Far Side* book as a Christmas gift that year. On Christmas Day, I showed a few sketches to my dad. He thought they were hilarious, and he also became a fan. Dad's favorite *The Far Side* cartoon shows a pair of snakes lying in bed. The snake on the left has thrown off the covers, revealing a knot in the middle of his body. With an anguished expression, the snake shouts, "Charley horse!" A favorite of mine shows a man in his living room with shards of broken glass on the carpet. He reads a note saying,

Bricks thrown thru your window?

Call

Al's Glass

555-1232

Gary Larson's *The Far Side* books introduced me to a style of comedy that resonated with me. More importantly, they allowed me to connect with my dad on a different level through shared laughter. That was something new for me because until then I hadn't related to my dad as a peer. A new chapter in our relationship was beginning. My ability to make Dad laugh by leveraging our mutual appreciation of Gary Larson's work exemplified the changing dynamic in our relationship. This demonstrates that a bookstore is more than just a place to buy books; it is a space where serendipity makes joyful, life-enhancing discoveries and shared experiences possible.

Musicland

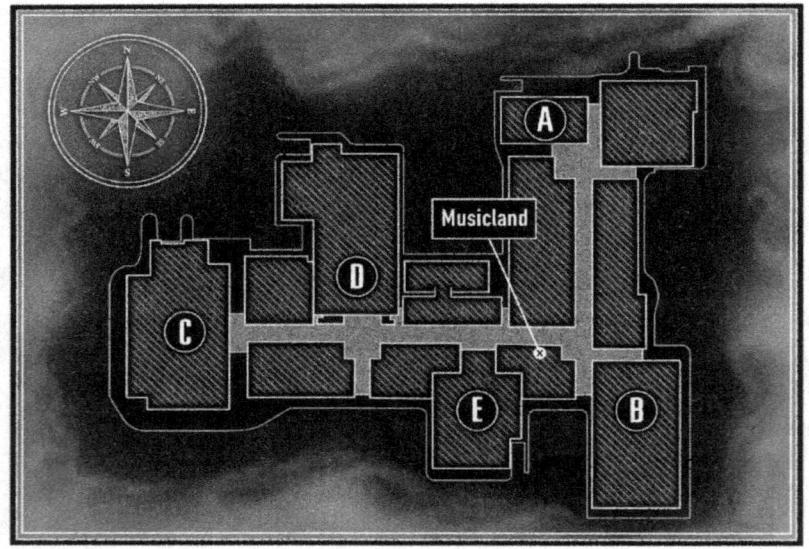

Like fog enveloping the Olympic Peninsula, a raw new sound descended on America in 1991. That year, one of history's most influential rock bands emerged from Aberdeen, Washington: the legendary Nirvana. Led by vocalist Kurt Cobain, Nirvana became a cultural phenomenon with the release of their second album, *Nevermind*. The first track on that record, "Smells Like Teen Spirit," became the de facto anthem for Generation X. Embodying the essence of Seattle's grunge scene, Nirvana found a receptive audience with America's disaffected youth.

Nirvana is that rare band that captured the spirit of a generation. "Smells Like Teen Spirit" epitomizes the angsty, cynical, anti-establishment traits for which Generation X is known. The song gave shape to our emerging generational identity. Nirvana disbanded in 1994 following Cobain's untimely death, but the band's popularity endures. In 2019, the video for "Smells Like Teen Spirit" hit one billion views on YouTube, which is impressive for a song from the Pre-Internet era.

Music stores are a popular mall destination for teenagers. Four music stores once operated in El Con Mall—Record Bar, Musicland, Sam Goody, and Tracks. My first music-listening experiences were in my pre-school years. Alex and I had a child's portable record player made of plastic. It played 33s and 45s. We had stacks of these records, 1970s era hand-me-downs from our mom and teenage uncles. It was a hands-on, tactile introduction to the music world. I couldn't read, but I learned to identify songs based on the designs and colors of the record labels. The sound of the needle crackling as it made contact with the spinning record is unique to the vinyl format. These are my earliest associations with music.

My Uncle Andy played a significant role in shaping my early music preferences. He mainly listened to rock 'n' roll, but his taste in music was diverse. I loved looking through his album collection, which in the early 1980s included bands like The Moody Blues, Billy Joel, ZZ Top, Tom Petty and the Heartbreakers, Journey, Toto, and ABBA. Album cover art plays a crucial role in the musical experience. The cover art tells a story about the music inside. Two album covers from Uncle Andy's collection stand out: *Long Distance Voyager* by The Moody Blues and *Asia* by Asia. The former, a blue-tinted version of

Thomas Webster's "Punch" painting, reveals a scene from late nineteenth-century England; the latter, a fantastical illustration of a sea serpent pursuing a white orb. Seeing either of those covers takes me back to my childhood.

As people mature, their taste in music often changes too. That happened to me at the start of adolescence. In the mid-1980s, skateboarding entered my life. With its heavy influence on the skateboarding subculture, punk rock music also found its way into my life. A friend, Vince, introduced me to punk music, which embodies skateboarding's rebellious counter-culture ethos. Vince listened to bands like the Sex Pistols, Social Distortion, Suicidal Tendencies, Red Hot Chilli Peppers, Agent Orange, Dead Kennedys, Circle Jerks, and J.F.A., a local punk band from Phoenix. By then cassette tapes were the dominant music format. Wherever we skated, we took a ghetto blaster to play our punk music cassettes.

For Gen X teens, a day at the mall meant trips to the music store. Music has always been a tool for identity exploration and self-expression. Finding an artist or band that plays music you resonate with is like finding a long-lost friend. You learn something about yourself and experience the satisfaction of knowing someone else gets you. The greatest record store of all time, Tower Records, had a famous slogan: "No Music, No Life." Nothing could be truer for people like me who would feel lost without music.

I'm grateful to Uncle Andy for connecting me with music early on. I'm also thankful to stores like Musicland and Sam Goody at El Con for connecting me with new music that formed and shaped my adolescent identity.

Champ's Sporting Goods

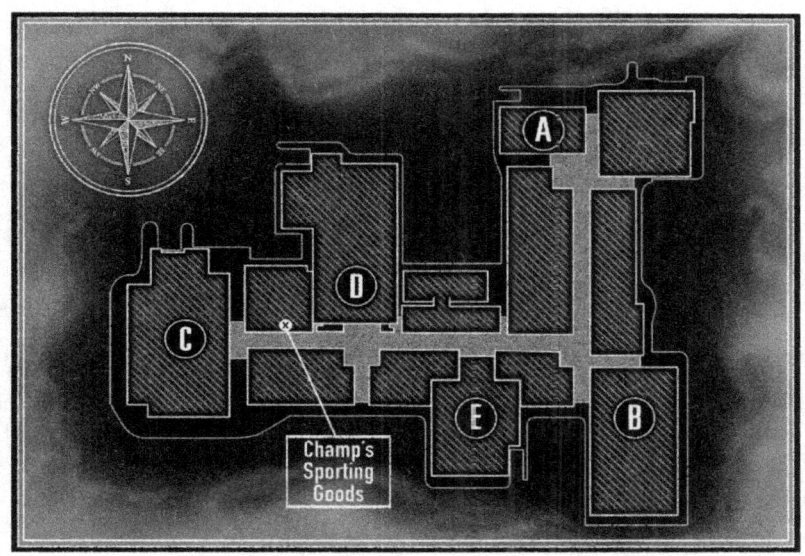

It happened on January 27, 1989, at the Arizona Veterans Memorial Coliseum, known affectionately by the locals as the "Madhouse on McDowell." Here's what unfolded. The Phoenix Suns were hosting a regular-season NBA game with the New York Knicks. With 5:05 remaining in the fourth quarter, the Suns stole the ball and began a fast break. Tom Chambers, the Sun's six-foot, ten-inch all-star power forward sprinted down the court on a give-and-go with Kevin Johnson. Mark Jackson was the lone Knicks defender standing between Chambers and the basket. Chambers got the pass from Johnson and went for a dunk. What happened next was a moment in Suns history worthy of legend.

Rather than going around the defender, Chambers went over him. He elevated from just inside the free-throw line, jumping so high that, at one point, his knees rested on Mark Jackson's shoulders. At the apex of his jump, Chambers' shoulders were parallel with the rim. The sequence ended with a thunderous two-handed slam dunk, with Chambers ducking at the last moment to avoid hitting his head on the rim. It still ranks as one of the best dunks in NBA history.

My Uncle Peter introduced me to Suns basketball. Uncle Pete is the youngest of ten kids on my mom's side. His life revolved around sports, and the Phoenix Suns were among his favorite teams. Uncle Pete lived with his parents until my nana passed away in 1985. He was twenty-four years old. Following Nana's death, Uncle Pete moved into a studio apartment and visited our house often. He loved listening to Suns games on KTUC 1400 AM radio. After work, he'd park his Toyota minitruck in our driveway, open a bag of sunflower seeds, and sit listening to Al McCoy's play-by-play broadcast. I frequently joined him, and before long I became a Suns fan.

The late 1980s and early 1990s were exciting times for Suns fans. The Suns were an up-and-coming team coached by Cotton Fitzsimmons and stacked with good players like Kevin Johnson, Jeff Hornacek, Eddy Johnson, Mark West, Dan Majerle, and Tom Chambers. My favorite was Tom Chambers, an underrated but elite NBA player of that era. The "Tommy Gun," as fans called him, was an offensive machine. He had the height to play inside, the shooting ability to play the perimeter, and the ball-handling skills to excel in transition. Chambers was stoic and played with a quiet confidence that I admired.

The teams and players we support become part of our identity. Buying our team's gear was a way to express that. To purchase authentic Suns gear in the 1980s, we went to the stadium's pro shop or a sporting goods store. In 1972, H. Cook Sporting Goods opened a shop in the new air-conditioned section of El Con Mall. In 1981, Oshman's Sporting Goods announced its purchase of all H. Cook stores. Oshman's moved into the H. Cook store at El Con. In July 1989, Champ's Sporting Goods announced it was taking over Oshman's store at El Con. Champ's retained this El Con store until the mall closed. I got my first Suns gear at this El Con Champ's store, a purple baseball cap and a #24 Tom Chambers jersey.

Suns power forward Charles Barkley once famously said athletes are not role models. I agree, but athletes can be powerful examples of what's possible when you work hard, develop your talent, and refuse to quit. Tom Chambers broke the wrist on his shooting hand in high school. He turned the setback into an opportunity by learning to shoot with his left hand, a skill he utilized throughout his professional career. I heard this story during a Suns game broadcast in the late 1980s, and it taught me to treat obstacles as opportunities for growth. Athletes may not be role models, but they can teach us a lot about life.

It is natural for teenagers to seek role models. At a time when identity is in flux, adolescents often look to athletes and celebrities for guidance. There's also a benefit to being a member of large groups, like the fan base of a sports team. With the products they carried, stores like Champ's Sporting Goods allowed teens to champion players they identified with and teams they supported. I will never forget the #24 Chambers jersey I got from Champ's Sporting Goods. Whenever I see the #24 on a basketball player's jersey, it brings back memories of my Uncle Peter, listening to Suns game broadcasts on

KTUC radio, and my earliest sports hero, Phoenix Suns legend Tom Chambers.

Sanger-Harris

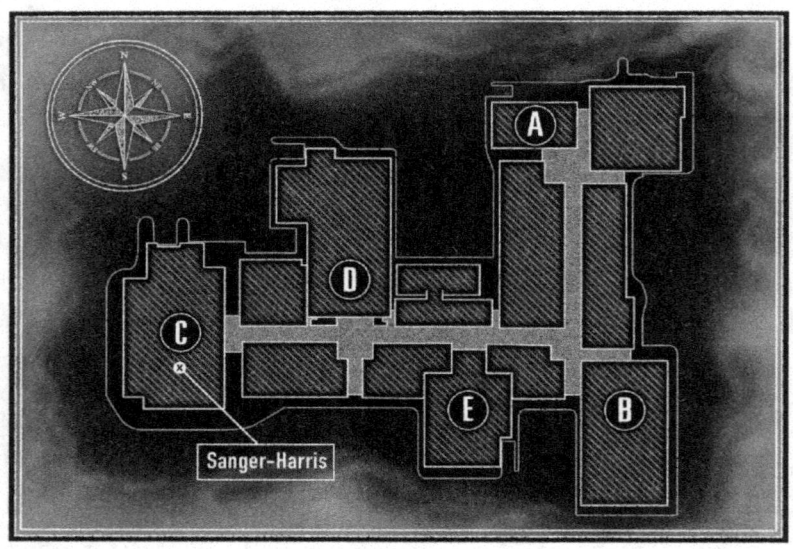

Every Gen X teen remembers shopping for clothes at the mall. While the stores varied from one mall to another, malls were the best place to go for the latest fashions. The 1980s were a decade of dubious fashion. Sometimes I wonder what we were thinking when I look at pictures from that era. Big hair, shoulder pads, spandex, acid-washed jeans, leg warmers, harem pants, fanny packs, and neon colors typify the fashion of this era. Thankfully, some elements of 1980s fashion are still popular today, like Swatch watches.

Switzerland has a celebrated history of watchmaking. Before 1960, watches were primarily mechanical, and Switzerland owned 95 percent of the watchmaking market. Then in 1969 Japan introduced the quartz watch, sparking what is known as the "Quartz Crisis." Quartz watches were more precise and required less maintenance than mechanical watches. As quartz watches gained popularity, Swiss dominion over the watchmaking industry diminished.

By the mid-1970s, Japanese quartz watches cost less than mechanical watches. Many Swiss watchmaking companies went out of business. On the brink of collapse, Switzerland's two largest watch companies, SSIH and ASUAG, combined. Under the leadership of Nicolas G. Hayek, the newly merged ASUAG-SSIH company worked to develop a product that could compete with Japan's inexpensive quartz watches. Hayek rightly guessed that people still saw the value in owning a watch with "Swiss-made" movement. Still, Hayek had to find a way to make mechanical watches competitive with quartz watches.

With everything riding on its next move, Hayek's ASUAG-SSIH company engineered a fifty-one-piece quartz-regulated watch made from injection-molded plastic. Unlike other Swiss watches, these weren't handmade. The watches were assembled on automated production lines, allowing the manufacturers to mass-produce them cheaply. Because the watches were inexpensive, consumers could afford more than one; hence, they named the line "Swatch," a contraction of the phrase "second watch."

With its debut in 1983, Swatch saved the Swiss watchmaking industry. Swatch had the goods to compete with quartz watches from Japan. Swatch watches were inexpensive and well-engineered. Though quartz-regulated, Swatch watches retained the highly desirable Swiss movement for which Switzerland's mechanical watches were famous. On top of all that, Swatch watches were incredibly stylish.

Swatch incorporated bold colors and designs into their watches like no other watch line before. Every Swatch element was a canvas for artistic expression—the straps, case, crystal, face, hands, and indices. Swatch even collaborated with artists like Kiki Picasso and Keith Haring to create art-inspired designs for their watches. Oxford Languages defines fast fashion as "inexpensive clothing produced rapidly by mass-market retailers in response to the latest trends." In 1983, the watch became fast fashion for the first time in history, thanks to Swatch.

Guess, Awatch, and M-Watch emerged with their fast-fashion watch lines, but Swatch stood head and shoulders above the competition. Swatch advertised on MTV and popular fashion magazines, including *GQ, Glamour,* and *Seventeen.* The company's savvy marketing and colorful, artistic, ever-evolving watch designs fueled Swatch's viral growth. Every year, Swatch introduced two watch lines in various design categories. For example, Swatch released its "Granita de Frutta" (Italian Ices) line in the spring of 1984. It included watches with pink, yellow, and light blue straps scented like raspberry, banana, and ice mint, respectively. [124]

Swatch was a massive success in the United States, generating $3 million in total US sales in 1983. By 1985, that figure increased to $135 million. Department stores like Sanger-Harris in El Con Mall struggled to keep pace with demand. During the 1985 Christmas season alone, Sanger-Harris averaged 400 Swatch sales weekly. The

El Con Sanger-Harris was one of 470 department stores in the US to have a Swatch Shop, an area devoted exclusively to selling Swatch-related merchandise. In addition to watches, the Swatch Shop sold crystal-protecting bands (Swatch Guards), sunglass holder straps (Chums), alpine ski-inspired sunglasses called Shields, umbrellas, wall clocks, and clothing.

A Swatch watch in the mid-1980s cost about $30. Because Swatch watches were inexpensive, people bought more than one and used them as fashion accessories. It wasn't uncommon to see people wearing more than one Swatch at a time. "I go to the UA [University of Arizona], and the new style is to wear four Swatches on one arm and three on the other," [125] said Beth Bougopoulous, a sales clerk at Diamond's department store in Park Mall. Swatch wasn't just a fad with teens and college students; it appealed to people of all ages, including kids and seniors. "I sell them from 9 years old, all the way up over the hill," [126] said Anna Bell, a sales clerk at the Sanger-Harris store in El Con.

Swatch watches were popular when I entered middle school in 1986. The cool kids at my school had more than one. That was the year my brother and I got Swatches at Sanger-Harris in El Con. Alex got the Nautilus GK 102 V1. It had a translucent blue-and-green wrist strap with an image of nautical instrumentation on the watch's face.

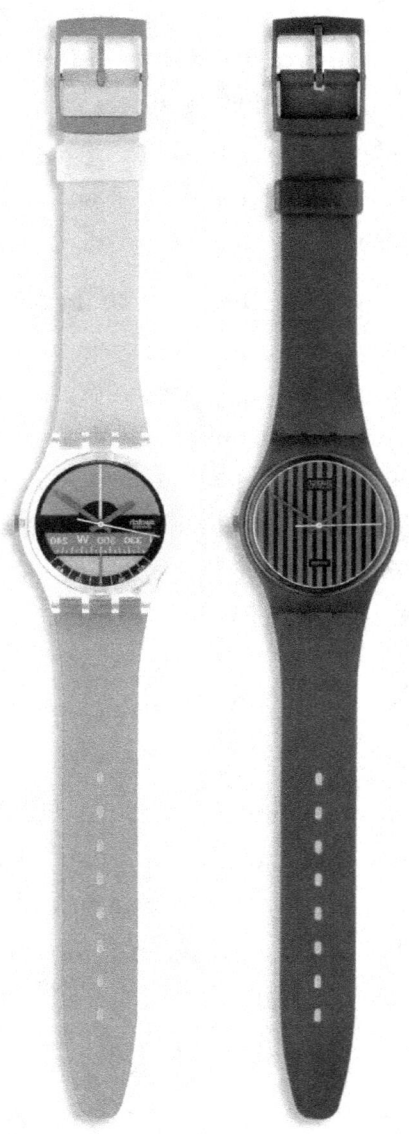

Nautilus GK 102 V1 (Image courtesy of Swatch) Left

Pinstripe GA 102 model (Image courtesy of Swatch) Right

I entered the store that day intending to buy a Jellyfish, Swatch's celebrated see-through watch. The Jellyfish was one the most popular Swatch models of all time. It was a safe pick because the Jellyfish was well-liked, and other kids at school already had it. Something I wasn't expecting happened that day, though. While looking over the array of Swatches, I felt compelled to choose one that nobody at school had. It was risky, but I wanted my Swatch to be unique. I ended up getting the Pinstripe GA 102 model. It was solid black with black and gray pinstripes on the watch face. The minute and hour hands were red, and the second hand was yellow. It was the only Swatch I've ever owned, but to this day, I'm pleased with my choice. Unlike many fashion items from the 1980s, it aged well and doesn't look out of place today.

Swatch remains an iconic watch brand. It is satisfying to witness the continued success of a company that was so much a part of my Gen X youth. Swatch is a memorable part of the 1980s and one of the rare examples of fashion that transcended the decade and achieved timeless status. As a teen, buying a Swatch was one of the first times I exercised fashion to be unique and do my own thing.

Conclusion

This chapter took us on a nostalgic teen-led tour of El Con Mall in the 1980s. We revisited the mall stores where Gen Xers commonly shopped, the items we bought, the trends we followed, and the ways we entertained ourselves. There are several stores we didn't cover, like Cele Peterson's, The College Shop, Dave Bloom & Sons, El Continental Barber Shop, El Con Custom Cobbler, Grunewald & Adams, and Steinfeld's. These are some of the most celebrated stores in El Con's history, but most Gen X teens didn't have these stores on their radar. Today, malls are no longer the social centers they once were. People still shop at malls, but they have been replaced by the Internet and social media as the primary space for social interaction, evoking a sense of nostalgia for the mall experience of the past.

We now live in the digital age, an era "in which many things are done by computer and large amounts of information are available because of computer technology." [127] The Internet has been around since the 1960s, but it wasn't until the mid-1990s that Internet usage became common in American homes. The first social media platform, SixDegrees.com, was formed in 1997. It was followed by Friendster (2002), MySpace (2003), Facebook (2004), Twitter (2006), and many more. With these applications, there was no longer a need to meet at the mall; kids could socialize from anywhere using their phones. This development, combined with the convenience of online shopping, ended the shopping mall's supremacy in consumer culture.

Like so many other things, the mall experience I had growing up is now a relic of the past. While writing this book, I have done a great deal of reflection on Generation X. Civilization is approaching a tipping point with technology. Many factors that led to the undoing of malls are also weakening the social bonds that humans need to thrive. As one of the last generations to come of age in the pre-Internet era, Generation X has a valuable storehouse of wisdom to draw from. It is our responsibility to preserve this wisdom and pass it on to future generations, ensuring that it is not lost in the digital age, hence my impulse to write this book.

INTERLUDE

George Romero's *Dawn of the Dead* (1978) is a cult classic film about the zombie apocalypse. Four human survivors take refuge in an abandoned shopping mall overrun by zombies. Realizing that the mall has everything they need to survive—food, medicine, supplies, and so on—the quartet resolves to hole up there for a time. Romero's film was shot in the late 1970s when malls were a staple element of American culture. In 2010, one could be forgiven for mistaking El Con Mall as a post-apocalyptic sequel to *Dawn of the Dead*. After years of steady decline, El Con had become a dead mall. The second half of this book tells the story of El Con's demise, but in this interlude, I'll share a unique experience I had at El Con during its "dead mall" phase.

My fascination with the topic of dead malls began accidentally during a three-month project in 2010. Like the protagonists in *Dawn of the Dead*, I took refuge in a dead mall for several weeks to work on this project. Two years later, the final remaining section of the enclosed mall was demolished, and El Con became a retail power center. My quest to understand why El Con died led me to the larger phenomenon of dead malls. This opened me up to an entire community of people who share this interest. For example, check out the subreddit r/deadmalls, a community where people post "pictures, articles, videos and discussions of malls from the past . . . and current malls in their dead, dying, abandoned or currently being demolished state." With 204,000 members, it ranks within the top 1 percent of Reddit's largest communities—demonstrating the wide-ranging interest in dead malls.

On July 26, 2021, this question was posted to the r/deadmalls community: "Why do we have a fascination with dead malls?" [128] Fifty redditors joined the conversation, doing their best to answer. Their collective posts made two things clear. First, something about dead malls is difficult to put into words. They embody ineffable qualities that people intuit but have difficulty articulating. Second, dead malls are fascinating. This interlude is my contribution to the discussion about what makes dead malls fascinating. As a dead mall enthusiast, I want to share the insights I learned while working in a dead mall. I'll identify four reasons people are intrigued by dead malls, each supported with evidence collected during my three-month project at El Con.

2010 Writing Project

The year 2010 was transformative for me. Gifted with a window of free time, I pursued my dream of writing fiction. I had been writing a story intermittently for years, but the project always stalled. Having resolved to write, I began looking for an optimal workspace. It had to be functional with access to restrooms, coffee, and food. I didn't want to pay anything, which ruled out bookstores and coffee shops. To minimize distractions, I avoided places with internet access. That eliminated libraries. One day in late February, I left my apartment and went for a walk that took me past El Con, which I hadn't been to in years. The mall had been in a prolonged decline since 2000, so I avoided going there. Curious, I decided to drop in and take a look.

That decision resulted in my first experience of a dead mall. After passing through El Con's main entrance, I discovered the post-apocalyptic scene described in the introduction to this book. Half of El Con, the original north-south wing, had been replaced with three new entities—Century 20 Theaters, Home Depot, and Target. Only the east-west wing of the mall remained. I knew El Con was struggling, but I had no idea until I entered how bad it was. The mall was clearly on its last legs. Still, something about the atmosphere resonated with me, even though I couldn't say what. In retrospect, one reason I felt drawn to the mall in that state was that it embodied elements of a restorative environment.

The Dead Mall as a Restorative Environment

The American Psychological Association defines a restorative environment as "an environment—often a natural setting—that rejuvenates a person and can help restore depleted attention resources or reduce emotional and psychological stress." [129] Nature is a good example. Just think of a time when you felt recharged after spending time outdoors. For an environment to be restorative, it must exhibit the following four characteristics: [130]

1. Being away
2. Fascination
3. Extent
4. Compatibility

The setting I encountered at El Con in 2010 was unlike anything I'd experienced before. All but a handful of stores were abandoned; their interiors empty, dark, and barred shut. It felt as if I'd wandered onto a set of the *Walking Dead*, a TV series about the zombie apocalypse. After emerging from a coma in the hospital, Officer Rick Grimes discovers that the world has been taken over by zombies. Several episodes in the series show Rick and/or members of his group breaking into abandoned buildings and using them to escape from the invaders. The empty buildings became a refuge from the world. In a similar fashion, each time I arrived at the mall to write it felt like stepping into another world, creating the "being away" quality of a restorative environment.

The second quality, "fascination," describes the ability to "hold your attention without you having to focus or direct it in a certain way." [131] There are two kinds of fascination, hard and soft. Hard fascination absorbs your attention so completely that you're unable to think about anything else. An example is being engrossed in a movie at the theater. Soft fascination is stimulating enough to absorb your attention but not enough to hinder reflection and introspection. An example is a walk outside to relax. I experienced soft fascination at El Con during my writing project in 2010. A big reason for that was the mall's dystopian vibe.

While in a dead mall, it feels like you're the last person on Earth. Even though nearly all the stores were vacant, El Con was still a functioning mall in 2010. The Poster Warehouse, El Con Custom Cobblers, El Continental Barber Shop, and JCPenney still operated in the mall interior. A steady trickle of people came to El Con all day, some to walk laps in the air-conditioned setting and others to shop. Most people came to shop at JCPenney. Also, despite the empty stores and anemic traffic, the floors were waxed, the plants were cared for, and the temperature remained at 70°F. Something about the juxtaposition of abandoned stores and the maintained space created a magical effect, as if time had stopped and I was the only one who knew.

The third quality of restorative environments is "extent," a feeling of being at ease and comfortable. For an environment to be restorative it must be predictable, and to be predictable it must be familiar. That doesn't mean that extent is limited to places you've been to; however, the new environment must be "similar enough to places you have been that you are not feeling uncomfortable, confused, or out-of-place." [132] When an environment is familiar, you can let your guard down and relax. But familiarity isn't the only factor of concern. Restorative environments must also be comfortable.

Only when an environment is familiar and comfortable can you allow your mind to wander.

Like all malls, El Con was a predictable environment, designed for safety and comfort. This held true throughout El Con's dead mall phase too. Despite all the vacant shops, the mall continued to employ cleaning crews to keep the space looking good from open to close. Security guards monitored the parking lot and the mall's interior, so I never felt unsafe writing there in 2010. A security guard named John actually befriended me. He made conversation with me one day while I was working. I told him I was writing a book, and he jokingly asked if I'd name a character after him. From that day forward, John made it a point to check in with me.

The fourth quality of restorative environments is compatibility, a measure of how well the space works for you. If you're in an environment out of necessity or because you have no other options, it's unlikely to be restorative. However, if you're in an environment because you want to be there, and you like it, it has restorative potential. In short, "The compatibility component is all about feeling enjoyment and congruence in your environment." [133] There must be congruence between what the space offers and what you're using it for.

The day I decided El Con would be my writing workspace, I spotted a row of tables outside the abandoned Carol's Yogurt Shoppe. There were four tables with chairs. I chose the second table as my writing station. Each day of the project I walked to the mall, set up at the second table, and wrote. Here's a picture of the table where I worked (bottom-left corner):

My café table workstation at El Con Mall

(Image courtesy of Jason Damas and Ross Schendel of Labelscar.com)

As you can see, it was clean and comfortable and made for a great writing space. One of the best things about the workstation was that it didn't cost anything. In bookstores and coffee shops, you have to make purchases to justify your presence there. After a few hours, you start feeling like you've worn out your welcome. Although you likely won't get kicked out, there's a socially acceptable amount of time to work in such places. After two hours or so, the pressure to leave mounts. That's not the case at a dead mall.

I like to hear activity happening around me when I write, or I start feeling restless. The voices of mall patrons echoing in the empty corridors provided white noise throughout the day. Mall walkers and JCPenney customers provided the right amount of activity to keep my mind stimulated. While the mall's interior was dead, the stores on its perimeter, including Target, Starbucks, and Chick-fil-A, offered the food and coffee I needed to get through the day. On days when writing became particularly frustrating, I packed up my things and walked over to Target where I'd treat myself to a Snickers bar, a bag of Peanut M&M's, or a dark-roast coffee from Starbucks. El Con provided everything I needed, making it a highly compatible environment for writing my book.

The Dead Mall as a Contemplative Space

A second reason dead malls are fascinating is that they embody elements of a contemplative space. In his dissertation, "Immersive Experience: Evoking the Elements of Contemplative Space in Japanese Architecture," Dr. Brian Corr defines a contemplative space as "a constructed spatial environment which, through its structure, material composition and aesthetic expression, provides the opportunity for transformative psychological, emotional, perceptual or spiritual experience." [134]

Defining what makes a space contemplative or not is difficult because it involves mystery. How does one quantify the transformative psychological, emotional, perceptual, or spiritual effectiveness of a space? The answer is, you can't. Ultimately, it comes down to how a space makes you feel, how the elements within a space work together to put a person in the frame of mind where transformative experiences are possible. Thanks to the pioneering work of Dr. Corr and other researchers, we have a language to talk about contemplative spaces and identify the elements that contribute to them.

Contemplative architecture is an emerging practice focused on environments that allow people to transcend the distractions of everyday life and to experience awakening. Traditionally, places like churches, cathedrals, monasteries, mosques, synagogues, museums, and libraries have provided these opportunities. A building need not be religiously affiliated to function as a contemplative space. More and more, architects incorporate elements into their building design that raise the contemplative potential of secular spaces. To be clear, most shopping malls were never built with contemplative potential as a guiding factor. Rather, most malls only gain the potential to become contemplative spaces as a byproduct of the emptying out that occurs as they die.

Three key elements of any contemplative environment are lighting, sound, and space. Uncluttered, open areas are key elements of contemplative spaces. While the entirety of El Con Mall fit this description in 2010, the food court stood out. El Con hadn't had a dedicated food court for thirty-nine years. As part of the mall's revitalization plan, a food court was built on the former site of the El Con 6 theater in 2001. The 30,000-square-foot food court sat vacant for years. No tenants moved into the space, so few people went to that part of the mall. It was usually empty, as seen here:

El Con Food Court

(Image courtesy of Jason Damas and Ross Schendel of Labelscar.com)

Sometimes I'd go to the food court, sit with my back against the wall, and write on the floor because it was the only place where I could find electrical outlets. If my computer battery was running low, and I wasn't ready to quit for the day, that was my only option. On one occasion, afternoon sunlight streamed down from the gazebo windows above, filling the empty court with a warm glow. I was alone, but I could hear the muffled voices of mall walkers as they traversed the main concourse. For the first time, I detected an element of the holy within the mall, a feeling not unlike being in a quiet church.

The absence of people and activity in a dead mall allows you to slow down, creating the conditions that make awareness possible. For example, during my writing project, El Con contracted a painter to create a new mall directory. Ten yards away from my table workstation was a blank wall, which the painter used for the new directory. Here's a picture of the painter at work.

Painter working on El Con Directory

(Image courtesy of Jason Damas and Ross Schendel of Labelscar.com)

Watching the painter stenciling and painting the store names for the new directory was a unique experience that never would've happened if the mall had been full of people. In the absence of crowds, noise, and constant activity, the mind is free to wander. Dead malls give you the time and space to stop, look, and observe what's happening around you because they contain elements of a contemplative space.

Dead Malls and Place Attachment

Another reason for fascination with dead malls is place attachment. This is a concept from environmental psychology that deals with "the person-to-place bonds that evolve through emotional connection, meaning, and understandings of a specific place and/or features of a place." [135] To illustrate, consider this example. When I was ten, my dad left a respiratory therapist position at Tucson Medical Center to start a landscaping/yard cleaning business with two of my uncles. He called the business Triple C, which represented the last name of each of the co-owners—Callahan, Cuesta, and Cuesta. Not long after they started, my uncles found other work and left the business.

Dad had more work than he could handle, but he couldn't afford to drop any customers. To help, my brother Alex and I worked with Dad in the summertime. Cleaning yards in Tucson during the summer is no easy task. Oddly enough, I didn't mind doing it. I took pride in the realization I could work hard and that I was doing my part to help the family. Some of my fondest adolescent memories involve summer work with Dad and Alex, but one day stands out in particular.

It was during the summer monsoon season, and we were working at the Discovery Inn. It was a difficult job, requiring two people to mow grass for most of the morning. Alex and I mowed while Dad edged the lawns and trimmed the hedges. That day, mowing was even more difficult because the grass was overgrown and wet from recent rains. The heat was stifling. By the time we broke for lunch, Alex and I were already worn out, but hours of work lay in wait for us. Toward the end of the day, dark clouds rolled in and smothered the sun. With an hour of work left, we raced to finish before the rain arrived. I remember how cool the wind felt as we finished cleaning the last section of the property. The sense of shared purpose I felt as we packed up the truck to go home is a treasured memory.

Such experiences bonded me not only to Alex and Dad but also to the job sites as well. Over many summers helping Dad, a handful of properties emerged as places that are special to me, thanks to experiences like the one at Discovery Inn. Now I understand that this was a result of forming place attachments. Personal experiences and memories are key factors in place attachment. As the article "Place Attachment Theory: Exploring Our Emotional Bonds with Environments" notes, "The places where we've had significant life events—both positive and negative—often become deeply ingrained in our psyche." [136] Length of exposure to a place plays a role as well. "The more time we spend in a place, the more likely we are to develop an attachment to it." [137] With all the memory-making potential they offer, is it any wonder that people like me feel a connection to the malls where we spent much of our youth?

The Dead Mall and Ruinenlust

Another contributing element to the appeal of dead malls is *ruinenlust*, the obsession with ruins. The term *ruinenlust* refers to "the feeling of pleasure taken from spending time amidst ruins." [138] Something about ghost towns, crumbling structures, and abandoned spaces ignites the imagination. Perhaps it's morbid fascination, the kind that makes us look as we drive past the scene of a car accident. We all know we're going to die someday, and that scares us, if only at an unconscious level. Perhaps our morbid fascination is nothing more than an attempt to approach life's edge and peer into the abyss, to catch a glimpse of what lies on the other side. Whatever the case, to spend time in a ruin is to linger in death's presence. You cannot help but reflect on mortality.

In telling El Con's story, I have tried to share some of my city's story as well. Tucson is a city with a rich Native American and Mexican culture. This is reflected in the art around town. For example, on South Fourth Avenue between East 24th and East 25th street is this mural, created by Wagon Burner Arts:

(Photo by author with permission from Wagon Burner Arts)

It's a close-up of La Catrina, a calavera in female form. The calavera is a colorfully decorated representation of the human skull, often used as part of the Mexican holiday known as "Dia de los Muertos" or "Day of the Dead." Celebrated every year on November 1 and 2, Dia de los Muertos is a time to honor the memory of loved ones who have passed on. The image above accurately captures the dynamics at work in ruins. Through the medium of a physical object, we are brought face to face with death.

Ruins bear witness to the life force that once occupied a space. When you visit a ruin, you encounter faint echoes of this life force. The wistful nature of dead malls often encourages self-reflection. In a *ruinenlust* blog at emotionalgranularity.com, Jonathan Cook offers this profound assessment: "Who among us is not ruined? When we enter a building that has fallen apart, we offer the wrecked portions of our personalities a mirror in which they can finally step to the fore. We acknowledge the towers that have fallen from our own fortresses, and we take reassurance in the certainty that those who now boldly announce their immortal vitality will soon stand where we stand." [139]

The experience of writing for six hours a day in a dead mall for three months was cathartic for me. It came at a time when I was approaching midlife, and deeper questions about what's important in life and how I want to spend my remaining time were entering my consciousness. Seeing the mall in its stripped-down state, so different from what it used to be, forced me to acknowledge that I too was getting older.

The saying "misery loves company" often carries a negative connotation. But in this case, experiencing the mall in its diminished state was comforting to me. It sparked an extended period of reminiscing and reflection that eased me through the midlife transition. As described by Cook in the quote above, the mall became a mirror through which I perceived my own brokenness. Every day I worked at El Con, the mall was quietly working in my subconscious, planting the seeds that would one day sprout into the idea for this book.

Conclusion

This is my contribution to the ongoing discussion about our fascination with dead malls. Nostalgia certainly plays a big role. Nostalgia is defined as "a sentimentality for the past, typically for a period or place with happy personal associations." [140] The Ghost Directory chapter offers numerous examples of the link between nostalgia and dead malls. Had the topic not been addressed in the previous chapter, I would have brought it up here. Hopefully, the four ideas I mentioned—restorative space, contemplative space, place attachment, and ruinenlust—will add to meaningful dead mall discussions like the ones on the r/deadmalls subreddit.

I began this section referencing the *Dawn of the Dead* film, and I will end that way too. After landing atop the Monroeville Mall, Stephen, a helicopter pilot, and Francine, his girlfriend, are seen observing the zombies through a rooftop window. "What are they doing? Why do they come here?" Francine asks.

"Some kind of instinct," Stephen replies. "Memory of what they used to do." "This was an important place in their lives." [141]

If I had to think of one statement to explain people's fascination with dead malls, this is it. Ultimately, the popularity of dead malls is proof that malls played an important role in many people's lives. Despite their maligned reputations, malls are more than temples of consumerism where people go to shop till they drop. Malls fulfill a critical role by providing a community gathering space for entertainment and social connection. Like the zombies wandering Monroeville Mall, this is why people join online communities to share pictures, videos, and memories about dead malls. Because above all, the mall was an important place in our lives.

CHAPTER 5

THEATER OF WAR

Theater of War

L ong before they came to El Con's doorstep, big-box stores were creating controversy in towns and cities throughout America. In 1996 a property owner in Hazlet Township, New Jersey, obtained approval for a 129,000-square-foot building on the southbound side of Route 35. For more than six months, the property owner refused to confirm the identity of the building's tenant. Neighboring residents feared it was Home Depot, citing concerns about increased noise and traffic. Vernon Manning, who lived near the proposed building site, wrote to the local newspaper: "They don't want to admit [that it's a Home Depot] because they know people are going to get upset," Manning said. "You are talking about a residential neighborhood. Beers street has a school, a playground, a medical office and a hospital at the end of the street." [142]

It turns out the proposed building was Home Depot. Neighborhood residents were not informed until late in the approval process. Adding insult to injury, developers sought to rezone an adjacent 3.5-acre lot to build additional satellite stores. Neighborhood residents were up in arms. In addition to traffic concerns, they feared for the safety of children in the area. "By the time they [children] go to school, traffic is in full swing," Marcy Mason said. On May 21, 1996, the township committee met to discuss the requested rezoning. Roughly seventy people attended the meeting, armed with petitions containing 400 signatures in protest.

While they could not keep Home Depot out, the protesters did halt rezoning on the 3.5-acre lot, preventing the intrusion of satellite stores. The township committee agreed the area could not handle the traffic load that these additional retailers would generate. "It's a quality-of-life issue for the people in that area," Deputy Mayor Mary Jane Wiley said. [143] Despite opposition from neighborhood residents, The Hazlet Home Depot, store #926, opened on January 30, 1997. Little did they know it, but 2,400 miles away in Tucson, AZ, residents of the neighborhoods surrounding El Con Mall were about to engage with this very threat.

For its first fifteen years, El Con Mall thrived as a shopping center without equal in Tucson. Beginning in 1975, however, competitor malls emerged, and El Con lost ground. By the 1990s, El Con was a run-down mall sorely in need of renovation. In October 1996, concurrent to the drama playing out in Hazlet, a string of events set in motion that ultimately brought the big-box controversy to El Con Mall. It began with an announcement that Park Mall, El Con's nearest competitor, had been purchased by a well-funded mall management operation. Soon afterwards, in 1997, El Con's owners demolished the mall's north wing to make room for a twenty-screen theater. This left acres of mall property available for construction. Then rumors surfaced that El Con's owners were courting Walmart to fill the empty space.

The possibility of a Walmart so close to their homes alarmed residents of El Con's surrounding neighborhoods. Then, a second bombshell dropped: Home Depot would be coming too. By the late 1990s, Tucson, like many other American towns and cities, was under assault by armies of big-box stores. Recall that "big-box" refers to a large discount store, over 100,000 square feet in size. Such stores were popping up everywhere, including locations near established neighborhoods. News of the two superstores coming to El Con sparked a fire of dissent from nearby residents. Part of their opposition amounted to self-interest. People who lived in these neighborhoods stood to lose the most in terms of the increased traffic, noise, and crime that inevitably comes with superstores. But this wasn't the only motivation spurring the opposition.

Despite its fall from grace, El Con was beloved by the midtown community. Many people cared about El Con and wanted to see the mall restored to its former glory. They disagreed with El Con's owners, who appeared to be taking the mall in another direction, at odds with its established character. By courting Walmart and Home Depot, El Con's owners were putting the mall on a path to become a retail power center. James Chen, former director of investing and trading content at Investopedia, defines a power center as "a large (250,000 to 750,000 square ft.) outdoor shopping mall that usually includes three or more 'big box' stores. This type of property might include smaller retailers and restaurants that are either free-standing or located in strip plazas and surrounded by a shared parking lot. Power centers are built for the convenience of motorists." [144]

The threat of Walmart and Home Depot sparked a war between the neighborhoods surrounding the mall and El Con's owners. The former wanted El Con to remain an enclosed mall; the latter sought to transition it to a power center. The neighborhoods battled fiercely to save the mall, but El Con, as you will see, was fighting a war on two fronts—one with Park Mall, the other with invading superstores. This chapter illustrates the factors that drew El Con into the war and the threats the mall faced on both fronts.

Joseph Kivel: Competing Interests

The seeds of El Con's undoing were sown early—two years before the mall opened to be exact. Chapter 2 introduced Joseph Kivel, one of El Con's principal founders. Recall that in 1958, Joseph Kivel, a stakeholder in Kivel Interests and Magna Corp., announced the start of construction on Tucson's first-ever regional shopping center, El Con. In addition to owning the land upon which El Con was built and investing in its construction, Joseph Kivel was instrumental in lining up tenants for the new shopping center. As reported in the *Arizona Daily Star*: "At the time, downtown was the totally dominant retail center. Its stores included Steinfeld's, Levy's, Sears, JCPenney, Jácome's, Myerson's, Dave Bloom & Sons, and Grunewald & Adams. Malls were virtually unknown, and moving east to the new shopping center was considered chancy by many of the conservative, risk-fearing merchants." [145]

Undaunted, Kivel persisted in his efforts to lure tenants to El Con. According to some reports, Kivel repeatedly visited some downtown stores until he convinced their merchants to sign a lease. [146] As a testament to Kivel's negotiating skills, all but three of the stores listed above (Sears, Jácome's, and Myerson's) signed with El Con.

Having a persistent, growth-minded investor like Joseph Kivel leading the charge for El Con seems like a good thing, right? To an extent, it was. Unfortunately, Kivel's desire for a Tucson shopping center wasn't exclusive to El Con. In 1958, the same year construction on El Con was announced Kivel sought zoning on a land parcel just 2.9 miles east of El Con to build a second shopping center. Securing zoning rights for this land proved difficult, but Kivel persisted. When he set his mind to something, he was relentless. Many residents of the Rogers Elementary School area were opposed to a shopping center in their neighborhood. To win them over, Kivel donated nine acres to the city for a park and agreed to build a buffer wall between the neighborhoods and the future shopping center. [147]

After four years of tough negotiations, Kivel obtained the rezoning rights he needed to build Park Mall Shopping Center, which became in time El Con's rival. Sears department store opened for business in 1965, followed by Furr's Cafeteria in 1968. For the next six years, no stores were added to Park Mall Center. This, in part, was because Joseph Kivel was holding out until the right opportunity presented itself. In a five-part, *Arizona Daily Star* series called "The Mall Maker of Tucson," merchants describe Kivel as a "stubborn, tough negotiator." As they explained, "His tactics are simple. He refuses to bend. He states a price and will let his property sit vacant until he gets it." [148] C. Roger Fulton Jr., author of the *Mall Maker of Tucson* series, notes the Broadway-Hale Stores of Los Angeles (later Carter Hawley Hayes Stores, Inc.) expressed interest in building a store at Park Mall as early as 1969. Three years later, they were still tied up in negotiations with Kivel.

Eventually, a deal was reached, and two new department stores joined Sears as anchors at Park Mall—Diamonds and The Broadway. Diamonds opened its doors on August 5, 1974, and The Broadway opened on August 26, 1974. By December of 1974, additional tenants began filling in the T-shaped mall space, connecting the three anchors. At 800,000 square feet, Park Mall was smaller than El Con (1 million square feet). Still, when Park Mall was dedicated on May 3, 1975, it created a seismic shift in Tucson's retail landscape. The city had not one but two regional shopping centers separated by just three miles. The week-long dedication ceremonies featured music by the Tucson Boys Band and mariachis, a balloon release, dignitary appearances (including a visit by blues legend B. B. King), a "Century of Fashion" pageant, and performances by the Fred Cowan Puppets, a bilingual puppet troupe. [149]

The shock waves created by Park Mall's grand opening were felt immediately at El Con. When Park Mall opened, El Con was fifteen years old and midway through its own expansion and enclosure project. It added new stores, connecting the east-west and north-south wings, while enclosing the mall's original north-south section. Despite the exciting improvements planned for El Con, nothing could overcome the buzz created by a new mall. When Diamonds opened in 1974, Kivel boasted that Park Mall was "in the very heart of the most densely populated and rapidly developing area of Tucson." [150] El Con now had to compete with Park Mall for these customers. Some people, like Henry Quinto, President of Levy's, were optimistic. "We are delighted the city has grown to a point where it can house an additional retailer," Quinto said. "We are happy to welcome them." [151] Others, like Joe Pesci, executive director of the El Con Merchants Association, were more sober in their assessment. "Park Mall will definitely present new competition for El Con," Pesci conceded. "We will see some slowing for awhile, but I think we can recapture any losses eventually. It will take more promotion, more hustle and more advertising." [152]

Joseph Kivel was sole owner of Park Mall and part-owner (33 percent stake) of El Con Mall. The question arises: why would Kivel build a competing shopping center so close to El Con? It's a question that the Papanikolas family of Magna Investment & Development Corp., co-owners of El Con, surely asked as well. Having a major competitor three miles away on the same street cut into El Con's customer base. Furthermore, some argued that Kivel deliberately sabotaged El Con's development to benefit Park Mall, where he kept 100 percent of the profits. "I think the way Joe saw it was that, 'A dollar is 50 cents for me at El Con, but a dollar is a dollar for me at Park Mall,'" an anonymous merchant said. [153] Kivel denied interfering with El Con's development, but some remained skeptical. "Time and again we had major corporations calling and saying that their real estate people were interested in leasing at El Con, but that the resident partner (Kivel) only talks about some other center." [154]

Kivel's decision to build Park Mall caused a permanent rift with Gus Papanikolas, Magna Corp. president and co-owner of El Con.

Communication ground to a halt, and important business decisions were delayed because Kivel and Papanikolas disagreed on everything. The situation got so bad that the El Con Merchants Association threatened to file a lawsuit that would force the warring partners to agree on a management policy for El Con Mall. In a *Mall Maker of Tucson* article, C. Roger Fulton Jr. provides a vignette showing how bad the situation was. It happened at a meeting with Charles E. Conner, El Con's attorney:

> During one argument in Conner's downtown offices, Kivel and Gus Papanikolas had to be separated by the office staff and relatives, and in other meetings the two developers would speak to each other only through intermediaries. Said Leon Levy, former owner of Levy's, 'Kivel and Papanikolas fought all the time . . . I separated them myself, a dozen times . . . they just wouldn't speak for long periods of time.' [155]

Kivel downplayed the acrimony between himself and Gus Papanikolas. "We may have had heated arguments, but never a physical fight," Kivel said. "Gus was the kind of guy who thought everyone was trying to take advantage of him. It was really tough trying to talk to a guy like that." [156]

The two sides eventually reached an informal agreement. The Papanikolas family would manage El Con Mall, and Kivel would collect 33 percent of the profits. Kivel insisted his business interest in Park Mall never influenced his decisions about El Con. No one can say for sure, but it's hard to believe Kivel didn't secretly have a rooting interest in Park Mall. Kivel stood to gain more from Park Mall's success, so he likely favored it over El Con. Regardless, Kivel's decision to build a competing shopping center clearly weakened El Con Mall. El Con faced competition from other malls later but none so directly as Park Mall. C. Roger Fulton Jr. characterized the problem this way: "Joseph K. Kivel's Park Mall was to be 2.9 miles east of its forerunner, and on the same street–East Broadway. The proximity of the two sites guaranteed that El Con would lose a huge chunk of its sales." [157]

With experienced players like Magna Corp. and Kivel Interests guiding El Con's development, management should have been an area of strength. Early on, Kivel's persistence and unwillingness to accept no for an answer secured many of El Con's first tenants. Kivel enjoyed his privacy and avoided publicity whenever possible, but behind the scenes he was always working. Consider this story from Joe Pesci, former executive director and manager of El Con: "A security guard called me at home to tell me he found a little guy wandering through the El Con after the mall had shut down for the night. I asked the guard to put him on the phone after the description sounded familiar. It was Kivel. I told the guard to let him go, he owned the place." [158]

Turns out, Kivel habitually stopped by his malls at night for impromptu walk-arounds. He did so because he thought it was a good idea to check in on the guards. Imagine that: the owner of the mall checking in regularly on the guards. That's dedication. Just imagine how El Con might have fared had all of Kivel's attention been focused on it instead of being divided with Park Mall.

Tucson Mall

Nobody knew what effect Park Mall would have on El Con when it opened in 1974. Because Park Mall was so close, it had the potential to cut into El Con's customer base. [159] A much bigger threat emerged on Tucson's northwest side: the Old Pueblo's third regional shopping center, Tucson Mall. Tucson Mall opened on March 22, 1982. Unlike El Con and Park Mall, The Tucson Mall was built by a well-funded organization that specialized in urban and suburban shopping mall development, Forest City Rental Properties. At a cost of $77 million, the double-level mall boasted five department stores and over 1.35 million square feet of retail space. Tucson Mall also featured a dedicated food court called "Picnic Place." Food courts were the popular trend in malls at the time, and neither El Con nor Park Mall had one.

I rarely shopped at Tucson Mall because it was a twenty-minute drive from my home. On the few occasions I did, the mall amazed me. It was in a league of its own, more modern than El Con and Park Mall. It didn't take long for Tucson Mall to usurp El Con as the premier shopping center in town. Part of the reason El Con took a back seat to Tucson Mall was because, from 1979 to 1996, El Con's owners had avoided making any meaningful improvements to the mall. It was the same story over at Park Mall. Following its grand opening in 1974, Joe Kivel was reluctant to invest money in the upkeep of Park Mall. Over the course of two decades, Park Mall fell into disrepair and became dated. El Con underwent a significant renovation in the late 1970s, but it, too, fell behind Tucson Mall. From the mid-1980s onward, El Con and Park Mall fought it out for second place.

The First Front

By the mid-1990s, El Con and Park Mall were long past their prime and sorely in need of an overhaul. In 1996, Paul Schloss, a retail specialist with Grubb & Ellis Co, criticized the outdated malls. Park Mall and El Con "by mutual agreement have chosen not to upgrade and move with evolving trends," Schloss said. "They're like a can of Coke that has been left out overnight. The fizz is gone." [160] The push that El Con and Park Mall needed to overcome their complacency came on May 25, 1995. On that day, Joe Kivel passed away at age eighty-five. Kivel's estate transferred to his wife, Esther, and two sons, Lee and Foster. It included a 33 percent ownership interest in El Con Mall and 100 percent ownership of Park Mall. Despite the checkered history between the Kivel and Papanikolas families, Mike Papanikolas honored Kivel by describing him as "very astute and extremely knowledgeable about real estate." [161] Kivel's facility with predicting real estate trends didn't extend to mall management, though. For nearly two decades, Kivel apparently allowed El Con and Park Mall to languish. As noted in the *Arizona Daily Star*, "Retail experts say Park Mall has suffered under years of benign neglect from the Kivel family, which also is a part-owner of nearby El Con Mall. Without the threat of competition, the Kivels decided to maximize cash flow instead of reinvesting profits in the malls." [162]

El Con and Park Mall continued their detente after Kivel's death, but the fortunes of both malls were about to change. On October 7, 1996, General Growth Properties (GGP) announced its purchase of Park Mall. The Kivels sold the mall to GGP for $50 million, half in cash and half in shares. [163] As one of the most successful mall developers in the country, GGP had the capital and industry knowledge necessary to transform Park Mall into a premier shopping mall. In 1996, GGP had ownership interests in forty-seven malls and managed sixty malls. Purchasing struggling malls and transforming them into successes was GGP's bread and butter, and the organization had the financial firepower needed to bankroll expensive renovations. Foster Kivel said the family chose GGP over other prospective buyers because, "We concluded they were best suited to carry out our father's wishes for the mall." [164] GGP's chief financial officer, Bernard Freibaum, said they were keen to invest in Tucson because it was a strong market. [165]

The sale of Park Mall shifted the balance of power between the city's three major malls. Soon after it opened, Tucson Mall became the undisputed ruler of the mall scene in the Old Pueblo. El Con, Park Mall, and Foothills Mall posed no serious challenge to Tucson Mall from the mid-1980s onward. As noted in the *Tucson Citizen*, "Tucson Mall has dominated the city's retail scene for more than a decade. In large part, that's because the ownership at El Con Mall and Park Mall either didn't have the capital or chose not to invest it in improving their centers." [166] That all changed when GGP, the number-two mall management and development firm in the country, purchased Park Mall. With a well-funded developer like GGP, money would not be a limiting factor in Park Mall's renovation. In addition, the likelihood that Park Mall would emerge from its makeover as a modern, thriving mall was virtually assured with the industry experts at GGP guiding the project.

Before construction started, Park Mall was already being talked about as a challenger to Tucson Mall. As noted in the *Tucson Citizen*, "New

Park Mall owner General Growth Properties, like Tucson Mall developer Forest City Enterprises, is one of the country's major mall developers and managers. That gives Park Mall the financial clout to mount a serious challenge to Tucson Mall's supremacy." [167] Tucson Mall officials projected confidence in the face of Park Mall's reversal of fortune. Mitch Stallard, president of Forest City Southwest (the company that developed Tucson Mall), argued that Tucson was capable of supporting more than one successful mall. "We don't think we will get hurt," Stallard said regarding Park Mall's renovation. "Although we may lose a few sales here and there." [168] Despite attempts like these to put on a brave face, it's clear that officials at Tucson Mall had taken notice of their resurgent eastside challenger.

General Growth Properties vaulted Park Mall into the top tier of city malls and threw El Con into existential crisis. When the dust from the Park Mall sale settled, attention shifted to El Con. What would it do to stay relevant? Park Mall had always been a thorn in El Con's side, but the GGP sale turned that thorn into a deadly knife. In place of a middling competitor, El Con would soon have a lethal competitor three miles down the road. Barry O'Connor, Park Mall's general manager, was clear about Park Mall's intentions: "We want to be the dominant shopping center on the eastside," [169] O'Connor said. "The finite detail we haven't come to terms with, but it's going to be of multimillion (magnitude) depending on the scope of what is approved." [170]

Details of Park Mall's planned renovation leaked out for months, and with each revelation, pressure on El Con to respond increased. Some local retailers expressed doubt about El Con's viability. As noted by

Ernie Heltsley, writer for the *Arizona Daily Star,* "El Con, caught between two modern and larger malls, could be left out in the cold without a sweeping update, or so the reasoning goes among some retail-industry analysts who asked not to be identified." [171] For the second time, El Con Mall was put in a precarious position by Park Mall. The first was in 1974 when Joe Kivel opened a rival mall three miles away from El Con. The second was in 1996 when Joe Kivel's family sold Park Mall to a mall developer with the wherewithal to put El Con out of business.

Turn-of-the-Century Theater

El Con's owners publicly downplayed the significance of Park Mall's good fortune. Even before the deal with GGP was announced, there were rumors that two of El Con's anchors, Foley's and JCPenney, would move to Park Mall if new owners emerged. El Con's general manager, Mike Papanikolas, acknowledged the possibility in a news article. "We aren't just going to sit back and take it," he vowed. Though he struck a defiant tone, what Papanikolas said next didn't inspire confidence in the direction El Con was headed. "It's no secret we've been taking a good hard look at remodeling. But our position is that (El Con's retail mix) will stay pretty much the same." [172] It was a head-scratching comment to say the least. Park Mall was bought out by the second most powerful mall developer in the country, and El Con's plan was to stay the same? Just imagine how retailers at El Con felt. Papanikolas' statement couldn't have inspired confidence that El Con's management understood the threat and were taking meaningful action to address it.

What would El Con do to counter Park Mall's resurgence? Many in Tucson's retail community expressed doubt about El Con's viability. David Dolgen, former president of Forest City Southwest (the developer of Tucson Mall), warned that without major changes, El Con would continue to deteriorate. "Unless El Con is substantially enhanced, it probably will not survive as an enclosed regional mall," [173] Dolgen said. To keep pace with its rival, El Con basically had two options. The first was to match Park Mall's effort. That would require El Con's owners to spend tens of millions of dollars on renovations, attract new anchor stores, and breathe life back into the mall's anemic core. The second option called for El Con to differentiate itself from Park Mall and Tucson Mall. El Con would have to reinvent itself as a niche mall, providing stores and services that other malls didn't offer.

With a well-funded, professional outfit like GGP in the other corner, El Con had no chance of winning a head-to-head fight with Park Mall. Option one was a no-go. El Con's only path forward was option two—reinvention. Mitch Stallard, president of Forest City Southwest, summarized El Con's plight in a statement to *Tucson Citizen* business writer William Clemens: "El Con needs to be rehabbed and repositioned in the marketplace. It can't just stay the way it is. It's going to take some capital investment and only the owners know what is planned." [174] Stallard was right; only El Con's owners knew the direction in which they planned to take the mall. El Con and Park Mall played their cards close to the chest, revealing little about their renovation plans. Then, in September 1997, the first glimmer of El Con's future surfaced; it centered on a movie theater.

The first theater at El Con Mall, the El Con 6, opened on August 15, 1979, to a packed house. It was Tucson's first six-screen movie theater. Tickets sold for 99 cents, and the opening night proceeds were donated to the March of Dimes. Following a ribbon-cutting ceremony at 5:00 p.m., there was a cocktail party at El Con's Tequila Mockingbird restaurant for a select few. Roughly 3,000 people showed up to see six films: *Watership Down, The Enforcer, Winds of Chance, Murder by Decree, Agatha, and Movie, Movie,* with showtimes of 7:30, 9:30, and 11:30 p.m. Construction on the theater continued up to the last minute—literally. Doors were scheduled to open at 7:00 p.m., but as the first moviegoers arrived, the doors were still being installed. At 6:30 pm, workers were still putting the finishing touches on the cashier's window. But the show went on as scheduled. [175]

Opening night at the El Con 6 Theater (Copyright Arizona Daily Star)

For the next eighteen years, the El Con 6 Theater served as a primary entertainment hub for the mall. But like the rest of the mall, by the mid-1990s the theater was really showing its age. El Con 6 Theater, renamed AMC Theater, closed its doors for good on September 1, 1997. The next day, Foster Kivel, part-owner of El Con, said he would make a major announcement regarding the mall's future the following day. "The closing of the theater is a small part of the announcement," [176] Kivel teased. Reporters pressed for more information, but Kivel remained tight-lipped. The following day, he announced that AMC Theater had closed to make way for a new, multi-million-dollar theater complex. The new twenty-screen theater would serve as the "first anchor" in the "large scale renovation" of El Con Mall. Finally, eleven months after GGP purchased Park Mall, El Con had the beginnings of a response centered on a massive new theater. "It will be unlike anything in Tucson." [177] Kivel said. He went on to describe the new theater complex as "the first step in our ongoing large-scale renovation of El Con." [173]

To clear space for the new theater, El Con 6 Theater and the northeast end of El Con Mall were demolished (see below).

Demolition of El Con 6 Theater

(© Tucson Citizen – USA TODAY NETWORK via Imagn Images)

Construction of the new theater began on November 12, 1998. The theater complex was built and owned by San Francisco-based Century Theaters. When El Con announced it was getting a new theater, Century already owned two other theater complexes in Tucson—Century Gateway 12 on Speedway and Kolb and Century Park 16 on West Grant Road and I-10. Century 20 El Con Theater would be roughly five miles from the other theaters, ensuring they wouldn't compete for the same customer base. The El Con site was carefully chosen. Nancy Klasky, spokesperson for Century Theaters, said her company followed a proven formula before investing in new markets. "We do a tremendous amount of research. We wouldn't do it if we didn't project the numbers to make it successful." [179]

Theater construction neared completion by June 1999. The buzz around El Con's megaplex was palpable. El Con management was counting on the theater to turn the mall's fortunes around. Century 20 was "the centerpiece of the first phase of the [El Con Mall] redevelopment," said Brenna Lacey, vice president for the Volk Co. (a commercial real estate company). "In our plans to reposition El Con Mall, we felt an entertainment component was critical to make it a success in today's retail environment." [180] The thinking was the theater would attract more people to the mall. After the film, moviegoers would spend time shopping in the mall and eating in the food court. "This is the wave in retail: entertainment and retail," Century spokeswoman Nancy Klasky said. "We want people to say, 'Let's spend the day at El Con.'" [181]

The Century 20 El Con Theater held a pre-grand opening fundraiser on June 29, 1999. Over 4,000 people attended. In a gesture of goodwill, Century 20 provided free admission with the donation of a canned food item. The opening day event was dubbed the "Canned Film Festival," a reference to the famous Cannes Film Festival in France. The items collected were donated to the community food bank. [182] The following day the theater officially opened. It was an instant hit with moviegoers. *Tucson Citizen* film critic Chuck Graham wrote a glowing review. Here is an excerpt from his column: "That lobby ceiling just keeps going up, up, up in the new Century 20 El Con multiplex. Everything feels bigger here. The hallways are longer, the rake in each theater is steeper, the sound is fatter, the seats thicker. Watching a movie here is a superior experience." [183]

Many Tucsonans were anxious to experience the much-hyped theater. In his review, Chuck Graham noted that El Con's parking lot was full. "All day in the parking lot outside, all the close-in spaces stayed perpetually filled. Every time one car pulled out, three cars rushed over." [184]

El Con had engineered a winning strategy, but its success was short-lived. The plan failed for two reasons. One was beyond El Con's control. The first signs of trouble surfaced seven months after Foster Kivel announced El Con was getting a new theater in an April 2, 1998, news article entitled "Park Mall Ready to Expand by 50%." What came next must have been a bitter pill to swallow for El Con officials. "A bigger Dillard's, a food court, more parking, additional stores and restaurants, and a new theater complex are in the plans for Park Mall announced today." [185] The article announced what was likely El Con management's worst fear: Park Mall was getting a theater too. Details about Park Mall's theater remained unknown, but the unwelcome news assured that Century 20 El Con would have a competitor three miles down the road.

Construction on Century 20 El Con Theater hadn't even finished, and already the central pillar of El Con's redevelopment efforts was under attack. More bad news for El Con surfaced in May 1999. In an article titled "Park Mall's Fresh Look," the *Arizona Daily Star* revealed that Park Mall would be changing its name to Park Place, remodeling, and adding new venues. Among its planned additions were a food court and a twenty-screen theater. [186] Barry O'Connor,

Park Mall's general manager, projected that the food court and theater would be open in time for the 2000 holiday shopping season. This article ran six weeks before Century 20 El Con Theater's opening day. Before a single movie screened there, Park Mall had already stolen El Con's thunder by announcing it too was getting a twenty-screen theater.

The worst news, however, emerged on September 20, 1999. In a section of the *Tucson Citizen* called *Street Talk*, the name of the theater chain opening in Park Mall was revealed. Keep in mind that this announcement came less than two months after Century 20 El Con Theater opened. The article began with praise for El Con's theater: "Century Park Theaters at El Con Mall are an impressive display of modern technology. With 20 screens, digital sound and comfortable, stadium-style seating, they are enough of a draw for Tucson moviegoers to overcome their slightly higher price." [187] Then came the gut punch: "Rumor has it that the mega theater planned for Park Mall will be another Century theater complex." [188] Cue the record scratch sound. Come again? Century Theaters, the chain El Con partnered with to create the cornerstone of its redevelopment effort, was building a rival theater three miles away at Park Place. This was a stunning turn of events for El Con, one that left many people scratching their heads. With all the emphasis Century placed on market research, how did it make sense to build a rival theater so close to the El Con location? As stated in the *Street Talk* article, "Apparently the chain doesn't believe that having two major theater complexes within several miles of each other is bad." [189]

In this case, what was good for the goose was not good for the gander. While Century Theaters may have stood to gain, the rival theater at

Park Place was a disaster for El Con. Century 20 Park Place opened on Friday, August 10, 2001. It had all the amenities El Con offered and more. Adding insult to injury, Nancy Klasky, marketing director for Century Theaters, emphasized Park Place's advantages over El Con. "This theater will meet and surpass El Con," she boasted. "We're very excited." [190] This was the same marketing director who had promoted El Con's theater two years earlier. For the officials who worked with Century Theaters to bring a multiplex to El Con Mall, it must have felt like a betrayal.

El Con officials must have known what was coming next. When Century 20 El Con opened in 1999, Century Park 16 and Century Gateway 12 theaters reported attendance drops. [191] El Con Century 20 theater had been top dog in Tucson's cinema landscape for two years, but that changed when Park Place Century 20 opened. Moviegoers were swept off their feet by the new theater. "It's beautiful. It's fabulous," one patron remarked. No one can say for sure how many customers Century 20 Park Place lured from El Con, but Cara Rene of the *Tucson Citizen* identified at least two in her August 10 article. Their names are Z. Smith and John Ramirez. The pair were noted to "usually frequent Century's El Con theater, which also features stadium seating and top-quality sound, but said they would now go to Park Place." [192] El Con was outmaneuvered by Park Mall once again, this time with help from the very agent El Con hired to build the cornerstone of its own renovation effort.

The Second Front

El Con was doing everything it could to remain viable in the face of Park Mall's dramatic resurgence. The rise of Park Place was an existential threat to El Con Mall. As if this weren't enough, a second front emerged following the Kivels' decision to sell Park Mall to GGP. El Con's owners announced the first phase of the mall's redevelopment, construction of Century 20 Theater, in September 1997. By February 1998, another element of the owner's redevelopment plans materialized—bringing big-box stores to El Con. Before construction began on the new theater, the old theater and El Con's north wing were torn down. This left room on the northeast end of the mall for a new building.

On February 22, 1998, Ernie Heltsley, in an article for the *Star*, revealed the mall owners' intentions for the vacated space. After rebuilding the theater and food court, focus would shift to "rebuilding the northeast end . . . for another large retailer, persistently rumored to be Wal-Mart." [193] Cynthia Lyn, a spokeswoman for Walmart, confirmed that Walmart was indeed "considering the site." The store would be the "traditional size" of 125,000 to 130,000 square feet.

When residents of the surrounding neighborhoods learned Wal-Mart might open a store, El Con's big-box controversy began in earnest. Days after the Walmart announcement, another article by Heltsley appeared, ominously entitled, "Potent Neighbors cast wary eyes on El Con." For the article, El Encanto Neighborhood Association president Rick Secrist met with Heltsley to discuss "some real concerns" shared by the mall's neighbors. "Among neighbors' concerns are the traffic, noise and lights that a possible 24-hour Wal-Mart or other store could generate," [194] Heltsley shared. Secrist, a real estate agent, also feared big-box stores at El Con could negatively impact property values. This was especially the case for homes on cul-de-sacs near the five-foot wall on Jones Boulevard. In addition to noise from semi-trucks on Jones at night, people parked by the wall to drink and party. They also threw trash over the wall into people's backyards and occasionally jumped the wall into the neighborhood. [195]

One prominent concern was the increased traffic Walmart would generate. El Con's main entrance was on the mall's south side, which faced Broadway. The mall's north side was accessed by three roads—Jones, Palo Verde, and Dodge Boulevards (see below).

(© Tucson Citizen – USA TODAY NETWORK via Imagn Images)

Residents feared El Con's new twenty-screen theater, coupled with a Walmart, would attract too many people, drastically increasing the number of vehicles entering and leaving El Con via the northside roads. Representatives from the mall and local neighborhoods began meeting to work out a compromise.

On May 5, 1998, Home Depot announced it was opening its fourth Tucson store in Marana. "Home Depot anticipates opening two other stores in the Tucson area in the next few years," Christina Valdez Diaz of the *Citizen* reported. "Locations have not been decided." [196] By late August, negotiations between El Con and the neighborhoods were at an impasse. The neighborhoods wanted all three north roads closed, restricting mall access to Broadway Boulevard. Mall owners offered to install traffic-slowing devices like speed bumps and traffic circles while insisting the roads remain open. Though repeatedly solicited for interviews, El Con's owners refused to speak with the press. Robert Gugino, El Con's lawyer, sent a letter to City Manager Luis Gutierrez, citing the need for all three roads to remain open. Gugino wrote, "For this reason, it will be necessary to enter into a recordable agreement, separate from the lease with the City of Tucson, providing that the City shall forever maintain Jones Boulevard, Dodge Boulevard, and Palo Verde Boulevard as public streets providing ingress and egress to El Con." [197]

On December 7, El Con representatives made a proposal to Tucson's City Council. It involved closing Palo Verde Boulevard but leaving Jones and Dodge Boulevards and implementing measures to reduce traffic. The neighborhoods wouldn't budge from their position that all three roads should be closed. The council scheduled a meeting on January 11 to discuss El Con's proposal. [198] When the meeting day came, the council voted four to three to close all three roads. It was a best-case scenario for the neighborhoods, but the council's decision was panned as a mistake. In late February, news surfaced that the city was working behind the scenes with representatives from the neighborhoods and mall to achieve a compromise. [199]

In March, the council voted six to one in favor of giving El Con's owners two months to work out a compromise with the neighborhoods. Negotiations ensued, and on June 7, 1999, the council met to vote on the newly brokered plan. More than 150 people attended the meeting. Some in attendance persisted with the argument that all three roads should remain closed. Others, like Jan Fry from the Miramonte neighborhood, agreed that it was important to keep some of the roads open. "In order for the mall to remain viable, there needs to be a way to get to the mall," Fry said. "Keeping those streets open will permit the mall to survive and provide jobs." [200]

The council remained poised to protect the neighborhoods, but since the January meeting it had become clear that closing all three roads was in no one's best interest. Eliminating northern access to the mall would cripple El Con. Before the vote. John Liosatos of the Tucson Metropolitan Chamber of Commerce issued a warning to the council: "We believe that if you do not come up with a solution that allows consumers to fully utilize the mall, you will be condemning El Con to a slow economic death." [201] By a six-to-one vote, the council approved a plan that called for Jones and Palo Verde Boulevards to close and Dodge Boulevard to remain open. In addition to the road closures, the following protections were granted:

- No delivery trucks on Dodge Boulevard
- Construction of sound absorbing walls on the mall perimeter
- Buffer landscaping between parking lot and residential areas
- Limits on lighting, truck deliveries, loading dock locations, and loudspeakers [202]

It was a victory for the neighborhoods, but the tension in their standoff with the mall owners was about to ratchet up even more.

The day after the road closure vote, an article by Norman Peckham in the *Citizen* revealed that, in addition to Walmart, "Home Depot, or a similar type of store, also has been mentioned as a possible new tenant." [203] Tension between the neighborhoods and El Con quickly escalated following this announcement. The combination of a multiplex theater, Walmart, and Home Depot signaled El Con's owners were taking the mall in a new direction. El Con was becoming a power center, defined as "a large outdoor shopping mall with three or more big-box stores and smaller retailers." This was a complete break from the enclosed mall concept El Con was known for.

Criticism for the power center concept came fast and furious. Chris Tanz, resident of El Encanto, wrote a letter to the editor on June 29 expressing mixed feelings. Though glad to see the mall coming back to life, "What the El Con owners want is not a renovation," Tanz said. "It has only recently emerged that they want to convert the mall to an entirely different entity: a 24-hour 'power center' of 'big-boxes' or 'superstores' like Wal-Mart and Home Depot." Tanz also noted that El Con, surrounded as it is by historic neighborhoods, wasn't an appropriate site for a power center.

"This shouldn't happen to any neighborhood," Tanz argued. "Power centers belong away from homes."

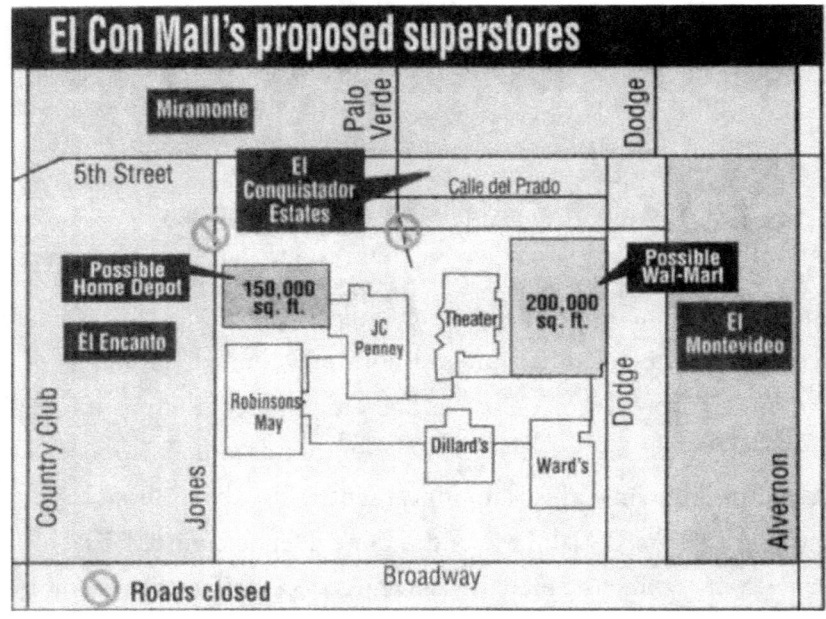

Proposed superstore locations (Copyright Arizona Daily Star)

To make matters worse, neither Walmart nor Home Depot would confirm their intentions. Walmart admitted to having discussions with El Con's owners, but they hadn't signed a lease. In keeping with its modus operandi, Home Depot held its cards close to the chest. El Con's owners followed suit, saying only that Home Depot was "a possibility." [204] In late June, the *Star* featured an article with a graphic identifying the proposed locations of both superstores (see image above).

The talk had become reality, ratcheting up the intensity. The El Con neighborhoods became increasingly vocal in their opposition to a power center. Residents feared noise pollution, increased traffic, higher crime, lowered property values, and an overall diminishment of life quality. The following statements demonstrate this.

"My big worry is property value. Why would anyone want to buy a house in this neighborhood with that mess over there?" [205]	–Ed Stellmacher, Miramonte resident
"Home Depots and Wal-Marts engage a big volume of customers and generate traffic. It's quiet and peaceful in (the neighborhood), and I think we'll lose some of it." [206]	–Ira Larsen, El Montevideo resident
"With a Wal-Mart open 24 hours, crime would go up. These stores just don't belong next to neighborhoods." [207]	–Marcia Spark, El Encanto resident
"We would have big diesel trucks with noisy, polluting engines all hours of the day and night, and forklifts on the dock beep, beep, beeping. No amount of mitigation could make up for that." [208]	–Dr. Jean-Paul Bierney, El Encanto resident

The neighborhoods also challenged the appropriateness of big-box stores at the mall. El Con had been part of the community for nearly forty years when the big-box controversy erupted. People had standards for the mall, and the conversion of El Con into a power center represented a lowering of those standards. In addition, many felt that putting discount stores in a prime midtown location like El Con was a waste. This is evident in the following statements:

"Locating a Home Depot at El Con Mall has to be —Anonymous
one of the most inappropriate uses for the central-city
shopping center. The mega-hardware store is a traffic
producer and is inconsistent with the elegance of the
stately nearby neighborhoods." [209]

"It is ironic that the owners do not recognize how —Ruth Beeker,
inappropriate such stores are at this site. Simply Miramonte
because the surface area is available for big-box resident
construction does not justify such insensitive land
use." [210]

"This is not the El Con that many of us have been —Jerry
using for decades or the El Con that many of the Anderson,
neighbors chose to call a neighbor. This version of in- Tucson City
fill is not anyone's preferred vision." [211] Council Ward
3 member

Following the Home Depot announcement, the neighborhood outcry grew so loud it got City Council's attention. Councilman Steve Leal brought the issue to the council, where it was discussed at a study session on August 2, 1999. [212] It was a hugely consequential meeting, an inflection point in the city's effort to articulate a policy for addressing the big-box challenge. That day, long-time El Encanto residents Chris Tanz and Jean-Paul Bierny announced the formation of T.U.C.S.O.N., an acronym for "The Union of Citizens to Save Our Neighborhoods." The group's mission was to restrict big-box stores. It included roughly 300 residents from various neighborhoods. [213]

The battle to save El Con proceeded along two fronts—the effort to keep pace with its resurgent rival to the east, Park Place, and the attempt to fend off invading superstores Walmart and Home Depot on its home soil. In the next chapter you will learn more about the neighborhoods around El Con and how they were uniquely suited to fight big-box bullies. You will also learn about the Big Box Ordinance, one of the bright spots that emerged from El Con's battle over the superstores. Finally, you will learn about some of the heroes that stepped forward to prevent El Con from becoming a retail power center and breathe life back into the beloved mall.

CHAPTER 6

RETAIL POLITICS

Retail Politics

He's known as "Walmart's No. 1 Enemy," the "Guru of the Anti-Walmart Movement," and "Mr. Sprawl-Busters." I'm speaking, of course, of Al Norman, leader of the Walmart opposition coalition. Al Norman has been a thorn in Walmart's side since 1993. He stumbled into this vocation after a friend enlisted his help to prevent Walmart from opening a store in Greenfield, MA. Norman had no desire to get involved. He wasn't concerned about Walmart, but because it was only a twelve-week commitment he reluctantly agreed. [214] After investigating Walmart's track record, Norman concluded the superstore would have a devastating effect on his small town, and he was determined to stop them.

Walmart successfully lobbied to change the zoning of its Greenfield site from industrial to commercial, a requirement for building a store there; however, a local citizen's group gathered enough signatures for a referendum vote. The referendum election took place on October 19, 1993. The motion to permit the zoning change from industrial to commercial was defeated by 9 votes, ending Walmart's bid to build a store in Greenfield. Norman's background in politics played a pivotal role in getting the zoning decision overturned. [215] He later published a book, "Slam-Dunking Wal-Mart!," that serves as a community playbook for keeping big-boxes at bay. Norman also created the website sprawlbusters.com as an organizational tool for communities who chose to take on superstores.

Since 1993, Norman has worked tirelessly to protect communities from the negative impacts of superstores like Walmart. He has traveled the world to help communities organize against unwanted commercial development. "I can safely say that I have helped stop more Walmarts than anyone on the planet," [216] Norman admits. Ask yourself, why would Norman go to all this trouble to fight Walmart? The answer: he discovered how the company operates and the devastating effects it has on local communities. "Even in the beginning I realized there was something dramatically wrong with this company," Norman says. "My goal was to make it one of the most reviled companies in America." [217] In this chapter you will see the tactics Walmart employs in its mission to secure new store locations. You will also witness the lengths to which Walmart will go to achieve its objectives. But more importantly, you will read about the heroic efforts undertaken by neighborhoods, local celebrities, members of City Council, and many others to save El Con Mall.

Stores like Walmart and Home Depot are accustomed to getting their way. When it came to El Con, however, they learned quickly that pushing their weight around was unproductive. In their attempts to secure locations at the mall, both superstores faced strong headwinds. To fully appreciate the drama that plays out in this chapter and the next, you need to understand the context in which this big-box showdown occurred. Section 1 (Headwinds) identifies four factors underpinning the intense opposition to superstores at El Con Mall. Here you will learn about Randolph Park, Reid Park, and the historical neighborhoods surrounding El Con Mall. Section two (Retail Politics) provides a detailed account of the neighborhood-led resistance to superstores at El Con. You will also learn about one of the signature accomplishments of the opposition movement: Tucson's big-box ordinance.

Headwinds

El Con Mall is ideally located in the heart of midtown Tucson. South of the mall, on the other side of Broadway Boulevard, are two amazing assets—Randolph Park and Gene C. Reid Park. Together, these parks are Tucson's equivalent of Central Park in Manhattan, often described as "the green jewel of midtown Tucson." Randolph is a sprawling 300-acre park and golf complex. Once measuring 460-acres, the park was rededicated in 1978 by the city, and a third of it was named for the retiring parks director, Gene C. Reid. Since then the portion of the park extending west of South Randolph Way has been known as Gene C. Reid Park. It's home to the Reid Park Zoo, a swimming facility, and Hi-Corbett Field. The park includes baseball fields, a rose garden, an outdoor performance center, a few ramadas, playground areas, and two man-made lakes. Community events are hosted on its grounds, like the annual Oktoberfest and the Music Under the Stars summer concert series.

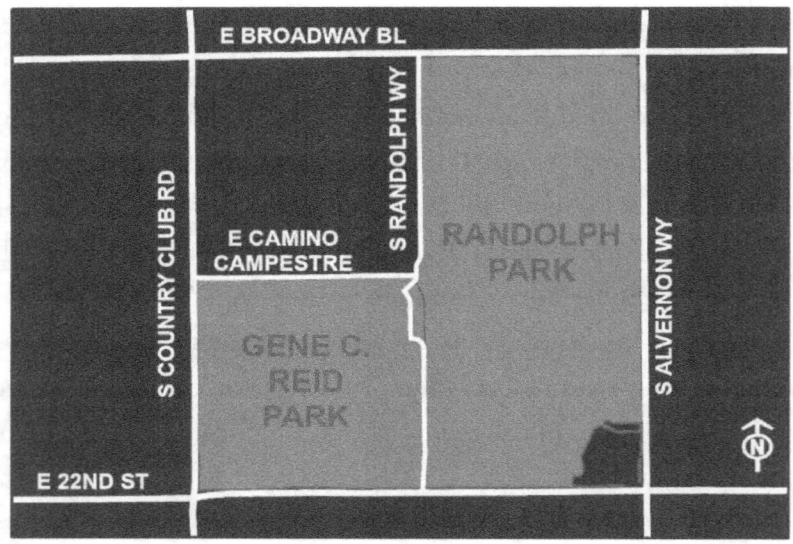

Map of Randolph & Reid Parks (Photo credit: City of Tucson Parks and Recreation)

I have so many memories from these parks. When I was a kid, my parents took the family on after-dinner walks there. After feeding the ducks, we'd go to the playground, which had swings, seesaws, and a towering 1960s-era rocket ship slide. One time my mom's younger brother, Andy, came along with us. Uncle Andy was in his late teens, but he agreed to play hide-and-seek with my brother and me. Ever the prankster, Uncle Andy brought a latex goblin mask with him to the park. He waited for my brother and me to hide in the concrete play tunnels, then put on the mask. I was crouched in the middle of a tunnel, as far from the exposed sides as I could get. I heard footsteps on the roof of the tunnel and leaned toward one end to get a look. Suddenly, a figure jumped from the roof, then landed and spun to face me. To my horror, I was face to face with a shrieking goblin who chased me out of the tunnel. Uncle Andy eventually took the mask off, but not until he scared Alex and me out of our wits. I may not have appreciated it then, but it's a memory I treasure now that I'm older.

Reid Park concrete play tunnels on a rare fog day in Tucson, 6 P.M. on December 29, 1970

(© Tucson Citizen – USA TODAY NETWORK via Imagn Images)

Countless Tucsonans have stories like this thanks to Randolph and Reid Park. Something is always happening at the parks—people playing golf, visiting the zoo, jogging the bike path, watching a baseball game at Hi-Corbett, celebrating birthdays at a ramada, swimming laps at the aquatic center, or taking ceramics classes at the recreation center. The parks provide a social hub for the community and give that part of midtown Tucson that special "something" few other areas of town can match. From the moment it opened in 1960, El Con Mall has benefitted from having these parks directly across the street. The mall and the parks complemented each other perfectly. Each one offered entertainment and community events that consistently brought in the crowds.

When El Con's owners announced their plan for revitalization following the sale of Park Mall, the ears of midtown Tucson perked up. This community had a vested interest in the vision El Con's owners were laying out for the mall. El Con wasn't just any mall. It was Tucson's first mall, heir to the legacy of the El Conquistador Hotel. The mall was perfectly situated in Tucson's historic midtown area, with the bucolic appeal of the parks directly across the street. No other mall in Tucson was adjacent to such a huge, communal gathering space. El Con's proximity to those parks is a big part of what makes it special.

People talked about El Con getting an overhaul in the late 1990s, but others expressed reservations. If El Con had to change, the community had high standards for what an acceptable replacement might be. For many, tearing down the enclosed mall and replacing it with big-box stores was not an acceptable use of this valuable space. This is one reason the neighborhoods resisted Walmart and Home Depot coming to the mall. You will see this reflected in many statements throughout this chapter and the next.

Historic Neighborhoods

The parks aren't the only interesting feature about the mall's location. El Con is surrounded by residential neighborhoods as well. The mall is bordered by the El Montevideo neighborhood to the east, El Conquistador Estates and Miramonte to the north, El Encanto to the west, and Colonia Solana to the south (see image below).

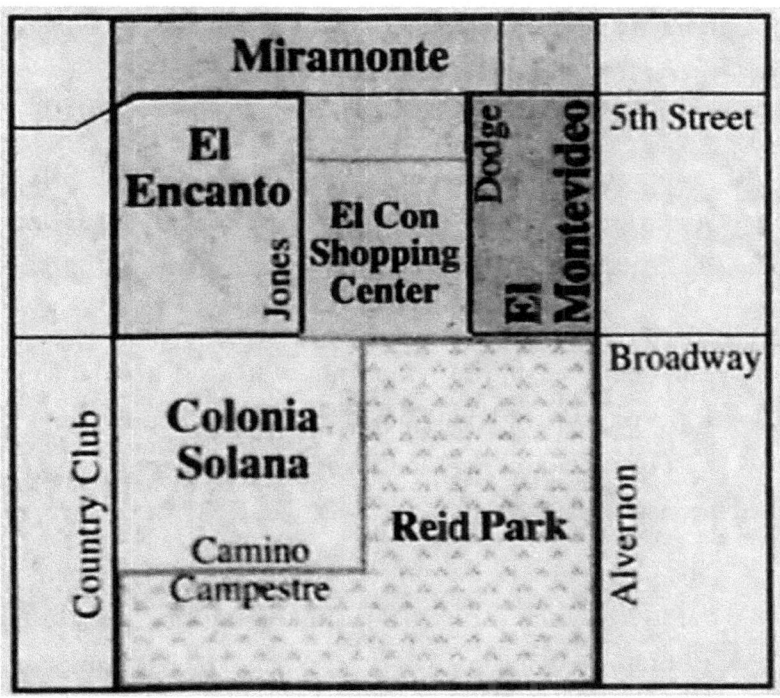

Map of El Con Neighborhoods (Copyright Arizona Daily Star)

There's a lot of Tucson history in these neighborhoods. Three of them—El Encanto, Colonia Solana, and El Montevideo—are on the National Register of Historic Places. This section examines one of them, El Encanto, more closely.

El Encanto, Spanish for "the enchanted," was the closer of the two neighborhoods to the El Conquistador Hotel. In 1928, ex-Ohio lawyer and legislator William E. Guerin Jr. purchased a 114-acre lot adjacent to the hotel on its west side. On May 12, 1928, Guerin and a group of investors formed El Encanto Estates, Inc., with the goal of developing the land into a subdivision. "The new company intends to start immediately subdividing and improving the tract in order that it may be open for public sale by the time the new hotel opens in the fall,"[218] the *Arizona Daily Star* reported.

All El Encanto streets have Spanish names. That's because on July 8, 1928, Guerin announced a naming contest for all streets in the subdivision. An advertisement appeared in the paper with the contest rules.

> Tucsonans will have an opportunity to assist in subdividing a 113 tract of land lying north of Broadway boulevard and west of and adjoining the El Conquistador Hotel property.. . .
>
> The Company [El Encanto Estates, Inc.] desires to name the streets with Spanish names in keeping with the words 'El Encanto' which means 'the enchanted.' The names must be easily pronounced. For each name accepted $5 will be paid or a total of $55.[219]

The contest began on July 9 and ended on July 14. The results (next page) were announced on July 29 in the newspaper.

Street Name	Meaning	Winner
Calle de Felicidad	Happiness Street	Everett Sibley
Calle Portal	Entrance Street	Everett Sibley
Calle Claravista	Clear View Street	Juan Lujan
Calle Primorosa	Neat Street	Milton Cohen
Calle Conquista	Conquest Street	T. C. Diaz
Calle Mirasol	Sunny View Street	T. C. Diaz
Calle Encanto	Enchanted Street	H. J. Blacklidge
Calle Resplendor	Splendor Street	Margaret Galvez
Calle de Amistad	Friendship Street	F. M. Maxey
Camino Miramonte	Mountain View Road	Bessie Strohmajer
Calle Corta	Short Street	R. M. Scruggs
Calle Belleza	Beauty Street	Henry Meyer

In January 1929, El Encanto awarded the building contract to George B. Echols Building Co. Inc., and construction began on three houses. The contractor's announcement in the paper included the following plug: "El Encanto Estates are planned to be one of the most attractive properties in the entire southwest, with no expense spared to make them so."[220] Incidentally, the second home built was owned by Ralph E. Ellinwood, editor and co-owner of the *Arizona Daily Star*. Ellinwood also gave the El Conquistador Hotel its name.[221]

In addition to lavish homes and perfectly manicured landscaping, El Encanto is known for its unique layout. El Encanto was the first Tucson neighborhood to deviate from a traditional grid layout, opting for a hub-and-spoke pattern instead.

Its six main streets lead from an oval outer drive to a landscaped circle in the center (see below).

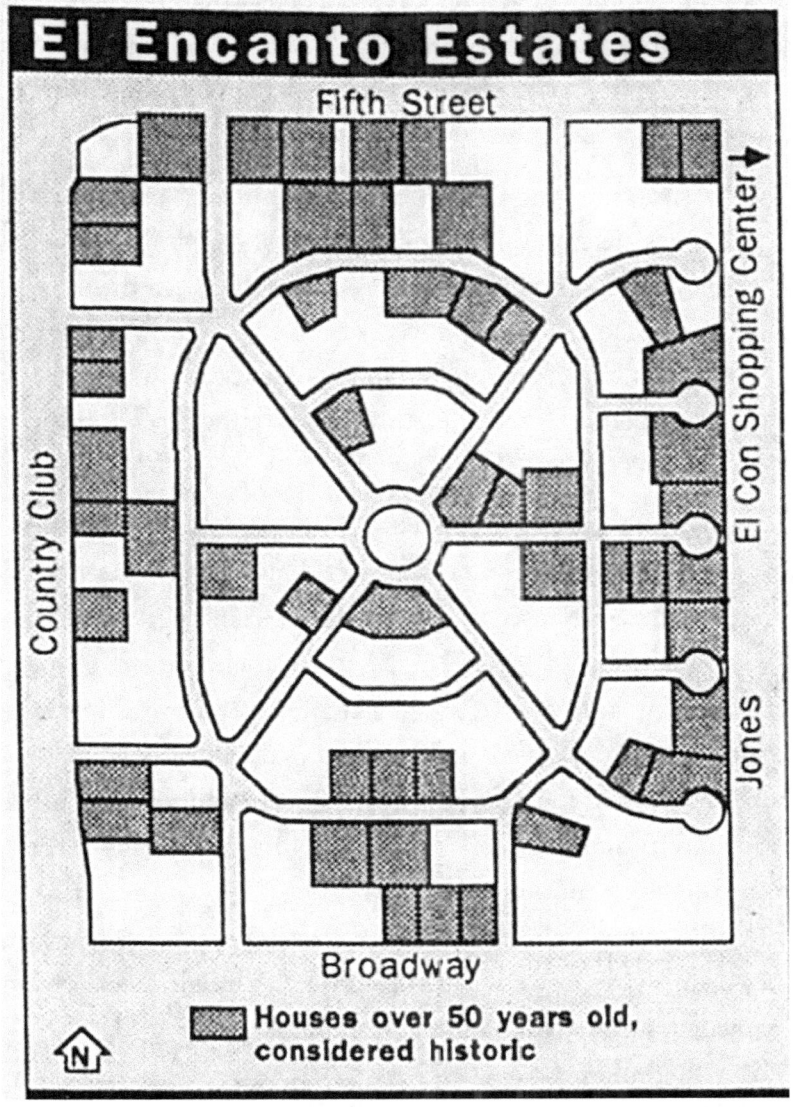

Map of El Encanto Estates (Copyright Arizona Daily Star)

While driving through El Encanto, you experience the magic of its unique layout. Each house feels like a discovery, hidden away in nooks and crannies of the subdivision. The streets are lined with towering palm trees, planted in 1929. This, in addition to the lush desert landscaping, gives the effect of an oasis. As George Mercedes of the *Tucson Citizen* noted in May 1988,

> Visitors entering the neighborhood from the surrounding streets are enveloped by the landscaping and immaculately gardened lots in a serene, cozy atmosphere. All the inner roads lead to a center circle park of 157 saguaros. Colorful flowers, now in spring bloom, wink back as if they're letting you in on their secret method for cheating the scalding Arizona sun and dry desert.[222]

Unlike many neighborhoods in Tucson, houses in El Encanto benefit from a cohesive architectural scheme. This is due to strict deed restrictions that governed the subdivision from the start. Anyone building a home in El Encanto had to get their plans approved by Merritt Starkweather, the overseeing architect. Starkweather is one of Tucson's most renowned architects, the designer of many local schools, shops, and the historic Arizona Inn. In addition to designing them himself, Starkweather reviewed architectural plans for all El Encanto homes throughout the 1970s. This ensured that the neighborhood maintained its cohesive theme. Early houses were built primarily in the Southwestern Revival style, although later exceptions were made for ranch-style and modern homes.[223]

The historic neighborhoods surrounding El Con are another factor underpinning the opposition to superstores at the mall. As the big-box controversy raged, some argued the residents of these neighborhoods had nothing to complain about. "You bought your home fully aware of the mall next door, so deal with it," was the prevailing sentiment. But this line of reasoning didn't account for one key consideration: there is a qualitative difference between living across from a mall and a retail power center. For one thing, malls open and close at reasonable hours, which is not the case with all superstores. Many Walmart stores are open twenty-four hours. For this reason, neighborhood residents express similar concerns about the possibility of a future with a superstore next door. These concerns include noise pollution, increased traffic, decreased quality of life, higher crime, and lower property values.

Power and Influence

In the late 1990s, the residents of the El Con neighborhoods were among the wealthiest in Tucson. Prominent doctors, lawyers, politicians, architects, CEOs, and local celebrities lived there. As noted by *Star* journalist Ernie Heltsley, "El Encanto and the other neighborhoods . . . have perhaps the wealthiest and most powerful collection of neighbors surrounding a shopping mall in Tucson." [224] The high status of these neighborhoods is partly why the resistance to superstores proved so effective. Big-box controversies were common in Tucson during this period. Nevertheless, it took a big-box controversy at El Con for the city to finally pass restrictions on big-box stores. Why? To put it bluntly, money talks.

The El Con neighborhoods had influence owing to their wealth and standing. "Power comes to the residents [of El Con neighborhoods], real estate tycoons, attorneys and judges, not only from money but from politics and social prestige as well," [225] Ernie Heltsley explained. Because the El Con neighborhoods were powerful, City Council took notice when they made a fuss about Walmart and Home Depot. Their voices carried a lot of weight. As Heltsley put it, "What they really want, they usually get." [226] The prestige of these neighborhoods was also bolstered by local and national celebrities who called them home over the years, including writer Erskin Caldwell, singer Linda Ronstadt, actress Elizabeth Taylor, and politician Robert Dole. Such high-profile residents increased the power and influence of the El Con neighborhoods.

Old Hands

There's one more reason the El Con neighborhoods were able to fend off superstores so effectively. To use a local expression, it "wasn't their first rodeo." Most neighborhoods are at a disadvantage against big-box bullies. They haven't dealt with commercial developers, so they get steamrolled when a company like Walmart shows up, looking to build a store. Not so with the El Con neighborhoods. Two of these neighborhoods, El Encanto and Colonia Solana, had previous experience fighting commercial development. El Encanto and Colonia Solana were old hands at this. They knew how to defend themselves because they had defeated developers twenty years before. Consider the following example.

Deed restrictions are largely the reason El Encanto and Colonia Solana have remained the gems they are today. These restrictions held prospective buyers to established standards and ensured that all new homes matched the character of the neighborhood. However, I'd be remiss if I didn't mention the darker side to the restrictions. The original deed restrictions established by El Encanto Estates, Inc. included racial restrictions. Like many other Tucson subdivisions prior to 1950, minorities were not allowed to buy homes in El Encanto. The master deed restriction included a provision stating, "No lot shall be sold, conveyed, rented or leased, in whole or in part, to any person not of the White or Caucasian race." These racial restrictions remained in place until the 1950s when they were struck down by a city ordinance. [227]

Aside from the race-restricting elements (which ended earlier), El Encanto's deed restrictions expired in December 1978. This left El Encanto vulnerable to commercial development along its periphery. El Encanto is framed by three major streets: East 5th street to the north, N. Country Club to the west, and Broadway Blvd to the south. El Con Mall constitutes the neighborhood's east border. Seeking to profit from the lapsed restrictions, developers bought vacant land and houses along the Broadway frontage and the lucrative corner lots on N. Country Club Road. With rezoning, these properties would be developed into banks, office buildings, and retail stores. Colonia Solana, El Encanto's sister neighborhood on the south side of Broadway, faced the same threat as its deed restrictions expired in 1977.

Ten months before El Encanto's restrictions expired, James R. Wyckoff of the *Tucson Citizen* published an article detailing what was coming. The opening line captures the panic El Encanto residents felt upon realizing their cozy hamlet would soon be vulnerable to commercial development: "In the subdued, tree-lined ambiance of two of Tucson's poshest old neighborhoods [Colonia Solana and El

Encanto], homeowners are scrambling for cover because they're losing 50-year-old protection against outside influence." [228]

Desiring some measure of control over their destinies, the two neighborhoods teamed up and devised a plan for dealing with the threat.

The two things they feared most were commercial properties encroaching on their neighborhoods and homeowners subdividing their land into smaller lots, which could then be sold and developed. [229] These were not idle threats. In Colonia Solana, Union Bank proposed to build a branch on the southeast corner of Broadway and Country Club. Another developer sought to build professional offices in Colonia Solana along the Broadway frontage. In El Encanto, there were proposals to build offices, shops, a restaurant, or savings-and-loan establishments on its corners.

Like Colonia Solana, it too faced calls for professional offices along the Broadway frontage. [230] All this depended, however, on developers to secure rezoning for the land.

To thwart the developers' plans, both neighborhoods petitioned the city to downzone, a process whereby land is rezoned for less intensive use. They did this to prevent lot splitting, wherein their larger R-1 lots could be split into 7,000-square-foot parcels and developed for profit. Colonia Solana requested downzoning to RX-1, requiring a minimum lot size of 36,000 square feet. El Encanto had smaller lot sizes to begin with, so it requested RX-2 rezoning, which required a minimum lot size of 16,000 square feet. [231] Next, the neighborhoods pooled their resources and hired an architectural and planning firm, Brooks & Associates, to create a neighborhood plan. [232] With restrictive zoning and a neighborhood plan in place, sufficient protections would be in place to prevent high-density development.

In June 1978, the neighborhoods got good news. City Zoning Examiner David Lim recommended against zoning for a bank on the southeast corner of Broadway and Country Club. Lim also advised City Council to stop considering zoning requests from developers until the neighborhood plan was complete. [233] Roger Brooks of Brooks & Associates finished his neighborhood plan. It called for professional offices on the two corner lots and medium-density, owner-occupied townhouses on the frontage properties. [234] Union Bank eventually dropped its rezoning request. In March 1979, however, Arizona Bank petitioned the city for commercial zoning to build a branch on Colonia Solana's corner lot. Once again, David Lim advised against rezoning until City Council approved a land-use plan for the neighborhoods. [235]

At a meeting on June 6, 1979, the Citizens Advisory Planning Committee urged City Council to adopt the neighborhood plan designed by Roger Brooks. The committee urged the Council "to 'retain the character of the neighborhoods' by allowing only residential building along the periphery of the area." [236] A public hearing on the neighborhood plan was scheduled for June 25. On the night of the hearing, residents, property owners, and developers took turns arguing their position. The Council vote on the two neighborhood plans resulted in a three-three tie. Mayor Lewis Murphy, the seventh council member, could not vote because he owned a house in Colonia Solano. The matter wouldn't be considered again until sometime after November, as 1979 was an election year for the Council. [237]

Representatives for Arizona Bank were present at the Council meeting to request commercial rezoning for a corner-lot bank. Luckily, the bank's rezoning request was voted down five to one, eliminating a major threat to the neighborhoods. [238] On January 9, 1980, the owner of the corner lot where Arizona Bank was to build sued the city for $1.5 million. The litigants asserted the city had destroyed their property's value by prohibiting commercial development. [239]

On January 15, the Council met to readdress the issue of the neighborhood plan. Following the fall elections, the Council's makeup was different. What hadn't changed was the significance of the vote. A lot was riding on the Council's decision. Councilman Volgy described the matter as "symbolically, a very important case." On the surface the decision only affected the residents of El Encanto and Colonia Solana, but the implications were more far reaching. As

Volgy noted, the fight to protect El Encanto and Colonia Solana from commercial development was "a question of whether neighborhood residents should have a say in the future of their area." [240] This time around the Council approved the neighborhood plan six to zero. With that, the effect of commercial development in both neighborhoods was effectively ended.

In 1979, El Encanto began the painstaking work of photographing and documenting the architecture of its oldest homes to apply for historic designation from the National Register of Historic Places. Eight years later, the State Historic Sites Review Committee recommended El Encanto for Historic District designation on October 27, 1987. Finally, on January 29, 1988, El Encanto Estates was listed as a Historic District on the National Register of Historic Places. It was the sixth neighborhood in Tucson at the time to earn this distinction. Reflecting on the designation, Rick Secrist, president of the neighborhood association, said, "It gives a neighborhood prestige and protects a neighborhood." [241] Colonia Solana was added to the register as a historic district on January 4, 1989.

Experience matters. Walmart and Home Depot have decades of experience building stores in hostile communities. They have expert lawyers who can get around the legal roadblocks that hold projects up. They also have experienced public relations teams who employ every trick in the book to ensure their company comes out on top. To go against these giants, communities must be disciplined, informed, and aggressive in defense of their interests. Following the expiration of their deed restrictions, El Encanto and Colonia Solana were thrust into a conflict with developers that threatened their quality of life. To protect their interests, they had to seek rezoning, develop a neighborhood plan, and convince City Council to take their side. They applied for and achieved historic district status, further strengthening their case. As Councilman Volgy said, "These two neighborhoods combined have more financial, political, and professional resources than any other two neighborhoods in Tucson. They can do things other neighborhoods can't." [242] Volgy's statement was as true in 1999 as it was in 1979.

The next section picks up where the last chapter ended. Following the announcement that, in addition to Walmart, Home Depot was opening a store at El Con too, a group called T.U.C.S.O.N. was formed to resist the superstores. The group's membership was composed of residents from the neighborhoods. The action in the next section picks up from there.

Retail Politics

The formation of T.U.C.S.O.N. was a declaration of war on Walmart and Home Depot. As its first offensive, the members of T.U.C.S.O.N. presented a report to Tucson City Council at the 8/2 study session discussion on "big box (superstore) development impacts." The report detailed how other cities were dealing with big-box stores. Afterwards, Councilman Leal introduced a motion to ban the construction of stores over 100,000 square feet. The motion passed, and the Council ordered City Manager Luis Gutierrez to write the ordinance. [243] Right out of the gate, T.U.C.S.O.N. had scored a huge victory. As reported in the *Star,* if the ordinance passed legal muster and the Council approved it, "Tucson would be the first city in the country to ban superstores." [244]

Calls for a big-box ordinance set off a chain reaction of events. Citing a "breach of trust," El Con's owners revoked their $3 million mitigation package offer to the neighborhoods and sued the city to reopen Jones and Palo Verde Boulevards. [245] The El Con owners' attorney Bob Gugino blamed the neighborhoods. "A handful of vocal neighbors have killed the compromise." Gugino said. "The vocal few have overcome the work of the many." [246] In response to the withdrawn mitigation agreement, Chris Tanz accused El Con's owners of bad form. "The mall is having a legal tantrum," Tanz said. "Now that the mall owners are faced with not getting everything they want, they're trying to grab all their marbles back." [247] Meanwhile, Home Depot, which hadn't even confirmed its intentions, filed plans with the city to build a 107,580-square-foot building in the area vacated by El Con's razed north wing (see below). [248]

Home Depot coming to El Con (Copyright Arizona Daily Star)

Home Depot purported that the filing had nothing to do with the Big Box Ordinance, though clearly it did. By getting building permits approved before the Council vote, Home Depot could evade BBO restrictions. It was a huge setback for the neighborhoods. Then on September 14th, there was another unexpected development—this one positive. Walmart announced it was no longer interested in building a store at El Con. "We thought that an agreement could be worked out between the owner and the neighborhood, but as things moved forward, we didn't feel that the transaction was appropriate," Daphne Davis, Walmart's community affairs director, said. "We have alerted city officials that we are not pursuing the location at El Con Mall." [249] It was a huge victory for the neighborhoods, but they weren't taking anything for granted.

The city wrote four ordinance proposals, ranging from a total ban on big-box stores to varying degrees of restriction. The Council vote on the BBO was scheduled for September 27, 1999. Days before the vote, T.U.C.S.O.N. brought a special guest to town to rally the troops—Al Norman. Five days before the vote, Norman flew to Tucson to testify at the city planning commission meeting and meet with local activists. The following day, T.U.C.S.O.N. hosted a "Thinking Outside the Box" rally and presentation, led by Norman.

T.U.C.S.O.N was doing everything it could to inform people of the issues. On September 27, 400 people showed up at the Tucson Convention Center to participate in a public hearing for the big-box ordinance. Many in attendance voiced their arguments for or against the superstores. Following the hearing, the Council voted five to two in favor of an ordinance restricting big-box stores. [250] In addition to meeting seventeen construction standards, all future big-box stores plans would have to be discussed at a public hearing before the city zoning examiner and City Council. "It's definitely a victory, but not a great victory," T.U.C.S.O.N. member Jose Rincon said. "We won the battle, but not the war." [251]

The Big Box Ordinance (BBO) was set to take effect on November 11, 1999; however, Home Depot's building permits were approved on November 8, which meant it was exempt from BBO restrictions. But the neighborhoods caught a break thanks to Miramonte resident Leo Pilachowski, who filed a lawsuit claiming the city zoning administrator had improperly reviewed Home Depot's plans. On November 9, a Superior Court judge issued a stay on Home Depot's building permits until the matter was decided. [252]

After bowing out in mid-September, Walmart reemerged a month later with an effort to force a public vote on the BBO. On October 16, a Walmart-funded group called "Consumers for Retail Choice Sponsored by Wal-Mart" began collecting signatures for a referendum vote. To get on the city election ballot, Walmart had to collect a specified number of signatures from registered voters by November 10, thirty days after the BBO was signed. The number of signatures needed equaled 10 percent of the votes cast in the November 2 mayoral election. On October 21, the *Star* reported city officials had warned Walmart it was using the wrong forms. Walmart was using state petition forms instead of city forms. Kathy Detrick, the city clerk, cautioned Walmart that the oversight could invalidate its referendum effort. Walmart pressed on using the state forms because it was too late to start over. [253]

On November 9, Walmart announced plans to turn in 12,000 signatures to prevent the BBO from going into effect November 11. The city refused to accept the signatures because they were gathered on the wrong petition forms, which contained referendum language different from the city. [254] Walmart sued the city, placing the issue in the court's hands. The BBO went into effect on November 11, but it was on shaky ground. If Walmart's suit was upheld and a sufficient number of valid signatures were collected, the BBO would be put on hold until a referendum vote in the spring. In the intervening period, Walmart and Home Depot could evade BBO restrictions and file for building permits at El Con.

On December 8, the El Con owners' suit to reopen Jones and Palo Verde Boulevards backfired. Not only did the roads stay closed, but the judge also ruled that North Dodge Boulevard would close on February 8 as well. "This is a significant victory and a significant commitment to keeping neighborhoods intact," [255] T.U.C.S.O.N President Chris Tanz said. One week later, however, the neighborhoods suffered a setback. On December 15, Tucson's board of adjustments ruled against Leo Pilachowski's city suit, affirming that the zoning administrator had acted properly. By delaying the building permits, however, Pilachowksi's suit effectively brought Home Depot under BBO restrictions. Home Depot could file for building permits, but it would have to abide by BBO restrictions. Instead, Home Depot opted to wait until a court decision was rendered in the city's lawsuit against Walmart. [256]

Momentum swung from the neighborhoods to the superstores in 2000. Tucson's newly-elected mayor, Bob Walkup, took matters into his own hands and brokered an agreement between the city and the mall owners. The broad outlines of the agreement were announced on January 21. The following key elements were included:

- North Dodge Boulevard to remain open
- Mitigation measures from original agreement restored (i.e., walls)
- Mall guaranteed freedom from future land-use restrictions

The new agreement was less restrictive than the BBO (see image below), although the city argued it matched the BBO's intent.

City-El Con proposal v. Big box ordinance

Proposal	Big box ordinance
NOISE WALLS SEPARATING NEIGHBORHOODS FROM CENTER	
Calls for walls 8 to 13 feet high.	Calls for walls 8 feet high.
LANDCSCAPING	
Calls for 8-foot-wide landscaping separating the center from neighborhoods.	Calls for 20-foot-wide landscaping.
LOUDSPEAKERS-LOUD MUSIC-NOISE	
Requires El Con to meet city noise ordinance and bans loudspeakers or loud music within 200 feet of homes.	Requires noise control plan and forbids idling trucks in the center between 6 p.m. and 7 a.m.
DELIVERIES-TRASH PICKUP	
Has no limits on hours.	Forbids trash removal from 4 p.m. to 9 p.m. and delivery and loading operations adjacent to residential areas from 10 p.m. to 7 a.m.
GROCERY STORES	
Has no limits on grocer size.	Forbids grocery area taking up more than 10 percent of a big box over 100,000 sq. ft.
OUTDOOR ACTIVITIES AND DISPLAY	
Prohibits outdoor activities within 200 feet of neighborhoods.	Bans outdoor sales display within 250 feet of neighborhoods

(Copyright Arizona Daily Star)

Walkup stressed the agreement hadn't been finalized and wouldn't be until the public had a chance to comment at the Council meeting on January 24. [257] The neighborhoods felt blindsided by the agreement, especially since it was announced so close to the Council meeting. "This big issue has been evolving over half a year, and now this information is tossed out to us with barely the time to look at it," [258] Chris Tanz complained.

On Monday, January 24, roughly 375 people attended a public hearing for El Con Mall's redevelopment. Knowing Mayor Walkup had the votes to pass his new agreement and bypass the BBO, Councilman Jerry Anderson made a motion to prevent the start of the public hearing. When the motion failed four to three, Anderson walked off the stage and left the convention center, accompanied by fellow Council members Steve Leal and José Ibarra. Since four council members had to be present for a meeting to be official, the hearing was canceled.

By walking out, the councilmen denied Mayor Walkup the opportunity to cut a less-stringent agreement with El Con's owners and circumvent the BBO. This ensured El Con's fate would be decided in court when a judgment was rendered on Walmart's lawsuit against the city. [259]

The walkout set off a firestorm. Some lauded the councilmen as heroes for standing by the neighborhoods. Others saw the walkout as a shameful stunt, characterizing the councilmen as deserters who neglected their duty.

Here's some examples of what people were saying:

"I am shocked that Mayor Bob Walkup and the present City Council are making moves to nullify the work and decision-making of the past Council with regard to placing constraints on big-box stores in urban areas.. . . If they do this, how can any neighborhood group take action on any issue without thinking that all they do—and remember this is always on top of and at the expense of their jobs and family lives—can be undermined in the immediate future." [260]

—Susan Phillips

"Those three childish, petulantly foot-stomping City Council members who picked up their marbles and walked out of that official meeting are a disgrace to the good name of Tucson, and should be ashamed ever to come to another meeting." [261]

—Randall Larson

"I would like to commend City Councilmen Jerry Anderson, José Ibarra, and Steve Leal for walking out of the Jan. 24 City Council meeting. I found their action a breathtaking example of integrity not often demonstrated by politicians. Each of them decided that they are responsible to the voters, and not to monied special interests." [262]

—Andrea Kennedy

"What an embarrassment for Tucson residents when three councilmen stormed out of the Jan. 24 meeting because they needed to spank the mayor and new Council member, Carol West, for their votes.. . . I know some third-grade students who probably could demonstrate techniques in conflict resolution to them, using appropriate vocabulary and behavior." [263]

—Wanda Marts

One week after the walkout, Councilman Anderson published a letter explaining his actions.

> On Jan. 24, I walked out of the City Council meeting along with Councilmen José Ibarra and Steve Leal to make a very visible point. To bring back the 'big-box' ordinance for reconsideration simply because two of the members of the Council have changed is an affront to those of us who worked long and hard for a solution. Further, to have the mayor involved in negotiations with the mall to the exclusion of the rest of us is an insult to the democratic process.
>
> The three of us walked out of last Monday's meeting in order to stop the reconsideration of the big-box ordinance. It sounds like an extreme action, but sometimes desperate times call for desperate actions. We passed an ordinance last year after months of meetings and discussions. Let's give it a chance to work. [264]

Regardless of which way you lean on the walkout, actions have consequences. Principles notwithstanding, the walkout wasn't a good look for the councilmen or the neighborhood. I love sports, football in particular. I've watched thousands of games over my lifetime. On several occasions, there arise moments in the game of significance when I realize my team has blown it. The outcome still hangs in the balance, but deep down it's clear that my team isn't going to come out on top. The "Walkup Walkout" was one such moment for the neighborhoods.

A photo of the councilmen taken after their dramatic exit captures this. You can see in their expressions a recognition that they'd lost (see image below).

Councilmen Steve Leal, Jerry Anderson, and Jose Ibarra (left to right)

(© Tucson Citizen – USA TODAY NETWORK via Imagn Images)

Superstitions aside, the walkout kicked off a string of setbacks for the neighborhoods. First, the January 24 Council meeting was supposed to include a vote to close Dodge Boulevard. Thanks to the walkout, that never happened, so Dodge would remain open. [265] Then on January 31, Pima County Superior Court Judge Robert Donfeld issued a ruling in Walmart's suit against the city, and it was a bombshell. Donfeld sided with Walmart, ruling that the city should've accepted Walmart's signed petitions for a referendum vote. This meant, as long as Walmart gathered enough signatures, the fate of the BBO would be determined by voters in a city election. State law mandates that when an initiative is put on the ballot, the challenged law is put on hold until the election, which likely wouldn't happen until May at the earliest, or November at the latest. [266] In the intervening time, Walmart and Home Depot could pursue their objectives at El Con unhindered by BBO restrictions. It was a worst-case scenario for the neighborhoods.

Mayor Walkup wasted no time using Donfeld's ruling as a prod to get the neighborhoods to reconsider his brokered agreement with El Con. Since the city brought the suit, Walkup could have appealed Donfeld's decision, an option Councilman Leal supported. Walkup argued that the appeal would be a waste of city money and would slow the result. Besides, Walkup argued, "There are 14,000 people that want to vote on it." [267] While it's true 14,770 signed the referendum petition, there's a bit of deception here begging to be called out. This was not a citizen-initiated referendum. Walmart hired the group "Consumers for Retail Choice" to collect signatures for its referendum. As reported in the *Citizen,* campaign finance reports show the group spent $24,750 on the effort and "the group's sole contributor was Wal-Mart's corporate headquarters in Bentonville, Ark." [268]

The ensuing discussion here will show the lengths to which Walmart goes to get its way. They have the money to pay for a referendum drive, if that's what's needed to win. Tactics like this motivate people like Al Norman to speak out against Walmart. T.U.C.S.O.N. president Chris Tanz point out the unfairness of the referendum drive that happened in October 1999. "A corporation in Arkansas has all the money in the world to pour into our political process," [269] said Tanz. On February 1, 2000, the day after judge Donfeld ruled in favor of Walmart in the petition legality case, Tanz spoke out again. "It's a real distortion of the process when a big corporation can come in and set up a referendum," [270] Tanz said.

After the judge ruled Walmart could use state forms, focus shifted to verifying if Walmart had turned in the required number of signatures. The city argued Walmart needed 8,518 valid signatures, and Walmart claimed 7,073. Either way, Walmart submitted 14,770 voter signatures. Things weren't looking good for the neighborhoods. Two days later, on February 2, Donfeld made a surprise announcement: Walmart didn't have enough valid signatures to force a referendum. According to the judge, because Walmart used state petition forms, it was bound by state referendum rules. [271] According to the state's standards, Walmart needed 15,800 valid signatures to make the ballot, representing 10 percent of the votes cast in the 1997 City Council election. Walmart based its calculation on city standards, and therein lay the problem. As reported in the *Citizen*, "City laws, however, use the total number of *ballots cast* [emphasis added] in that election. Because city voters could vote for up to three City Councilmen on the November 1997 ballot, the number of votes was more than double the number of ballots cast." [272]

Walmart's gambit to use state petition forms apparently backfired. If the BBO referendum effort failed, it couldn't be retried because referendum campaigns could only be initiated within thirty days of law passage. As you might expect, Walmart immediately appealed the decision.

On February 6, Mayor Walkup wrote an extensive guest comment letter for the *Star*. In it Walkup provided his rationale for brokering a development deal with El Con, the merits of the agreement, and Judge Donfeld's recent ruling concerning Walmart's referendum petition. "This decision [that Walmart didn't collect enough signatures] will be appealed, and the matter will remain in the courts for the near future," [273] Walkup said. Then the mayor laid out his "temporary reprieve" argument.

> This [Walmart's case tied up in court] has significant ramifications on the situation at El Con. We have been granted a temporary reprieve while the question over the signatures is sorted out.. . . However, as I said, this is a temporary reprieve. Sooner or later, we will either have a referendum on the current big-box ordinance [i.e., if Walmart's appeal succeeds] or the City Council will have to rescind or amend it significantly. Therefore, I see the next few weeks as a window of opportunity. [274]

Walkup planned to reintroduce the El Con development agreement at the Feb. 14 City Council meeting. To create support for it, Walkup used the letter to highlight the realistic possibility that the neighborhoods could lose everything if they didn't act quickly.

Two days later, Chris Tanz of T.U.C.S.O.N wrote a response to Walkup's guest comment. The neighborhoods were arguing from a position of strength and Tanz's response reflects this. Because Walmart didn't get enough signatures, the BBO remained intact.

With the threat of a referendum vote looking increasingly unlikely, it appeared the neighborhoods were safe. Tanz begins by articulating why the neighborhoods weren't on board with Walkup's proposal.

> Under the new development agreement, the mall will have a Home Depot and a mystery big-box. Approving that, sight unseen, is totally against the spirit of the big-box ordinance. The agreement also stipulates that no other new law, including the big-box ordinance, would apply to the mall for 20 years. This was all rushed onto the table at the Jan. 24 meeting. We want to know: Why should El Con be exempted? Why should it have a special deal? We want the law to apply to the mall as it does to other commercial developments. [275]

Then Tanz presents Walkup and the mall owners with a different proposal. Take the mall's development in another direction, something more in keeping with El Con's character and surroundings: "We must seize this opportunity for Tucson and persuade El Con's owners to look at alternative solutions that have brought financial success to mall owners in other cities, while contributing to the surrounding community rather than eroding it." [276]

Tanz ends the letter by announcing an upcoming forum that would include a presentation by Dover, Kohl & Partners, an urban planning firm from Miami, FL. The presentation would offer a community enriching, financially viable alternative to El Con's anticipated big-box development. "El Con's owners, who are long-time residents of the community, are the inheritors of a portion of the heart of

Tucson," Tanz pleads. "They could do something glorious with it." [277] The forum was scheduled for 7:00 p.m. on Feb. 11 at Our Savior's Lutheran Church. Tanz's letter ends on a high note, brimming with optimism for the direction El Con's future could take.

The good cheer didn't last, though. The day Tanz's letter appeared in the newspaper, Judge Donfeld issued another ruling with devastating consequences for the neighborhoods. Donfeld declared the ordinance would be placed in abeyance—on hold—until the matter was decided in court or by an election. This was necessary because Walmart used state petitions for the signature drive, not city forms. Under state law: "A government decision that's being challenged through referendum petitions is held in abeyance as soon as the petitions are filed, rather than after the petition signatures are counted and certified, as required by the City Charter." [278]

As a result, the BBO could no longer be enforced. Walmart and Home Depot could apply for building permits at El Con immediately, unrestricted by the ordinance. This new wrinkle gave Mayor Walkup all the ammunition he needed to coax the neighborhoods to the negotiating table. It was either accept the brokered agreement with the city and El Con, or risk getting nothing.

It was a dark moment for the neighborhoods. Donfeld's February 2 ruling had given them hope, but four days later he snatched it away. Despite the distressing turn of events, the forum, called "Alternative Solutions for El Con Redevelopment," went on as scheduled. The event was co-sponsored by a pair of local legends—Linda Ronstadt and Cele Peterson. Linda Ronstadt is Tucson's most famous singer.

"Ronstadt is known for hit songs like "You're No Good," "Blue Bayou," and "When Will I Be Loved?""

Cele Peterson is known as Tucson's "First Lady of Fashion." Peterson's fashion line, Station Wagon Togs, once garnered nationwide attention. In addition to her success at keeping Tucson stylish, Peterson hosted a local radio show while also devoting her talents and treasure to many philanthropic endeavors. Both women lived near El Con—Ronstadt in Colonia Solano and Peterson in El Encanto.

Tucsonans owe Ronstadt and Peterson a debt of gratitude for hosting this forum because it yielded the most compelling vision yet for how El Con Mall should have been redeveloped. The forum site, a church, overflowed with eager listeners on the evening of the event. Cele Peterson started the meeting saying, "I hope we can see the alternatives, see the possibilities and see the potential of how we can keep Tucson really Tucson." [279] Peterson's statement framed the issue well, rightly characterizing El Con as part of what makes Tucson special. Ronstadt urged El Con's owners to use "enlightened greed" by taking the ideas presented seriously and changing their development strategy. [280] The meeting was then handed over to the presenter, urban planner Victor Dover.

Victor Dover's firm—Dover, Kohl & Partners—was known for taking dead or dying malls and developing them into vibrant town centers. Their work utilized principles of new urbanism, a movement which promotes "smaller shops, public transit, pedestrian-friendly landscapes and the blending of commercial and residential properties." [281] Dover's firm had several high-profile mall transformations to its credit, including a recent one in Chattanooga,

TN. That project, like El Con, required mediation between the neighbors, developer, and city officials. All three parties came together for a two-week, consensus-building effort called a "charette." The project was so successful it won an award from the White House. [282] The goal for El Con was to turn the mall into a pedestrian-friendly, mixed-use town center complete with shops, offices, and housing (i.e., apartments, condos). "These are realistic, commercially viable alternatives to the big-boxes," [283] said Jean-Paul Bierney, Chris Tanz's husband.

During the presentation, Dover presented the attendees with a challenge: "Will Tucsonans build the shining city in the desert that's an example for others to follow, or will you just build more of what they're building everywhere else?" [284] It was a question the mall's owners needed to hear, but El Con refused the invitation to attend the forum. Two days prior, El Con released a statement saying it had no intentions of converting the mall to a town center. To his credit, Mayor Walkup attended. "I'd like to see the mall made the way it was presented here tonight," he said. "But then again, the process has been running on for two years." [285] Despite the promising ideas presented, a "too little too late" sentiment colored every statement Walkup made.

The elephant in the room was that, in three days, the Council would vote again on Walkup's development agreement. Councilwoman West said she'd consider delaying the vote if she heard a compelling reason, but it didn't look promising. [286] For this reimagining of El Con to have a shot, the neighborhoods needed more time to make their case to the mall's owners. Unfortunately, El Con refused to send a representative to the meeting. As reported in the *Citizen,* two days before the forum El Con issued a statement saying, "it had already worked for two and a half years to address neighbors [sic] concerns and has no intention of converting the property into a town center with apartments, offices and homes." [287] This was a missed opportunity for El Con and the community.

Cele Peterson (left) and Linda Ronstadt

(© Tucson Citizen – USA TODAY NETWORK via Imagn Images)

Three days after the forum, the El Con Mall Redevelopment Plan was introduced again at the City Council meeting on February 14, 2000. Approximately 250 people attended the two-hour meeting to voice their support or opposition to the agreement. After a contentious public hearing, the agreement was approved by a four-to-three vote. The three dissenters were Jerry Anderson, Steve Leal, and José Ibarra. Many were outraged by newly elected Councilwoman Carol West's decision to vote with the majority. [288] Despite the promise of the alternative development plan presented at the forum, the Council refused to further delay a decision on El Con. Resident Barbara Jamieson was in tears after the vote. "It's just not fair to do these things and make changes that are so unilateral and only benefit people who don't live here," she said, asking Councilwoman West, "How could you do this to us?" [289]

El Con's owners agreed to the $3 million mitigation plan they withdrew in the fall. Had they really wanted to stick it to the neighborhoods, they could've waited until the BBO was struck down and offered no protections. As previously agreed, Jones and Palo Verde Boulevards would close while North Dodge Boulevard would remain open. El Con's owners got approval to build a Home Depot store and an as-yet unnamed big-box store. One of the plan's perks that the neighborhoods found particularly irksome was that El Con was guaranteed no major rule changes on land-use for twenty years.

"We've made a lot of mistakes with land-use decisions in this city, and this is another one," Councilman Steve Leal said. "It's probably the biggest." [290] Councilwoman Shirley Scott, who voted with the majority, tried to spin the outcome as something positive. "This is the beginning, not the end," [291] she said. She was immediately shouted down with chants of "Twenty years! Twenty years!" [292] For neighborhood supporters who attended the meeting, it was a heartbreaking end to Valentine's Day.

Rio Nuevo

So, why did Mayor Walkup support superstores at El Con? The answer is likely connected to Rio Nuevo. As discussed in Chapter 2, El Con made a negative impact on the downtown area of Tucson from the time of its debut in 1960. For forty years, the city attempted to revitalize downtown, and Rio Nuevo was an effort to do exactly that. Rio Nuevo is a Tax Incremental District (TID) in downtown Tucson. A TID is defined as "a specific geographic area within a city or village that is targeted for development or economic revitalization." [293] In May 1999, the state legislature approved for Tucson a special funding advantage called Tax Incremental Financing (TIF). A TIF is a financial tool that allows local governments to fund their redevelopment projects. Through Tax Incremental Financing, the city could divert a portion of the sales taxes generated within the TID to fund Rio Nuevo's redevelopment.

On Jul 9, 1999, City Manager Luis Gutierrez introduced an innovative proposal to extend the TID boundaries beyond Rio Nuevo—from downtown all the way up Broadway Boulevard, terminating at Park Place Mall (see below).

Rio Nuevo Tax Incremental Finance District Boundaries (Copyright Arizona Daily Star)

This meant a portion of the sales taxes from all the commercial properties lining Broadway—from downtown to Park Place—could be used to fund Rio Nuevo's redevelopment. El Con Mall was within the TID boundaries. [294] Recall, El Con and Park Place were themselves undergoing redevelopment at this time; however, Gutierrez rightly calculated that when they finished, both malls would become huge income generators for the Rio Nuevo Project.

On July 12, City Council voted five to two in favor of Gutierrez's proposal. Then voters approved the measure four months later when Proposition 400 passed in the November 2 election. The irony here is worth noting. On August 2, City Council directed Gutierrez to begin writing a big-box ordinance, a measure designed to protect El Con. Thirty days later, Gutierrez's Rio Nuevo initiative passed, making El Con and Park Place two of the major engines driving downtown's revitalization. Park Mall had no issue living up to that expectation, but El Con was a different story. The longer El Con's redevelopment dragged on, the less money it brought in for Rio Nuevo.

From the moment the proposal was announced, residents of the El Con neighborhoods noted the conflict of interest. The city, they argued, would be more inclined to relax its regulations on the kinds of stores to go up at El Con in a bid to get the mall up and running quickly. As Miramonte resident Leo Pilachowski explained, "Since they're including El Con and Park Mall [in the Rio Nuevo Tax District], they're counting on the revenue from those (malls). So if something is going to go wrong with those developments, the city is going to be tempted to make recommendations to enhance revenue from those malls." [295] The *Star* paraphrased Chris Tanz, president of T.U.C.S.O.N., as saying "the tax financing gives the city an incentive to allow, if not encourage, inappropriate superstore construction." [296]

With Rio Nuevo, it was in the city's interest for El Con to generate income as quickly as possible. El Con's representatives, including part-owner Michael Papanikolas, used Rio Nuevo to argue against the big-box ordinance. Consider this statement from El Con's attorney, Bob Gugino, the day after the Council approved the BBO: "And the Council, if it bans big-box stores, will hurt its own Rio Nuevo project. There might be a smaller El Con Mall [without big-box stores], and that's interesting because the Council passed Rio Nuevo relying on El Con sales taxes." [297] And here's another statement from Michael Papanikolas in a letter to the *Tucson Citizen,* defending El Con's opposition to the BBO.

The proposed ordinance seems to be a tool to control or possibly prohibit the successful, profitable redevelopment of El Con. This is a short-sighted course of action, considering the city included El Con in its extended Tax Incremental Financing District specifically to utilize sales tax revenues that would be generated only through substantial new retail development, to fund the $320 million Rio Nuevo project. [298]

It's not a stretch to infer that Mayor Walkup had an incentive to rush El Con's redevelopment agreement. Walkup attended the forum on the future of El Con in February 2000. At the end of the presentation, attendees begged Walkup to postpone the Council vote that would bring Home Depot to El Con. Walkup said the presentation was "very compelling" and that something similar was planned for the city's Rio Nuevo redevelopment project. The writing was on the wall. Like El Con's owners, the city couldn't wait for the mall to postpone redevelopment any longer. [299] In my opinion, Mayor Walkup rushed the El Con redevelopment agreement because kick-starting El Con with profitable big-box stores was in Rio Nuevo's interest. As *Star* writer Macario Juarez Jr. noted in 2002, "The wheels of Broadway and Rio Nuevo don't spin without Park Place and El Con." [300]

When downtown Tucson deteriorated in the 1960s, I'm sure many people thought it would never come back. Today, downtown is brimming with vitality thanks to successful redevelopment projects like Rio Nuevo. Many blamed El Con for killing downtown Tucson. When the Rio Nuevo Tax District plan was proposed, some Tucsonans rejoiced at the prospect of diverting money from El Con to pay for downtown's renewal. One Tucson resident, Carol D.

Culbertson, wrote a letter to the editor expressing her delight with Gutierrez's Rio Nuevo Tax District plan. "It seems legal—and also very just. After all, it was El Con Mall that precipitated the exodus from downtown. Now, some of the state sales tax generated by El Con will help pay for the damage." [301] Today, downtown Tucson is thriving thanks to the Rio Nuevo Project. I hope one day the favor will be returned, and the city will find a way to restore El Con.

Big-Box Breakthrough

On May 26, 2000, the Arizona Court of Appeals announced it had rejected Walmart's appeal of the Pima Superior Court's ruling, stipulating that Walmart lacked sufficient signatures to qualify for a BBO ballot measure. According to the ruling, although the city's petition form was stricter than the state's, the city was within its rights to use its own referendum rules. [302] By this point, there was nothing to stop Walmart from building a store at El Con. The City Council had already approved Walkup's development agreement. That didn't stop Walmart from taking matters further, though. As reported in the *Star*, Walmart wanted to "void" the BBO "not only because it wants to develop large stores in the city but because Walmart fears it could encourage other towns to adopt similar restrictions." [303]

Unsurprisingly, Walmart appealed the Court of Appeals ruling to the Arizona Supreme Court, but the appeal was rejected in October 2000, ending any possibility of a referendum vote on the BBO. [304] Days later, Walmart sued the city again, arguing the BBO protected local grocery stores from competition. In addition, the suit claimed the city violated state open meeting laws when Council members made amendments to the ordinance before approving it without publicizing those changes in advance of the meeting. "I think they're grasping at straws," [305] Councilman Steve Leal said. Apparently, the Pima County Superior Court thought the same thing because Judge Charles S. Sabalos dismissed the suit in September 2003—four years after the ordinance passed. [306]

Pete Kanelos, a Walmart spokesman, expressed the company's disappointment but added, "We are reviewing all of our options in our effort to allow Tucson citizens to shop in the store of their choice without restrictions." [307] It wasn't the last the neighborhoods heard of Walmart. Home Depot moved forward with its plan to build a 107,000-square-foot store at El Con. To its credit, Home Depot worked closely with the neighborhoods throughout the entire process. "They've gone out of the way to meet the concerns of neighbors," [308] said Bill Du Pont, president of Colonia Solana Neighborhood Association.

Given the choice, the neighborhoods would have preferred no big-box stores. "If everyone was given their druthers, the first choice of a lot of people would be for El Con to become an urban village, and Home Depot would not be there," [309] said Ruth Beeke of Miramonte. Carolyn Emerine, an area resident, captured the "make-the-best-of-it" attitude many had of the situation. "Now it's [Home Depot] here, so how do we deal with it," Emerine said. "We have to put aside our differences and live with them." [310] Tucson's sixth Home Depot, store #486, opened at El Con Mall on June 28, 2001.

CHAPTER 7

OPTIONED OUT

Optioned Out

In 2000, El Con went into a twelve-year tailspin from which it never recovered. The mall, which had turned forty in 2000, wasn't adjusting well to midlife. A resurgent competitor, Park Place, forced El Con to reinvent itself. The problem was, El Con's owners couldn't decide in which direction to take the mall. The redevelopment dragged on for over a decade, a stretch that witnessed El Con's descent into dead mall status. Poor decisions on the part of El Con's owners, combined with long stretches of indecision, led to mass store closures in the mall's interior. El Con became a ghost town.

When General Growth Properties purchased Park Place in 1996, El Con was backed into a corner. To remain competitive, El Con's owners had to invest as much in El Con's redevelopment as GGP invested in Park Place—more than $50 million. El Con's owners also had to match GGP's knowledge and expertise in mall development, which was a tall order. By 2000 one thing was clear: El Con couldn't remain the mall it had been. Park Place's GGP-backed redevelopment assured its standing as Midtown Tucson's premier enclosed mall.

Faced with these constraints, El Con's owners rightly decided to take the mall in a new direction. El Con had two paths forward. We'll call them Option E and Option C. Miramonte resident Ruth Beeker captures the essence of Option E in her June 1999 letter to the editor: "The reality is that Park Mall already has positioned itself as the regional shopping center on East Broadway, securing many prime leases. El Con is left with its 'big-box' concept, hoping to lease to national chains that provide value shopping with volume, noise and hours incompatible with its surrounding residential neighborhood." [311]

As Beeker explains, El Con couldn't compete with Park Place as a traditional mall. To stand out, El Con could transition from a mall to a power center. Love them or hate them, big-box stores are huge revenue generators. By packing the central midtown property with as many big-box, fast-food, and chain stores as possible, El Con's owners could quickly turn the center into a cash cow. Option E, which involved the mall transitioning into a power center, would allow El Con to escape from Park Place's shadow. The "E" in Option E represents "expedience." But expedience, as we know, has a cost.

Going with Option E required El Con to forfeit its role as a beloved community center. That's because, although power centers attract hordes of bargain-hunting consumers, they're soulless places that people only go to get what they need and then leave. Power centers are the antithesis of a town square.

In contrast to this was Option C, which would distinguish El Con from Park Place in a different way. As in the previous example, the crux of the argument behind this plan is evident in the observation of a community member. In a September 2005 letter to the editor, Mick Mathieu says,

> If you think about the land around El Con—the historic neighborhoods, Randolph golf course, tennis center, Hi Corbett, Broadway Village and area hotels—you know this is a special place, what I viewed at one time as the heart of Tucson. If you look at what's at the mall now, the heart of Tucson is broken.
>
> The owners need to come up with a plan that fits with Tucson and surrounding areas. Let's bring back the heart of Tucson and do the right thing at El Con. [312]

By the 2000s it was clear El Con couldn't attract high-end department stores like Nordstrom, Saks Fifth Avenue, or Neiman Marcus. Without premier anchors, there was nothing to distinguish El Con from other malls. But rather than turning the mall into a power center, El Con's owners could redevelop it into something unique.

Taking cues from its unique surroundings, El Con could be creatively re-envisioned into a community shopping center based on principles of new urbanism. This was Option C, which called for El Con to transition to a mixed-use, pedestrian friendly community center, taking full advantage of its midtown location, the parks, and the historic neighborhoods surrounding it. The February 2000 forum hosted by Linda Ronstadt and Cele Peterson laid out a vision of what an El Con reimagined in this way could look like. The "C" in Option C represents "character." By choosing this option, El Con's owners would breathe life back into the shopping center by giving it a fresh mix of novel stores, offices, restaurants, and more, all the while maintaining El Con's character as a beloved town center.

As you might have guessed, El Con's owners went with Option E. For people like me who wanted more for the mall, the toughest pill to swallow is that El Con's owners took steps to embrace Option C initially. They promoted a redevelopment plan called "The Plazas at El Con," which would have been fantastic had they followed through with it. But El Con's owners never fully embraced the plan, and over time, their inaction led to El Con becoming a power center. This chapter is divided into three sections. Section 1 (Plazas at El Con) discusses the Plazas at El Con redevelopment plan. Section 2 (Optioned Out) explains why Option E was the eventual outcome. Section 3 (Walmart Returns) provides a detailed account of Walmart's bid to open a store at El Con.

Plazas at El Con

Following the approval of Walkup's redevelopment plan in February 2000, things looked bleak for El Con, but later that year, a glimmer of hope emerged, following the announcement of a new development plan for the mall. On September 13, 2000, the *Arizona Daily Star* published an article titled "'De-malling' of El Con." In it, the first details of a redevelopment plan emerged. El Con's redesign and renovation were being coordinated by a design company based in Coral Gables, Florida. "A new name, a new look, and new attractions are in store for El Con Mall," the article begins. First, El Con would drop the word "mall" from its name in exchange for a new moniker: "The Plazas at El Con." The new name signaled a change in El Con's retail strategy. According to Mr. Chapman, an architect with the design company, "The Plazas at El Con no longer will be a typical mall where shopping is the main attraction. Instead The Plazas at El Con will feature a mix of retail stores, restaurants and activities aimed at revitalizing the center, which has fallen on hard times as retailers have left and shoppers have moved on." [313]

The Plazas at El Con redevelopment plan would leverage El Con's history and central midtown location to create a unique community gathering place in the heart of Tucson. El Con's redevelopment plan called for a new look. El Con would be remodeled as a "Spanish colonial-style marketplace with arches and towers, walkways and lush gardens that connect shops, plazas, an open-air market and restaurants that offer outdoor dining on linen-dressed tables." [314] The Spanish colonial theme was an obvious nod to the El Conquistador Hotel.

The Plazas redevelopment plan called for new attractions at El Con. The word "plaza" is Spanish for "square," meaning an open area surrounded by a town, village, or city. As explained in the "'De-Malling' of El Con" article, the name "Plazas at El Con" was "meant to reflect the transformation of the mall into a retail center of plazas, or 'neighborhoods' with similar retailers, restaurants and services grouped together." [315] El Con was to be divided into seven to eight plazas, each with an eclectic mix of restaurants, entertainment venues, and stores. In response to Park Place's renovation, El Con would be transformed into a lifestyle center unmatched by any other mall in Tucson: "Plans call for adding services and amenities other shopping centers and malls don't have, such as multi-use space for performing arts and exhibits, an outdoor market on the northwest end of the center, and a gourmet food store on the east end. The possibility of having a public library and government offices has been discussed." [316]

Interestingly, the plan called for a museum row and artist studios. These two elements alone would have made the Plazas at El Con a popular destination for out-of-town visitors looking for something to do.

Here's a map (below) showing the locations of some attractions.

The Plazas at El Con

Due to a technical error yesterday, this graphic did not run correctly. Here is how it should have appeared. El Con Mall is proposing a new, Spanish Colonial-style concept for its retailers and customers. The 1.1 million-square-foot mall could be redesigned to include up to 10 retail, entertainment, service, dining areas.

The Plazas at El Con development plan (Copyright Arizona Daily Star)

Phase one of the Plazas plan was supposed to begin in early 2001. Part of phase one involved repurposing the former Dillard's anchor store to accommodate restaurant and entertainment venues. In September 2000, Chapman, the architect, shared that a billiard room, martini bar, and cigar bar were being considered for the vacant Dillard's building. "Tucson is an eclectic mix of people, and we want to find retailers and services that can appeal to that mix," Chapman said. "The idea is to have under one roof a broad selection of entertainment and food to appeal to a broad market, people from age

15 to 50 and over." [317] El Con was poised for a mix of tenants that would have made it different from any other mall in Tucson. It's not every day that you come across billiard rooms, martini bars, and cigar bars in a mall. No mall in Tucson featured such venues. Had El Con followed through with that plan, it would have been a hit.

Public reception of the Plazas plan was positive. The plan was lauded as a "welcome move" in the dispute over El Con's future and "far more in keeping with the character of the area." [318] The Plazas redevelopment plan was announced seven months after the City Council approved Mayor Walkup's redevelopment plan-the one that brought Home Depot to El Con. It appears to be based on concepts floated at the forum on the future of El Con. Had El Con's owners followed through with the Plazas plan, El Con may have remained the beloved community center it had always been. Though the owners occasionally rolled out elements of the plan, the Plazas never got off the ground.

Optioned Out

To understand why El Con's owners abandoned the Plazas plan, start with the Century 20 Theater. Recall the initial step that the mall's owners took to distinguish El Con from Park Place was the construction of a twenty-screen theater. The theater was the cornerstone of El Con's revitalization effort, but while it was still being constructed, Park Place announced that it too was getting a twenty-screen Century Theater. Once both theaters were in operation, the success of Century 20 Park Place highlighted two glaring mistakes that El Con made in its theater design process. The first involved a flaw in the layout of Century 20 El Con: the theater was not connected to the rest of the mall.

Like El Con 6, the Century 20 theater was built in proximity to the mall but not connected to it. None of its entrances or exits opened directly into the mall. Here is a 2007 map of El Con Mall:

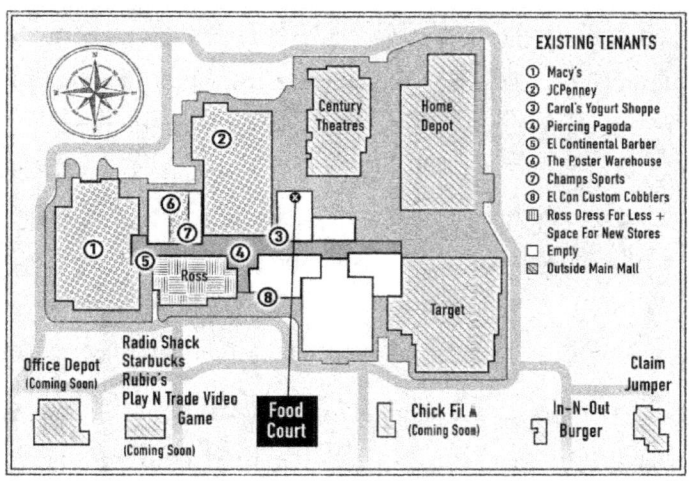

Food Court at El Con Mall, 2007

Note that the theater is disconnected from the mall's core. To enter the mall, you either had to drive around to the main entrance or walk south from the theater entrance to enter through the food court. The theater was created to attract people to the mall. By not connecting it to the mall's core, however, the strategy failed. People came to El Con to see movies, but they didn't stick around to shop in the mall. As time passed, more retailers left the mall until its core dwindled to a handful of stores.

El Con's second mistake was failing to connect the theater to its newly constructed food court. Like Park Place, El Con's renovation plans called for a new food court. By March 2001, El Con had begun construction on its first ever food court. An excerpt from Issue VII of the El Con Mall *Communique'* newsletter highlights the progress made on the mall's food court:

> The new Food Court floor is in the process of being resurfaced. Grinding is complete on the old flooring and the passageway through the Food Court from the mall to Century Theatres is now open. Temporary drywall facades have been placed in front of each proposed food court bay while the service corridors are being constructed. We are working with several local and national operators, and hope to announce new Food Court tenants in the near future. [319]

In May 2001, a *trompe l'oeil* mural featuring scenes with food vendors was painted on the vendor bays of the food court. A *trompe l'oeil* mural is a two-dimensional painting that creates the illusion of a three-dimensional object. Ironically, these paintings were the only vendors that the food court ever housed. This too was a consequence of getting upstaged by Park Place, which debuted its own food court two months later in August 2001.

In phase one of GGP's renovation, Park Place got a much-needed face lift. Its dated exterior was replaced with an eclectic mix of storefronts indicative of the "lifestyle center" concept or "a collection of shops, restaurants and entertainment venues designed with an emphasis on access and comfort." [320] Phase two of the renovation involved the theater and food court. Like El Con, Park Place never had a food court. In 1997, an anonymous Park Place shop manager described the mall as "absolutely dead, particularly in the evening." The manager cited the lack of a food court as the problem. "There's no place to eat, so there's no reason to stay." [321] Phase two of Park Place's renovation addressed this deficiency.

Park Place officials unveiled the new food court on August 8, 2001, just two days before the theater's grand opening. Roughly 5,000 people showed up for opening day, which included a ribbon-cutting ceremony and a gift bag give-away for the first 1,000 customers. Designed as a marketplace setting in a Spanish village, the food court featured seating for 800 people, twelve spaces for food vendors, and a kids' play area. The play area was a hit with parents and kids alike. "It's really neat," said Becky Thomson, one of many moms who visited the play area. "It'll be nice to keep the kids busy when we come here shopping." [322] The addition of a food court in Park Place was a home run, as evidenced by statements from three people who stopped in to experience it on opening day:

"This is the kind of thing people in Tucson have been waiting for a long time." [323] — Mayor Bob Walkup

"We really had no idea how many people would show up. We're very surprised. It really shows the pent-up desire for entertainment and a food court." [324] — Mike Hackstadt, Park Place general manager

"We used to drive all the way to Tucson Mall. Now we don't have to." [325] — Jeannette McCale, East Side Tucson resident

The south wing of Park Place fed directly into the food court, and it was deliberately packed with teen-oriented businesses. [326] Teens and mall food courts are a match made in heaven. In its strategic location, Park Place's food court received a constant flow of traffic from shoppers entering through the mall's south wing and people entering and leaving the movie theater. "The food court and movie theater will keep people in the mall longer, which translates to more spending," [327] noted Teya Vitu, business writer for the *Tucson Citizen*. And indeed, they did contribute to more spending. "On a scale of one to 10, [the food court and the movie theater] has to be a nine for the whole mall," said Larry Atkinson, owner of the Santa Fe Trading Co. store in Park Place. "Hopefully, this will expand the shopping experience." [328]

The food court and theater of Park Place were a potent one-two combo. By late 2001, El Con Mall had a food court too. As mentioned, though, El Con made a huge tactical error by not attaching the theater to the food court and the rest of the mall (see image next page). In addition, the food court was far too small. The food court of Park Place dwarfed the one at El Con. Judging from the size of it, the El Con food court was built to fit perhaps 100 to 150 people. You could fit eight El Con food courts in the Park Place food court, which could accommodate up to 800 patrons. The Park Place food court opened just as El Con was nearing completion of its own food court. The day after Park Place debuted its food court in August 2001, Susan Allen, the spokesperson for El Con, surmised how the new development would affect El Con. "The playing field will level off in a few weeks. We have loyal customers who have stayed with us during the transition [i.e., the redevelopment at El Con]." [329]

Theater (bottom-left foreground) and main north entrance of Food Court (Spanish-colonial themed structure in background) Note: Theater and Food Court are not connected

(Image courtesy of Jason Damas and Ross Schendel of Labelscar.com)

Allen's assessment was incorrect. El Con was unable to lure a single tenant to the food court. The disparity in the food courts at Park Place and El Con was glaring. More than eighteen months after completing the *trompe l'oeil* mural, the El Con food court remained empty. Management could no longer hide behind falsely optimistic statements, so they switched to damage control. "It would be unwise for us as developers and for any individual food operator to open by themselves," Susan Allen said. "A one-person food court doesn't do anyone a whole lot of good." [330] True, but why weren't vendors moving in? Why would any vendor risk leasing a spot in the food court when only a handful of stores remained in the mall's core?

El Con's owners committed unforced errors that sank its Plazas redevelopment effort. The discontinuity between the theater and the mall was a big mistake. Imagine the traffic Century 20 El Con could have generated in the mall's interior if moviegoers had had to walk past rows of stores to get to the theater. What if, like Park Place, El Con had had a massive food court just outside the theater entrance, luring people coming and going to the movies? Food gives people a reason to hang around, and when people linger in a mall, there's a high likelihood that they'll shop. "People don't go to the mall to eat," said Jim Gebhart, owner of the local food consulting firm Gebo Inc. Consulting. "They might stop, be shopping, and stop to rest their legs and grab a bite, or possibly eat before a movie. But it's not a destination." [331]

Another example of poor planning and execution was El Con's remodeled south entrance. One element of the Plazas plan that I found particularly meaningful was its acknowledgment and celebration of the mall's roots in the El Conquistador Hotel. One of the primary ways it achieved this was by incorporating elements of the El Conquistador Hotel into El Con's architecture. To their credit, El Con's owners began moving in this direction as far back as 1999 when the big-box controversy was just getting started. In an open letter published August 16, 1999, El Con co-owner Michael Papanikolas gave the community a glimpse of planned changes to the mall's south-facing exterior. An artist's rendering of the new main entrance revealed several architectural elements reminiscent of the El Conquistador Hotel. [332]

The owners never followed through on this redesign. A similar aesthetic was part of the Plazas at El Con redevelopment plan, which had the mall becoming an open-air center with Spanish-colonial architectural influences reminiscent of the hotel. This time, El Con's owners followed through with some aesthetic changes. In 2003, construction was completed on a new main entrance for the mall. The entrance was an homage to the porte-cochere and bell tower of the El Conquistador Hotel. This elaborate entryway featured a pair of forty-foot towers topped with copper domes (see image next page).

El Con's re-modeled south entrance, 2008

(Copyright Arizona Daily Star)

I give the owners credit for honoring the El Conquistador Hotel via aesthetic changes to the mall's exterior. That said, like the food court, the changes were executed in a ham-handed fashion. The Spanish colonial entrance stuck out like a sore thumb in contrast with the mall's 1970s-era exterior. As a result, the remodeled south entrance was largely panned. The Century 20 Theater, food court, and remodeled south entrance represented significant investments on the part of the owners to revive the mall's sagging fortunes. When all three efforts failed to attract vendors and shoppers to El Con, they became symbols of mall mismanagement instead.

The Plazas plan had overwhelming public support, but missteps like this eroded people's confidence in mall management. Longtime tenants became demoralized as more stores left due to the slow renovation progress. Many were loyal tenants who wanted to remain at the mall, but when they questioned management about its long-term plan, they couldn't get a straight answer. "They [the El Con management] share only what they want to share and then nobody in the mall that works here understands what's going to happen," Tucson retail consultant Marc Weiss said. "If you worked here and saw that they built this beautiful opening in the back side and then had a food court where there were no food stores, you'd begin to wonder." [333]

When the Plazas redevelopment plan was unveiled in 2001, El Con's prospects appeared hopeful. As time passed, however, it became increasingly clear that something was amiss. By 2004 there was no question that the Plazas redevelopment plan was off track. El Con's core withered, offering fewer and fewer reasons for shoppers to visit the mall. In September 2004, Doug Kreutz of the *Arizona Daily Star* penned an article titled, "Many Moods of the Malls." In it, Kreutz captures the personalities of five malls in Tucson after walking through them and asking shoppers and mall executives to weigh in. Here is what he wrote about El Con:

Tucson's first enclosed shopping center, El Con, at 3601 E. Broadway, has been around since 1960—and it's in the midst of a large-scale, but incomplete, redesign and renovation.

Shopping traffic could be described as "modest" in El Con's western wing—where stores such as Robinsons-May and Champs Sports are in full operation along half a dozen shuttered shops.

The mall's eastern reaches are devoid of shoppers. Vast stretches of retail space there await new tenants, and a spacious food court makes do with murals depicting food outlets in place of actual vendors.

"I would describe it as a depressing atmosphere right now," said shopper Miller. "It's a beautiful property, very valuable because of the location, but it needs a lot of help." [334]

By 2005 people were openly expressing their reservations about the lack of progress. That year, *Tucson Citizen* columnist Anne T. Denogean wrote an insightful article describing the plight of El Con with perfect clarity. She begins using the "green but untidy" lawn outside the main entrance of the mall as a symbol of an unspoken but widely recognized truth regarding El Con: "Somebody cares enough to keep it alive but not enough to make it thrive." [335] Denogean references the Plazas redevelopment plan, by then four years old. She describes the unique variety of retailers called for in the plan as "a mix that seemed right on the mark." [336] Like so many other Tucsonans, Denogean seemed genuinely excited about the vision for El Con laid out in the Plazas plan. "Today, the vision appears to be dead,"

Denogean says. "And no answers as to why are forthcoming from the only owners the mall has had in its 45-year life, Tucson's Kivel and Papanikolas families." [337]

Denogean invites the reader on a tour of the mall, a walk she describes as heartbreaking. "The center that at various times housed Cele Peterson's, Grunewald & Adams Jewelers, Dave Bloom and Sons, Goldwaters, Steinfeld's, Dillard's and Montgomery Ward is a midtown shopping wasteland." [338] Denogean notes the mall's awkward remodeled entrance, east end with big-box stores (Home Depot and Target) that don't open to the mall, and vacant food court. She interviews seventy-nine-year-old Louis Panos, owner of the Indian Arts & Crafts store. When asked if management is communicating its plans to tenants, Panos responds: "We don't see nobody. They don't say anything." [339]

Denogean closes by asking, "So what is in El Con's future?" Denogean admits she can't say because the mall's owners refuse to show their cards. Then Denogean uncovers a clue. "According to mall spokeswoman Susan Allen, the mall's owners, lawyers and management/leasing agent feel there's nothing to talk about, other than to say they are negotiating with prospective tenants." [340] Nothing to talk about? How could this be? The answer was there in plain view: there was no plan to talk about. The future of El Con would be determined by whatever tenants its owners signed leases with. Until then, Denogean rightly guesses, "El Con's owners are content to simply suck money out of their prime midtown property while adding little of value to the community that they call home." [341]

We may never know the real reason El Con's owners abandoned the Plazas plan, but it was likely a reaction to the costly failures of the early redevelopment efforts. The theater, food court, and remodeled south entrance were significant financial investments for the owners. When those investments didn't pay off, the owners became gun-shy. From then on they refused to do anything without a secured lease. This is evident in statements by El Con spokeswoman Susan Allen. Here is a sampling of statements Allen and others to support this theory:

"Retailers coming in have to be No. 1. You can't develop on spec. It's impossible." [342]	Susan Allen, 2002
"You can't set up a space not knowing who's going in there. It's not like building a house. I think the community sees El Con as dragging its feet. That's really not the case." [343]	Susan Allen, 2002
"The redevelopment, aimed at turning the midtown mall into a 'community center' with a village market atmosphere, can't move forward until El Con attracts more retailers willing to sign leases, mall spokeswoman Susan Allen said." [344]	Tiffany Kjos, *Arizona Daily Star* columnist
"Especially since its north side food court failed due to the lack of retailing mass inside, the owners of El Con aren't wild about building on speculation." [345]	Martin Rosales, Editorial Writer for the *Arizona Daily Star*

The consequence of this overly conservative approach was that El Con became a power center by default. Each year the mall's interior hemorrhaged more tenants, which were not replaced. Failed department store anchors were replaced with big-box stores. By 2006, El Con's owners had given up completely on the Plazas plan. This was never publicly communicated, but it was plain for all to see. In fact, an editorial written by Martin Rosales of the *Arizona Daily Star* basically confirmed what everyone suspected. "The mall's center has long needed a new identity, and discounters are its best hope of survival. El Con has decided it must differentiate itself from Park Place and Tucson Mall, and by placing Target on the east side, it set the tone for the rest of the mall." [346]

Rosales was spot on in his assessment. Had El Con limited its big-box holdings to Home Depot, the Plazas at El Con plan had a realistic chance of becoming reality. But after inking the Target deal, El Con was on a glide path to becoming a power center. The owners wanted this to remain a secret, but they weren't fooling anyone. Rosales exposed the truth when he summarized the situation this way:

> El Con has already halfway turned to discounters, already halfway turned to a pavilion-style outdoor shopping experience. It's time to go all the way. Target, Ross and the mall's peripheral chain food outlets could help attract other well-regarded low-price stores, allowing the chance to finally create a niche that the once-proud mall has lacked for years. [347]

In other words, by 2006 the transition from mall to power center was already well underway. While everyone else in Tucson scratched their heads, wondering why the El Con renovation was taking so long, the mall's owners knew exactly what they were doing. "Unlike General Growth, a national firm that plowed more than $50 million into Park Place, El Con's local owners have few established ties with retailers to assure them they'll jump in if things improve," Rosales explains. "So El Con is sitting back, waiting to see if Ross will come and what will happen with Robinsons-May [one of El Con's two remaining anchors at the time]." [348]

On January 5, 2007, seven new writers were introduced for the 2007 "My Tucson" column in the *Tucson Citizen* newspaper. Among them was Suzanne C. McLean, former vice president of planning and development for the Tucson Airport Authority. McLean had an extensive background in urban planning. In August 2007, McLean used her "My Tucson" column to write about the sad situation at El Con Mall. McLean begins by saying, "For 12 years, something has been going on at El Con Mall-but most Tucsonans still can't figure out what it is." [349] Her observation perfectly captures the bewilderment community members felt when witnessing El Con's prolonged fall from grace. Things were happening at the mall, but none of it amounted to anything.

The column featured an image of El Con's vacant core. The photo illustrates McLean's characterization of El Con as "the perfect setting for a creepy horror film." She goes on to say, "It's easy to imagine the living dead hiding in the dark behind all those boarded-up outlets." [350] McLean provides context for the plight of El Con by recalling its former glory days, when it was a thriving mall where everyone shopped. Next, she mentions the renovation efforts that have "occurred in dribs and drabs for years, with no recognizable plan or logic or sense of place." [351] McLean describes El Con's dilapidated state, juxtaposing it with the successful transformation of Park Place Mall:

> Both El Con and Park Mall's owners announced a "major overhaul" to their respective malls way back in 1995 when they were both due for some modernizing. Look at Park Mall—now Park Place—today. In just a few years, the owners turned the lagging mall around to become one of the most popular shopping experiences in town. They remodeled, enlarged, brightened and diversified the offerings to put Park Place on the map again. Where has El Con gone? [352]

It's the question we all wanted answered. By 2007, ten years after El Con announced its plan to build a twenty-screen theater, the prognosis for the mall was grim. El Con was still alive, but things weren't looking good. El Con didn't appear to be going anywhere. Rightly, McLean laid the blame on El Con's owners who "have been short-sighted in their quest to fill the space with anything." McLean ends her column with a damning statement: "El Con Mall is gone, and from the looks of it, it's never coming back." [353]

Three days after McLean's column, the *Tucson Citizen* published reactions to her piece written by members of the newspaper's online community. The "Your take" segment RealFAST online comments summarized the collective response this way: "RIP El Con. Few members of the Citizen's online community believe it will again become a prime shopping location. Bad management (the mall has been owned by Tucson's Kivel and Papanikolas families for all of its

47-year existence) gets most of the blame for the shopping center's demise." [354]

Some online commenters cited mistakes made by the El Con management. Joe Q., for example, argued that when the twenty-screen theater was built, "patrons should have been forced to walk through the mall to reach them, instead of creating exterior-only access." [355] Other commenters offered suggestions for what could replace the mall. One wanted to see it turned into a Castles and Coasters type attraction, another a workout gym, and still another an office space. The final comment struck me the most, though. A woman named Linda H. wrote, "Too bad they can't put the El Conquistador Hotel back. It was beautiful!" [356]

In January 2008 Martin Rosales published another editorial, this one expressing support for a redevelopment plan that aligned more closely with Option C. "Outside Macy's east entrance lies a withering, vacant mall core in which two teen-age boys were recently seen passing a football without hitting anyone or anything—and not because they have great aim," [357] Rosales says. He continues, expressing frustration about the mall's ongoing deterioration. Then Rosales proposes a solution:

> Our idea is that the continued erosion of El Con Mall be stopped with creative revitalization that is planned and implemented immediately. The 93-acre El Con property is prime central Tucson property, tucked among several of our community's most venerable neighborhoods. It sits across from Reid Park, golf courses, the zoo and the tennis center. [358]

If this sounds like a return to something resembling the Plazas plan, that's because it is. By this point, El Con's owners were too far into the surreptitious power center conversion to turn back. That Rosales returned to an Option C-style vision for the mall shows how attractive the Plazas redevelopment plan was. In contrast to that vision, Rosales describes the mall as it is. "The parking lot sits between Office Depot and Macy's and the core mall," he says. "As the mall's core withers, Target and Home Depot, separate buildings that have their backs to the mall and do not open into the mall, thrive." [359] The big-box stores, restaurants, and stand-alone stores on the periphery of the mall were the owners' focus. The enclosed mall was an afterthought.

Rosales ends his column with a seeming plea to El Con's owners: "Our community deserves better than an empty shell in what should be a jewel of the community. The highest and best use of this real estate is not vacant structures where watching paint peel is the main activity." [360] What nobody knew at the time was that an old enemy was waiting in the wings, ready to pounce. In what had to be the scariest of Halloween surprises for the El Con neighborhoods, an *Arizona Daily Star* article on October 31, 2007, announced that Macy's was leaving El Con. This created an opening for another big-box store and a potentially game-changing realignment for the mall. Walmart wasted no time. On May 4, 2008, the headline on the front page of the Arizona Daily Star Business section read: "Report: Wal-Mart eyes El Con space."

Walmart Returns

Following the dismissal by the Superior Court of Walmart's suit against the city in 2003, Walmart faded from El Con's view for several years. When Montgomery Ward announced it was leaving El Con in 2001, many feared Walmart would move in to replace it, but El Con was quick to snuff out such rampant speculation. "We don't feel Wal-Mart is an appropriate tenant," [361] El Con's spokeswoman, Susan Allen, said. A Target store replaced Montgomery Ward. Each year, more chain stores and fast-food restaurants went up around the mall's perimeter, places like Krispy Kreme, Claim Jumper, Rubio's, Starbucks, In-N-Out Burger, Radio Shack, and Office Depot. A portion of the enclosed mall near Macy's was torn down and replaced with a Ross Dress for Less store in 2007. El Con's slow, inexorable devolution into a power center continued, but still no Walmart.

Walmart reappeared in 2007 with another controversy that threatened to embroil the city. To get around the law, Walmart organized a voting initiative to repeal a provision in the BBO that limited grocery space to less than 10 percent of a superstore's overall floor space. The grocery limitation had been a requirement from the outset of the law in 1999. Two months earlier, the city waived this requirement for another developer, Eastbourne Investments Ltd., which requested an exemption through City Council. Walmart, on the other hand, bypassed the exemption process altogether and simply acted to repeal the provision using a voting initiative. [362] "This has to do with Walmart's desires to write local laws so they benefit the corporation . . . regardless of what the community desires," [363] Councilwoman Karin Uhlich observed.

Walmart hired a political consultant, Pete Zimmerman, to oversee its "Consumer Choice Initiative" petition drive.[364] Zimmerman got contractors to collect the required signatures. Needing 11,615 signatures, Walmart collected 21,934. On July 5, Zimmerman himself delivered the petitions to City Clerk Kathleen Detrick's office before the 5:00 p.m. filing deadline. He didn't get far. Detrick informed Zimmerman that land-use codes, like the BBO, were protected from initiatives under Arizona law. Were this not the case, key elements of the zoning process like public hearings could be circumvented. Detrick refused the petitions, forcing Zimmerman to lug the boxes out of City Hall.[365] To nobody's surprise, here is Walmart's response: "We're evaluating our next step and what our legal options are."[366] On July 13, Walmart wrote a letter to Mayor Walkup and City Council, announcing it wouldn't pursue legal action on the matter. "Engaging in a lawsuit with the city of Tucson wasn't the right alternative in this case,"[367] Delia Garcia, a representative for Walmart, said.

But Walmart had no intentions of dropping the issue quietly. On July 16, Delia Garcia of Walmart published a full-page "Open Letter to the Citizens of Tucson" in the newspaper. Garcia begins by noting the city clerk rejected the 22,000 signed petitions Walmart collected for its Consumer Choice Initiative. In doing so, the city "forced Wal-Mart into a position of having to file a lawsuit against the city to give its voters a voice."[368] Garcia shares that Walmart elected not to pursue legal action even though it had a good case. Then she argues that the residents of Tucson deserve to have their voices heard because the big-box ordinance prevents them from paying less for their groceries. In Walmart's view, the 22,000 signed petitions should be seen as a mandate for City Council to remove the grocery restriction from the ordinance. The letter ends with an injunction for the city to "do the right thing by revisiting this provision of the Big Box Ordinance and allowing Tucson's citizens the opportunity for open discussion." [369]

Walmart's open letter offers another good example of why the company is so often maligned. The fact that City Council waived the grocery restriction for Eastbourne proves that the city wasn't inflexible. Walmart just didn't want to play by the rules. "They want what they want, when they want it," Councilman Leal said. "It's more of an attitude problem than a legal problem." [370] Council-woman Uhlich agreed, observing that Walmart's propensity to challenge local laws appeared to be part of its corporate culture. "They'd rather dictate from afar," Uhlich said. "Wal-Mart is the only one that insists they need to change the rules in Tucson." [371]

Walmart had been repelled once again, but three months later the company became the recipient of an unexpected gift. On October 30, 2007, Macy's announced it was leaving El Con. "The El Con Center closure is a direct result of underperformance and the company has determined that it is no longer financially viable to keep it open," [372] Macy's spokeswoman Janet De Vor said. The failure of Macy's was a powerful indictment of El Con's failed strategy. The owners remained fixated on courting big-box stores and developing the perimeter of the property, to the complete neglect of the mall's core. "El Con has thrived on the outside in recent years while dwindling on the inside," observed B. Poole of the Citizen. "There are 29 empty stores inside, and eight active businesses." [373]

The Macy's announcement caught El Con's management off guard, as Macy's still had several years left on its lease. [374] It was a huge setback for the mall, leaving JCPenney as El Con's lone remaining department store. As the saying goes, "One person's loss is another's gain." After learning of the impending vacancy, Walmart entered negotiations with Macy's for the space. Near the start of May 2008, an El Con attorney broke the news to neighborhood leaders at an information session. These regular, informal meetings were called for in Walkup's development agreement. [375] El Encanto immediately hired an attorney, Bruce Heurlin, to fight Walmart. "If there is going to be some kind of action by Wal-Mart, I'm here, I'm ready to go, and we're going to object," [376] Heurlin promised.

Until then, the neighborhoods had successfully countered every Walmart move to gain a foothold in El Con. This time was different. Ernie Duarte, the city's development services director, explained that Walmart had found a potential loophole in Walkup's development agreement. "If any retailer went into that Macy's building and did just interior renovation, interior work . . . it would not trigger the big-box (ordinance)." [377] By skirting the BBO, Walmart wouldn't need the approval of the mayor or City Council to open an El Con store. In addition, unlike the BBO, Walkup's development agreement didn't include any restrictions on the size of grocery areas within a store. Walmart had found a way around the BBO, which it could use to outflank the neighborhoods and break into the prized midtown mall location.

If you're wondering why Walmart hadn't done this sooner, the answer is square footage. Macy's footprint was approximately 100,000 square feet, which was 80,000 square feet smaller than the typical Walmart supercenter. But Walmart figured out how to build a smaller supercenter. With a smaller store, Walmart could get around Tucson's BBO. *Star* reporter Josh Brodesky predicted this development would lead to an influx of new Walmart stores. "The Walmarts are coming," Brodesky warned. "Expect to see more and more Walmarts in town as the discount retailer makes a push into the Tucson market with a smaller store that will slide right underneath the city's big-box ordinance."[378] By October 2009, Walmart was pursuing these stores at three Tucson locations: Golf Links/Houghton, Valencia/Alvernon, and El Con Mall. "The smaller stores are coming,"[379] Brodesky warned.

On May 24, 2010, Walmart publicly announced its intention to build a store at El Con with an anticipated opening in mid-2012. As if this wasn't bad enough, days later Walmart announced that the El Con store would be open twenty-four hours. This was allowed under the zoning agreement signed in 2000, so the law was on Walmart's side again. City Council agreed to ask Walmart to reduce its hours of operation and change the orientation of the store at El Con. Walmart refused both requests. "Our plan is to offer customers the convenience of 24-hour shopping at the El Con Walmart,"[380] Walmart spokeswoman Delia Garcia said.

By 2011 only three tenants remained in El Con's deserted core: Poster Warehouse, El Continental Barbershop, and El Con Custom Cobbler. As bleak as things looked, many people hoped El Con would make a comeback. In April 2011, a spokesman for El Con extinguished that hope by revealing the pending demolition of the mall. The three tenants received notice that they would need to move. When the news broke, Tom Fetter, manager of Poster Warehouse, said he knew it was coming. "You can put two and two together when they have architects running around. You gotta figure they're gonna tear it down." [381]

On October 25, 2011, El Encanto sued the city of Tucson, claiming the Board of Adjustments was wrong to approve Walmart's move to El Con. The case was argued before Pima County Superior Court Judge Jeffrey Bergin in May 2012. Bergin gave no indication when he'd rule on the case. On June 20, 2012, demolition of the Macy's building (originally Levy's) began, making room for the new Walmart. Coincidentally, this was the summer solstice, the longest day of the year. From then on, days get shorter and nights longer. Like the solstice, the demolition of this store, once a centerpiece of the mall, signaled dark days ahead for El Con. This picture of the Levy's building demolition captures the virtual death of El Con Mall (see image below).

Demolition of Levy's Building, June 20, 2012

(Copyright Arizona Daily Star)

Though the outlook appeared bleak, the neighborhoods didn't give up the fight. On June 30, Chris Tanz, Cathy Davis, and Frank Babb wrote a letter to the editor that implored City Council to hold a public hearing on the issue: "Our neighborhood association (El Encanto) is waiting for Judge Jeffrey Bergin to issue a ruling on the Planning and Development Services Department's approval of a Walmart at the site. Our legal position is that any 'protected development rights' granted to El Con Mall in 2000 have expired. Therefore the big-box ordinance must apply." [382]

In July, Judge Bergin issued a ruling in Walmart's favor. Bergin found no cause to overturn the decision by the Board of Adjustment on Walmart, which matched City Council and the zoning administrator's judgments as well. Because the new store was being built within Macy's footprint, Walmart had every right to be at El Con. Walkup's development agreement with El Con—signed in 2000—included a provision allowing for development within El Con's plan. The law was on Walmart's side, and there was nothing the neighborhoods could do about it. "The judge's ruling is good news for Midtown Tucson residents who are one step closer to having an option for affordable, fresh groceries, general merchandise and pharmacy services closer to home," [383] Delia Garcia said in a written statement.

Walmart is known for its smiling, yellow-faced mascot, "Smiley." Walmart Chief Marketing Officer Tony described Smiley as "one of the most-recognized symbols of low price." [384] Walmart's friendly looking mascot belies a ruthless, unyielding corporation laser focused on furthering its interests. Walmart knew the neighborhoods weren't happy about the El Con store. As a gesture of goodwill, Walmart could have negotiated with the neighborhoods to reach a compromise. Instead, Walmart chose not to give an inch. Luckily for the neighborhoods, in March 2013, City Council voted to deny the El Con Walmart a liquor license. On July 11, 2013, the Arizona State Liquor Board upheld City Council's decision and denied Walmart the license. The neighborhoods played a role in the outcome, as some eighty midtown residents attended the hearing with charts and data to make their case against the license.

Walmart went silent after the decision as it considered its legal options. Walmart could appeal the decision or reapply for a license later, but both options carried risks. Walmart determined it was in its best interest to negotiate with the neighborhoods. In exchange for an agreement by the neighborhoods not to oppose the liquor license, Walmart agreed not to be a twenty-four-hour store. Councilman Steve Kozachik played a big role in securing the compromise. The deal, however, was contingent upon the State Board's approval of the license. When the El Con Walmart opened on September 11, 2013, it couldn't sell liquor. To everyone's surprise, the Arizona State Liquor Board denied Walmart's appeal on September 14, 2014. Walmart continued its twenty-four-hour operation. Kozachik brokered a second compromise the following year, which led to the unanimous recommendation for the license by City Council. The deal was contingent upon approval by the State Board.

While the outcome was still in doubt, Walmart spokeswoman Delia Garcia issued a statement. "It is encouraging that we have reached an agreement with neighborhood associations in the El Con Mall area. And we will continue to engage with stakeholders as we move toward application of a limited liquor license to better serve customers at this store location." [385] To me this is a perfect example of how Walmart operates. Garcia's statement gives the impression of a benevolent company—insert Smiley image—working toward compromise with the neighborhoods. In reality, Walmart only took the compromise route because it served Walmart's interests. The true nature of Walmart hides beneath the saccharine, boilerplate statements issued from the likes of spokespersons like Garcia. Had there been a way to get the liquor license and maintain its twenty-four-hour operation, Walmart would've done that instead. The Arizona State Liquor Board approved Walmart's liquor license on October 27, 2014.

So ended the fifteen-year neighborhood battle to keep Walmart out of El Con. Walmart prevailed, but the El Con neighborhoods and members of the community put up a valiant fight. Their efforts to block Walmart led to the creation of the Big Box Ordinance, which has protected the Tucson community from unmitigated superstore takeovers since 1999. In 2011, Josh Brodesky of the *Star* wrote an excellent piece that captures the shame-of-it-all feeling many had about Walmart coming to El Con. "Walmart and El Con's owners deserve each other. But this town, and these neighbors, don't deserve this," Brodesky said. He goes on to describe Walmart's many attempts to open an El Con store and neighborhood efforts to keep Walmart out. The article ends with Brodesky's summation of why the outcome was so unfortunate:

> What's sad here is El Con Mall could have been awesome. With Reid Park across the street, and surrounded by historic neighborhoods, it could have been the heartbeat of the city. But instead, it's a Big Boxville filled with depressing empty space and surrounded by fast-food chains. Its owners, the

Kivel and Papanikolas families, put no vision into it. Just another place. Walmart and El Con deserve each other. But this town, and these neighbors, don't deserve this. [386]

Well said, Mr. Brodesky. Well said.

The mall has been under new ownership since 2014, and there doesn't seem to be any movement away from the power center model, which still characterizes El Con today. Where the mall once stood is a collection of big-box stores, restaurants, and a movie theater, orbiting an empty core. When Stanley Kroenke, owner of Kroenke Sports & Entertainment, purchased El Con in 2014, he announced plans to make it into a "vital shopping destination." [387] Compared to the lively indoor mall that once occupied 3601 E. Broadway Boulevard, though, today's El Con is a shadow of its former self. El Con Center brings in plenty of shoppers, but it's a soulless void where people come only to get what they need and then leave. I'm not the only one who sees it this way either. Here's some El Con reviews posted on Yelp echoing the same sentiment:

During its [El Con Mall's] hey day it attracted most of the dull people in town until eventually they got bored. Now its empty but they have brought in some bland new tenants (Super Store USA crap). [388]

Ferdinand B. from New York, New York

I recently returned to Tucson to find its no longer a mall but really just an unwalkable generic plaza. Whoever reimagined El Con has no shopping experience whatsoever. This place had such potential. There was such history with El Con being the first "mall" in Tucson.. . . It's just an epic fail. The owner of the mall (who I understand is a sports person) has no idea what El Con meant to Tucson or its history. This could have been renovated into a beautiful, outdoor, brick-lined shopping experience. Now it's just another asphalt plaza mess that makes it even more miserable. There is still hope. Someone could come in and use that alley space now as the main corridor again. But I fear they never will. Tucson lost a bit of its history with the destruction of this place. [389]

N. M. from Tucson, Arizona

Trips to El Con these days are not what they used to be. I go there occasionally to shop at Home Depot. My wife goes to shop at Target or to get food for the kids at In-N-Out Burger, Chick-fil-A, or Portillo's. Still, the nature of every visit to El Con is in-and-out shopping: go in, get what you need, and get out as quickly as possible.

For most of my life, El Con was my first option among the malls of Tucson. Since El Con became a power center, I'm sorry to say I have optioned out of going there until something changes.

CHAPTER 8

HOPE STIRRING

Hope Stirring

The historic El Con sign was taken down in 1999. Like the "Welcome to Fabulous Las Vegas" sign in Nevada, the El Con sign was a local landmark. Standing forty-five feet tall on a pole shaped like a Spanish conquistador's spear, the colorful mid-century sign was familiar to everyone in Tucson. The sign contained six curved-diamond panels with letters spelling "EL CON." The third panel contained a stylization of a Spanish conquistador's face, as a nod to the El Conquistador Hotel. The El Con Mall sign had welcomed visitors to El Con since 1962. After being taken down, the sign was unceremoniously dumped into a storage area at the back of the mall.

In retrospect, the loss of the El Con sign was an omen of the mall's impending demise. The iconic sign symbolized El Con Mall in its heyday. For decades it had served as a beacon, proudly heralding the popular midtown Tucson gathering place. The decommissioned sign signaled the end of that era. In the previous chapter, I mentioned demolition of the former Levy's building began on June 20, 2012. Six months to the day later, the familiar midtown landmark reemerged from the shadows. On Thursday, December 20, 2012, crews reinstalled the original El Con sign after a thirteen-year hiatus. The fully restored sign reappeared in honor of the mall's fiftieth anniversary (see image next page).

This book is my attempt to bring a dead mall, El Con, back to life again through story. What would be even better is to see the actual mall restored to its former glory one day. Many Tucsonans want El Con to become the *place to be* again, as it was in its halcyon days. For El Con to rise again, three things need to happen, all of which are embedded in the mall's surroundings. In this chapter, we'll explore the three preconditions for El Con's restoration.

Restored El Con Sign, 2012

(Copyright Arizona Daily Star)

Altruism

For over three decades, El Con Mall was a beloved gathering space for the community. This is why the owners' decision to convert El Con into a power center was so devastating. While weighing Options E and C, El Con's owners held two different futures for the Tucson community in their hands. Would expedience be the priority, or would they prioritize character by redeveloping the mall into a rich community center? As we know, the owners chose expedience. To have done otherwise would have required them to put the community's needs ahead of their own. That would have been tough to do, but it was possible, and the rewards would have lasted well beyond a lifetime. For proof of this, just look across the street from El Con to Randolph and Reid Parks.

The stories of both parks began in 1919 when businessman W. E. Barnum obtained lease #04729 for a 480-acre parcel of state land south of Broadway. Barnum built a house on the plot, which at the time was a barren expanse marked only by desert scrub. In 1923 the city was looking to build a golf course. With its mild winter weather, Tucson has always been an ideal place to golf, a point that didn't go unnoticed by former Tucson golf professional W. B. Hutchinson. "The city needs a municipal golf course," he said. "There is little attraction here for the sportsman who is unable to join the local private club and the visiting tourists who are in the city for the winter months find little to amuse themselves." [390] Thanks to Barnum, Hutchinson's wish eventually became reality.

Barnum's lease was due to expire in 1924. City legal advisor Ben C. Davis identified Barnum's land as an ideal site for a golf course, but

Barnum renewed his lease, so the city had to look elsewhere. In 1925 the city accepted an offer of eighty acres on Leighton Kramer's property near Elm and Campbell. Clearing work began, but portions of the land were deemed unsuitable for golf. Then, unexpectedly, Barnum announced his willingness to give up the lease. Bidding for the land began at 11:00 a.m. on September 12, 1925. Fearing competition from business syndicates, City Council convened a special session in case it had to quickly authorize a higher bid. As the lease owner, Barnum had first shot at the bidding. Luckily, no one else showed up to the auction, and Barnum secured the bid. Then he sold the land to the city for the bargain price of $14,896. [391]

The city used the land to build a park and golf links, named "Randolph Park," in honor of Tucson's late railroad magnate, Col. Epes Randolph. The first course had only nine holes. Lacking irrigation, it featured dirt fairways and oil-sand greens. More than one hundred people attended the Randolph Municipal Golf Course dedication on October 24, 1926. [392] In 1927 the city built the Randolph Park Baseball Park, later renamed Hi Corbett Field. Hi Corbett was the spring training ground for Major League Baseball's Cleveland Indians from 1946–1992. It's now home to the University of Arizona baseball team. In 1939, city landscape engineer Charles Maguire created a master plan for Randolph Park, which prescribed development for 320 acres and included the following features:

- A small lagoon
- A botanical garden
- A native wildlife zoo
- Croquet courts
- Lawn bowling courts

- Tennis courts
- Baseball diamonds
- Indoor diamonds
- Baseball and softball diamonds for juveniles
- Outdoor basketball court
- Apparatus areas
- Picnic grounds
- A dance pavilion
- A music concourse for band concerts, lectures, and such
- A play area for small children
- A mall for kite and model plane flying
- A football stadium and track. [393]

Many of these features are present today in the portion of Randolph Park now known as Reid Park. In 1936, the golf course was upgraded with a sprinkler system and an expanded eighteen-hole golf course, featuring grass-covered tees, fairways, and greens. Barnum attended the opening of the expanded course on October 31, 1936, along with dignitaries such as US Senator Carl Hayden, Mayor Henry Jaastad, and golf pro Dell Urich. [394]

A second golf course, known today as Dell Urich, opened south of the original course in 1960. By then a lot of water was needed to irrigate the golf courses and park grounds. Enter Gene C. Reid, who served in the city's Parks Department from 1947–1978. Reid studied horticulture at the University of Arizona from 1932–1936. Four years later he went to work for the family business, Rancho Palos Verdes, Tucson's first commercial citrus grove. Reid began as the city park supervisor in 1947, putting his knowledge and training to work by managing Randolph Park's nursery. A highly resourceful man,

Reid often bartered his home-grown plants and trees for whatever the park needed (see image below).

Toward the middle of Reid Park are three of Reid's famous creations: the north pond, the south pond, and Barnum Hill (see image next page). Reid created the north pond as a storage basin for water to irrigate the golf courses. On May 2, 1960, City Council voted to name the pond after Reid in recognition of "his untiring effort in the development of parks in the City of Tucson for the benefit and pleasure of the citizens of the city and its visitors." [395]

Gene Reid

(© Tucson Citizen – USA TODAY NETWORK via Imagn Images)

Overlooking the north pond's southern bank is Barnum Hill, a man-made earthen mound featuring waterfalls, streams, grass, and Aleppo pines. After finishing the north pond, Reid felt like something was still missing. Inspired by the waterfalls at Los Angeles' Griffith Park, he worked with a local contractor to create a twenty-five-foot-high hill out of excess dirt from a street construction project. The mound was then covered with topsoil and planted. Reid repurposed large stones from an improvement project on Miracle Mile to make the waterfalls. Barnum Hill and the two ponds are the heart of Reid Park.

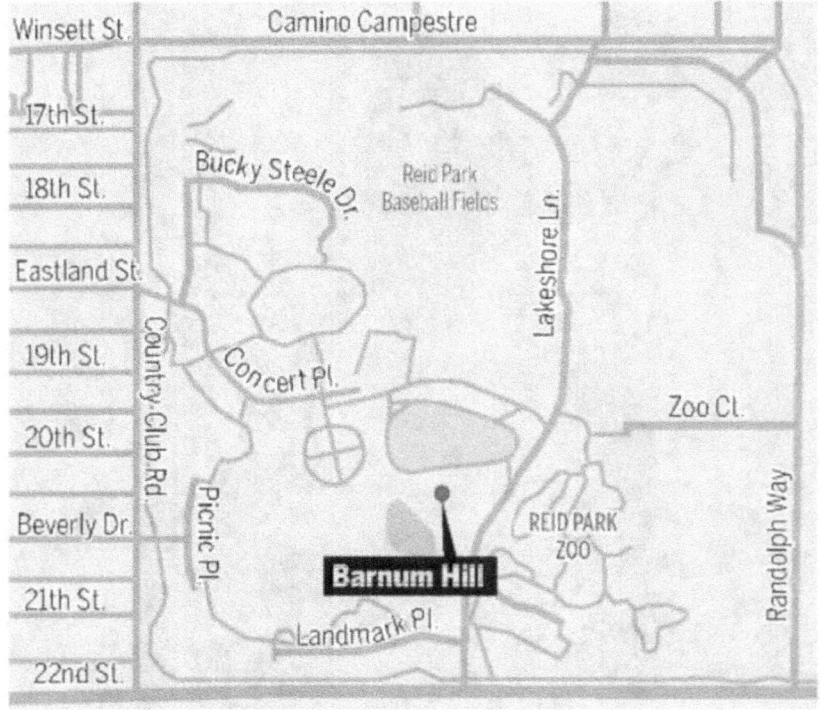

Map of Gene C. Reid Park (Copyright Arizona Daily Star)

Like many Tucsonans, I have lots of good memories in this area of the park. When I was a kid, my family went on after-dinner walks to Reid Park often. Mom always brought a loaf of bread for us kids to rip up and feed to the ducks. There's a photo of my brother and me standing on a picnic table by the north pond, surrounded by ducks and geese. As Mom explains it, moments before Dad snapped the picture, Alex and I were feeding bread to the ducks. Before we knew what was happening, they had surrounded us and were pecking at our hands. My parents swooped in and plucked Alex and me out before the frenzied, feathered mob overran us. That didn't stop us from feeding the ducks, but from then on we did so from the safety of the tabletop.

Autumn day in 1979: People feeding the ducks at Randolph Park

(© Tucson Citizen – USA TODAY NETWORK via Imagn Images)

Like El Con twenty-two years earlier, Reid Park found itself at the center of a firestorm in 2021. In 2017, voters approved propositions 202 and 203, allowing for a 0.1-cent sales tax needed to fund improvements at the zoo. In November 2020, the *Star* announced

Reid Park Zoo was about to begin a 3.5-acre expansion. The addition would subsume Barnum Hill and the south pond. [396] By January 2021 a full-blown controversy had erupted. Voters were not aware that the zoo's expansion would result in the loss of that treasured area of Reid Park. Work on the expansion was scheduled to start in February 2021, but members of the community organized a group called Save the Heart of Reid Park, staged protests, and gathered signatures for a petition to save Barnum Hill. "Barnum Hill is one of the most lovely sites in the park," co-chair Manon Getsi said. "It's the heart of Tucson's Central Park." [397]

On May 4, 2021, City Council voted six to one in favor of a plan directing the expansion northwest, away from Barnum Hill. Through the people's efforts, Barnum Hill and the south pond were saved. Why did community members go to all this effort to save 3.5 acres of land? The answer is simple: Barnum Hill is a beloved communal gathering space that holds memories for the community. Listen to this excerpt from a *Star* opinion piece, written in January 2021 when Barnum Hill's fate was in doubt:

> In an old central Tucson park, atop a hill shaded by a stand of giant Aleppos and cooled by a little waterfall, a grandfather and his grandson escape the summer heat. For hours they launch little boats into a stream, then follow them downhill to the natural shoreline of a pond teeming with frogs, shorebirds, ducks and other families keeping cool.

Thousands of Tucsonans . . . will immediately recognize this place as Barnum Hill and the south duck pond in the heart of Reid Park.

They will know it because it's a place they love–because they've walked there for years or sailed their own stick boats; because they've held family reunions and birthday parties there; because they've birded there, or sought solace when city life got too crazy.

It's a place where their kids always beg to go, or where they got engaged, or where they took their baby to see her first duck. Because for 50 years this beautiful 3.5 acres of public space has been a meeting ground for Tucsonans from all walks of life, who over and over have voted it the best park in town! [398]

Randolph and Reid parks are the byproducts of W. E. Barnum's altruism. Had Barnum refused to relinquish his lease, neither park would exist. Barnum's 480 acres were directly south of the soon-to-be El Conquistador Hotel. Though initially reluctant, Barnum gave over his lease to the Broadway land parcel. As reported in the *Citizen*, "It's unknown why he [Barnum] changed his mind, but it likely had to do with the tourist hotel—soon to be called El Conquistador Hotel—that was going to be constructed just north of Broadway. A public golf course and park nearby would help this hotel thrive and the Old Pueblo to become a winter vacation destination." [399]

Barnum's altruism gave the 480 acres of prime real estate for the bargain price of $14.50 per acre. Barnum could have asked for much more, as not long before, an agreement for a nearby land parcel designated that it should be sold for $200 an acre.[400] Barnum's modest price for highly prized land south of Broadway was an act of great generosity to the city. Many good things resulted from it.

REAL ESTATE TRANSFERS

W. E. Barnum and wife to city of Tucson, 480 acres of section 16, township 14 south of range 14 east.

Real estate notice announcing land transfer from W.E. Barnum to city of Tucson

I've looked through thousands of newspapers to find information about these projects on behalf of the community. Some news stories are more than one hundred years old. At the risk of sounding morbid, it has been sobering to discover people and pictures while knowing full well they're dead. This awareness has made me aware of my own mortality, causing me to ask, who do I want to be and how do I want to be remembered? I've reflected more on altruism and its impact on one's legacy. Go to Randolph or Reid today, and you'll find people from all walks of life enjoying the park—friends playing a round of golf, kids feeding giraffes at the zoo, families celebrating birthdays under a ramada, an old man giving bread to the ducks, and runners circling the David Bell Multi-Use Path. All these wonderful activities can be traced back to a discreet, long-forgotten notice of real estate transfer that appeared on page three of the *Arizona Daily Star* on September 29, 1925 (see image above).

The real estate notice documents Barnum's act of generosity to the city. One year later, the city opened its first municipal golf course. One year after that came Hi Corbett Baseball Field. Then came the calls from community members to develop the rest of the park. In 1939, the *Star* published landscape architect Charles Maguire's plan for what would eventually become Reid Park. "Tucson some day [sic] may have a park like this if a movement now under way becomes a reality," the caption read. "The above represents an architect's view of what could be done with 320 acres of city-owned land in Randolph Park." [401] And that's exactly what happened. Gene Reid, the city's parks supervisor, made Maguire's plans a reality. When Reid retired after thirty-one years of service in the City Parks Department, the city named a section of Randolph Park after him. All the while, Barnum's name and contributions were lost to history. No section of either park, or any facility within them, bore Barnum's name. Barnum's generous act, which made these two parks possible, was seemingly forgotten.

That changed on June 16, 1993, when J. C. Martin of the *Star* published a pair of informative articles on Reid Park, one detailing the park's features, the other its history. The history article discussed Barnum and his role in acquiring the land. The other article referenced a "nameless little hill" between the north and south ponds. [402] Six days later, a Tucson resident named Judy Hiner wrote a letter to the editor thanking the *Star* for the informative articles on Reid Park. She confesses that, before reading the article, she'd never heard of W. E. Barnum. Then Hiner makes the following keen observation:

Based on your article, it seems that a great deal is owed to the little-known businessman Willis Barnum, whose creative financing enabled the city to purchase the land in the first place. It seems that, without Barnum, the park would not exist today. And to think I had no idea that such a man ever existed. His name remains unknown, while almost everyone else associated with the park (Reid, Randolph, DeMeester, Corbett and Bossard) has an area or amenity named after them. However, this can be remedied. [403]

Hiner proposes to honor Barnum by naming the "nameless little hill" after him. "The water running over the rocks makes this place one of the most pleasant in the park," Hiner says. "What better way to pay tribute to the park's benefactor than to give the hill his name— Barnum Hill." Hiner petitioned Tucson's Parks and Recreation Commission to attach Barnum's name to the hill, and the city obliged. Thanks to Judy Hiner, the man whose generosity made Randolph and Reid Parks possible was finally recognized. Fittingly, Barnum's name now presides over an area considered by most to be the heart of Reid Park.

An altruistic investor is one who considers the social benefit of an investment alongside its financial benefit. Focus is directed toward the social good, and financial profits come second. Barnum's willingness to sell his land to the city at a discounted price is an example of altruistic investing. Barnum could have held out for a higher price, but he placed the good of the city above his own self-interest.

If El Con has any chance of rising again, its owners and the city need to prioritize the good of the community over profit. That will be extraordinarily difficult because today's power center is a cash cow. Any attempt to remake El Con into a vital community center would require a major shift in strategy, a strategy focused on quality over quantity, people over profit, and long-term over short-term benefits.

I'm optimistic that things can change, but I'm also a realist. Altruistic investing is risky because long-term financial rewards are not guaranteed. Still, Barnum's legacy proves that altruistic acts have social impacts that benefit multiple generations.

Barnum's Legacy

How many families have taken their kids to this playground? (Photo by the author)

How many kids have spent time with these turtles? (Photo by the author)

How many people have enjoyed these waterfalls? (Photo by the author)

How many people have picnicked on this hill? (Photo by the author)

How many people have come to Reid Park to feed the ducks? (Photo by the author)

Honoring the Past

Days before bulldozers demolished the venerable El Conquistador Hotel, an article appeared in the *Arizona Daily Star* that began with this observation: "El Conquistador Hotel—1928 to 1968. To newcomers it's an interesting relic beside the shopping center. To old timers, it's memories." [404] The article, written by Virginia Lee Hodge, contains a treasure trove of memories shared by former patrons and workers of the hotel. One story came from Genevieve Brown Wright, a former patron who attended the *Baile De Las Flores* dance at the hotel on February 9, 1929. Hodge writes that on the day of the dance, "Mrs. [Genevieve] Wright wore a blue velvet dress and was so starry eyed at the grandeur of the occasion and the magnificence of the new hotel that she almost fell down the stairs into the dining room." Later in life, Mrs. Wright taught deportment classes to youngsters at the hotel.

Another interviewee was Mary Abbot, who got a far-away look in her eyes as she recalled memories of the sumptuous meals at the hotel. "It was wonderful," Abbot said. "Cliff would take me out to dinner there and we would have a marvelous time."

In its heyday, the hotel managed a stable of fifty horses. Sally Rollings recalled riding one of those horses to a house at the edge of the hotel grounds where her friend, Margaret Knight, lived. Leionne Salter worked at the hotel. One of her duties was to paint desert plant scenes on the first-floor windows. She recalled springtime at the hotel, when riots of African daisies bloomed among the palm trees. "It's a shame to lose such a charming place," Salter said. [405]

Many people were saddened by the hotel's demise. "Every good time in my life was connected with the El Conquistador Hotel," Genevieve Wright said. She wasn't the only person speaking up. Carl Wilson wrote a letter to the newspaper to say he was "sadder than most Tucsonians about the passing of El Conquistador Hotel." For twenty-two years Mr. Wilson served as the hotel's chef. He left to work at a posh hotel in California, the Sir Francis Drake in San Francisco. Still, Wilson revealed that "his heart lies with El Con." Among Wilson's most treasured memories was a note written and signed by John J. Pershing, one of America's finest generals and a frequent winter guest at the hotel. It read, "To Chef Wilson: You are a fine cook." [406]

In failing to preserve the El Conquistador Hotel, Tucson squandered one of its architectural crown jewels. Many were angered by the hotel's unceremonious end, and when the mall fell on hard times in the 2000s, these people openly expressed their joy. An example of this is found in a letter to the editor from 2008, forty years after the hotel came down. It was written by retired educator named Margaret, who says:

> It is with a certain amount of glee that I view the potential demise of El Con Mall. I have never been able to understand how the El Conquistador resort hotel was allowed to be torn down to enable that mall to be built. The hotel was on par with the Arizona Inn. Perhaps there is some type of justice in the fact that the mall is in such trouble and has been for years. Of course we can't bring back the hotel, which is sad. [407]

The quote captures the indignation that many community members felt for El Con Mall's role in the hotel's demise. I never knew about the hotel and mall's shared history. I only discovered the connection while researching for this book. Now that I have a fuller understanding of El Con's past, I view the destruction of the El Conquistador Hotel as a turning point in the mall's history. From the beginning, El Con Mall's owners said they would incorporate the hotel into the mall someday. They broke their promise. Tearing down the venerable hotel was a travesty, and replacing the architectural gem with a department store was an even greater insult. If El Con is to ever make a comeback, it must do something to properly honor the hotel's legacy. For inspiration on how to do this, we turn again to El Con's surroundings for clues.

Ringling Bros. and Barnum & Bailey Circus comes to Tucson: June 24, 1975

Unloading the animals, Southern Pacific railyard in Tucson

(Copyright Arizona Daily Star)

In addition to being the man who made Randolph and Reid Parks possible, W. E. Barnum has another obscure claim to fame. He was a third cousin of P. T. Barnum, famed showman and founder of the Ringling Bros. and Barnum & Bailey circus. [408] Known as "The Greatest Show on Earth," the Ringling Bros. and Barnum & Bailey Circus was once the pinnacle of traveling circus acts. When the Barnum & Bailey train rolled into town, magic ensued. I experienced the magic one year when my family watched the circus animals being unloaded at the Southern Pacific rail yard near downtown Tucson. The circus always came to Tucson by train, and the spectacle never failed to draw crowds. A local newspaper describes when Barnum & Bailey arrived in Tucson on June 24, 1975:

> The Ringling Brothers and Barnum & Bailey circus train arrived at 8 a.m. in the Southern Pacific railroad yards south of Simpson St. and west of the Community Center. Within an hour, children were running around the cars, keeping the unloading crew busy with questions and, hoping for an advance show, calling for elephants to thrust their trunks out the doors. Unloadning [sic] the animals is itself part of the circus performance, said George Shafer, a night watchman who joined the circus in Phoenix four years ago. [409]

From the rail yard the animals walked to the Tucson Convention Center, where the circus performed. I remember sitting on a blanket with my siblings and cousins, watching in awe as elephants disembarked from the train. Many other families came to the rail yard to witness the animal unloading too. Due to declining ticket sales and controversy over animal cruelty concerns, the Greatest Show on Earth, which began in 1871, gave its last performance on May 21, 2017. The Ringling Brothers circus re-emerged in 2023, but the show no longer includes animal acts.

The main entrance to El Con is a street called South Randolph Way. Exiting El Con, if you follow Randolph Way south to East Camino Campestre, you'll see a curious memorial on the right side of the road.

Circular in shape, it contains a pair of bisecting railroad tracks that form a cross. At the terminal ends of each track are four train wheels, and the bust of a man's head emerges from the cross-shaped center (see image below). This memorial site is known as Epes Randolph Plaza.

Epes Randolph Plaza (Photo by the author)

I lived next to Randolph Park from 2008–2010. During that time, I went for daily walks along the Dave Bell Multi-Use Path. Those walks took me past the Epes Randolph Plaza, but I never understood its purpose. Now I know the plaza was created as a memorial to Epes Randolph, the namesake of Randolph Park.

Colonel Epes Randolph was a civil engineer, a railroad magnate, and a Tucson resident whose untimely death sent shockwaves through the American Southwest. Randolph was born in Virginia on August 16,

1856. He spent most of his career in the railroad industry, working his way into the highest levels of management. After contracting tuberculosis in 1894, Randolph and his wife moved to Tucson, a haven for sufferers of this disease due to the city's favorable climate. Randolph became superintendent of the Tucson division of the Southern Pacific railway line.

It's difficult to summarize the breadth of Randolph's contributions to the railroad industry, but you get a sense of his legacy in this tribute that appeared in the *El Paso Herald* after his passing on August 22, 1921: "He [Randolph] was rated with the biggest railroad men that ever operated in the west. E. H. Harriman [president of the Southern Pacific Railroad Company] once said that, give Epes Randolph his health, he would be the biggest railroader in the country." [410]

News of Randolph's death triggered a flood of telegram condolences from all over the country. The day after his passing, the state capitol flag was lowered to half-mast. On the day of Randolph's funeral, the Tucson Chamber of Commerce requested every business in Tucson to close at 4:00 p.m. out of respect. Similarly, at 5:00 p.m. that day, all activity on every railroad that Randolph was associated with stopped for one minute. [411] Such gestures make it clear that Epes Randolph was no ordinary man. He made a huge impact on the Southwest region, and he was one of Tucson's most beloved figures.

The day before his funeral, an article in the *Tucson Citizen* newspaper paid fitting tribute to Randolph with the following kind words:

> In the sudden death of Colonel Epes Randolph, Tucson and the entire southwest suffers the loss of one of the biggest figures in the history of the state, and his passing leaves a

gap in the affairs of big men that will never be filled. Arizona, and Tucson in particular, has reason to be proud of the man who has gone. He has carved a place in the history of the city and state that will live forever, and when future generations look down upon the history of the Baby State they will note foremost among the names of the state builders that of Colonel Epes Randolph. [412]

Having only recently learned about his legacy, I understand why Tucson's first municipal park was named in Randolph's honor. His contributions to the city and the entire southwest region of the country were immense. It's impossible to quantify all the good that's come of Randolph's work in the railroad industry. To illustrate the point, the railway system that Randolph created and managed allowed the circus to come to Tucson when I was a child. I got to experience the magic of the circus because of Randolph's legacy. The recollections from my own life in this regard are important. They enable me to properly honor people, places, and institutions I have not experienced but whose contributions have impacted my life for the better.

The people, places, and institutions that have made significant contributions to Tucson's growth deserve to be honored. It's not enough to name a park in Randolph's honor; his story should be told and celebrated. The same goes for important places like the El Conquistador Hotel. A vital part of Tucson's history, it played a major role in growing Tucson's population and gave our city a touch of class and sophistication. Architecture critic Lawrence Cheek once described the El Conquistador Hotel as "one of old Tucson's glories." [413] The decision to demolish the hotel and replace it with a department store was short-sighted and, frankly, negligent.

Other than adopting its name, El Con never sufficiently underscored its relationship to the hotel, nor did it ever atone for the role it played in the hotel's demise. This wrong must be righted before El Con can move forward on good standing. The architecture and theme of the El Conquistador Hotel were designed to reflect a Spanish colonial theme. Any future vision for El Con should include these elements, but we can take it a step further. Wouldn't it also be powerful to build the identity of a new El Con around a relic from the original hotel? They do exist, thanks to the foresight and effort of a few generous community members.

Before the hotel was demolished, developer George N. Genematas purchased the copper dome that graced the hotel's bell tower. Today it sits atop a thirty-five-foot tower in Casa Blanca Plaza, a shopping center on Tucson's northwest side. Chastain's Builders utilized many of the hotel's interior and exterior appointments for a home in the Catalina Foothills, dubbed the new "El Conquistador." Here's a detailed description of the elements that were preserved:

> They include some of her [the hotel's] doors and windows
> with their sunburst fanlight arches . . . Spanish masonry
> work that once framed a large picture window and a
> doorway . . . [and] such other salvaged and restored
> remnants of the El Con as a colored glass window, an
> antique walnut bench, decorative corbels, intricate iron
> railings, an exact replica of an El Con lobby fireplace. [414]

Local businessman Kelley Rollings saved the hotel's elaborately carved arch, a.k.a. the *porte-cochere* ("carriage porch"). Kelley purchased the arch in 1968 and had it moved to his home in pieces. It took ten trips. For the next eight years, the arch sat disassembled on pallets in Rollings' backyard. In the late 1970s, Christopher Sheafe, then-president of the Estes Co., found out about the arch when Estes purchased land from the Rollings family for a new housing community called Rancho Sin Vacas. Sheafe convinced Rollings to include the arch in the land package and then went about the difficult work of having it reassembled (see image below). [415]

Rancho Sin Vacas Gate House (Photo by the author)

What makes Sheafe's effort more heroic is that he proceeded with the work without a guarantee of success. He recalled the disassembled arch pieces in Rolling's backyard: "Weeds had grown up all around, and we weren't positive that all the parts were even there." [416] Contractors were unwilling to take the job because Sheafe couldn't guarantee all the parts of the arch had been saved.

Luckily, Sheafe got in touch with a contractor who had done previous restoration work with the University of Arizona. Though initially reluctant, the contractor accepted the project. It took three months and $30,000 in labor costs to resurrect the arch, but thanks to Sheafe it happened. Not a single piece of the arch was missing. [417] The former hotel arch now greets residents of the Rancho Sin Vacas housing community. Thanks to the efforts of Rollings and Sheafe, an important part of the El Conquistador Hotel survived.

It's wonderful that these elements of the hotel survived, but it's also unrealistic to think they'll ever return to El Con. The relics are scattered throughout Tucson, and each has become an ingrained part of the place where it currently resides. Luckily, El Con doesn't have to look far for an authentic link to the El Conquistador Hotel. There's one across the street on the other side of Broadway. Like the Epes Randolph Memorial, countless Tucsonans pass by it every day, having no idea what it is or how it came to be. I never knew the story behind this landmark either. Like the life of Epes Randolph, the structure has a fascinating story that needs to be told.

In 1983, Ron and Sue Hunter started a business called the Tucson Tour Co. They offered 1.5-hour guided tours of Tucson on a fifty-six-seat, double-decker "RT" bus from London. Passengers boarded the bus at 1:30 p.m. in the parking lot of Carlos Murphy's restaurant downtown. [418] The tour began with a drive through the historic downtown district, then on to Barrio Libre, the Armory Park Historic District, the University of Arizona, and other locales. Eventually the tour made its way to midtown. There, *Star* journalist Margo Hernandez, a tour participant in March 1984, reported the following: "As the group passes the [El Con] mall, Sue [the tour guide] points out that the prestigious El Conquistador luxury hotel used to stand where the mall is located. The only remnants of the hotel are a water tower across the street and a few palm trees in the parking lot." [419]

As part of the tour, Sue Hunter called attention to the last on-site relic of the El Conquistador Hotel—the El Con Water Tower across the street from where the hotel once stood. The El Con Water Tower was built in 1928 to provide water pressure for the Colonia Solana subdivision. Shortly thereafter, wealthy residents of Colonia Solana complained that the 50,000-gallon steel tower was an eyesore. So, famed local architect Roy Place was hired to design a facade for the tower in 1932. He built a ninety-foot-tall lighthouse-shaped shell to hide the steel tower. The tower's ornate exterior is composed of stucco and chicken wire supported by an interior metal frame (see image page 337).

Like the El Conquistador Hotel, the tower embodies the Spanish colonial revival architectural style for which Tucson is famous. The tower's upper portion features stained-glass windows, a tile roof, and a cast-iron weathervane, featuring a mining prospector leading a burro. Until recently, the El Con Water Tower was thought to have carried supplies to Colonia Solana, El Encanto, and the El

Conquistador Hotel. However, in 2002, Michelle Stewart of the *Star* raised this question in a "What's with that?" article:

> **Q:** Situated across from El Con Mall is the water tower built to serve the old El Conquistador Hotel. Two questions: Why is the water tower located so far from what was once the hotel? Who owns the water tower?

Here's the response to the first question:

> **A:** Though most believe that the tower also served the old El Conquistador resort hotel, once located across the street from the tower, Mitch Basefsky, public information officer for Tucson Water, said valve maps contradict that claim. Nor was it built to support El Encanto subdivision. "We have some of the old valve maps and we don't see any pipes crossing Broadway," Basefsky said. [420]

El Con Water Tower (Copyright Arizona Daily Star)

Since then, most descriptions of the El Con Water Tower note that it never serviced the hotel. This contradicts earlier accounts I've read in the paper, though. For example, a 1975 article in the *Citizen* states, "The tower was built in 1930 to fill water needs of the nearby El Encanto and Colonia Solana residential areas, along with the now demolished El Conquistador Hotel." [421] Several other articles make the same claim.

Whether the tower serviced the hotel or not, both landmarks shared a lot in common. Both were built around the same time, the tower in 1928 and the hotel in 1929. Like the hotel, the tower served double duty as an early ambassador for the city of Tucson. As Chris Limberis of the *Star* explains, "The tower did much to symbolize the city's first organized effort to lure winter visitors and those seeking the healthful environment of the desert." [422] In 1944 the city of Tucson assumed ownership of the tower. Facing costly renovations, the city twice considered demolishing the structure—in 1969 and 1975. On both occasions, vocal protest from community members saved the tower. In 1980, the tower was placed on the National Register of Historic Places. Eleven years later, City Council named it an official historic landmark. So, unlike the El Conquistador Hotel and El Con Mall, the tower's legacy is intact and protected from future threats. This is what should have happened with the hotel, but at least part of the hotel's legacy lives on in the water tower.

The significance of the El Con Water Tower can't be overstated. Though the term normally applies only to people, the water tower functions as a symbolic "remnant." The *Anchor Bible Dictionary* defines the remnant as "what is left of a community after it undergoes a catastrophe." [423] The El Conquistador Hotel and El Con Mall were both special places in the Tucson community. Forty years after the hotel was demolished, people who remembered it were still indignant. The same can be said for El Con Mall. Over time, community members formed "place attachments" with the hotel and the mall. "Place attachment" is a concept from environmental psychology that deals with "the person-to-place bonds that evolve through emotional connection, meaning, and understandings of a specific place and/or features of a place." [424] When places we're attached to disappear, their absence creates a psychic wound that we feel but can't articulate.

The El Conquistador Hotel, El Con Mall, and the El Con Water Tower are three separate entities; nevertheless, the mall and the water tower share symbolic roots in the hotel. Both got their name from the hotel. Their themes and aesthetics were shaped by the hotel's Spanish Colonial Revival style. And finally, both have a common shared history with the hotel. Of the three, the water tower is the lone remaining structure. From a cultural heritage standpoint, it's a blessing that the water tower survived. By its very existence, the water tower preserves the shared history of all three structures. Because the tower remains, the memory of the hotel and the mall endures. Like the reserves of water it once stored, the El Con Water Tower is now a container for hope—for the wistful aspirations of all who've ever dared to entertain thoughts that the hotel and the mall will make a comeback.

At the outset of this section, we established that for El Con to rise again, it must find a way to honor the memory of the El Conquistador Hotel. This can be accomplished in three ways. First, the theme and architecture of the new mall should match that of the hotel. All the structural elements should embody the Spanish Colonial Revival style. The thematic thread, woven through every element of the new El Con's design-naming conventions, décor, landscape elements, and art, would celebrate Spanish culture, customs, and traditions. The Plazas at the El Con redevelopment plan were on the right track. That's a good place to start.

Second, it would be wonderful to have a small luxury hotel onsite again, something along the lines of another famous local hotel, the Arizona Inn. El Conquistador Hotel was one of a kind, so efforts to replicate it are to be discouraged. Instead, the focus should be on creating a hotel with an enduring appeal, a building constructed with top-quality materials, attention to detail, and whimsical elements that infuse it with soul. In this way, the new hotel will evoke the legacy of El Conquistador Hotel.

Perhaps a room or gathering space within the new hotel could tell El Conquistador Hotel's story, using artifacts, pictures, and commemorative plaques. With the park across the street, historic neighborhoods, shopping, entertainment, and amenities offered by an onsite mall, the hotel could become a destination for Tucson. Others have made a similar suggestion. During the big-box controversy, several community members expressed their desire to bring back the hotel. This would be an outstanding way to honor El Conquistador Hotel.

Finally, in any collective revitalization effort, such as that of reestablishing El Con as a vital community center, the spiritual element can't be ignored. There's a lot of history at the El Con site. Though covered in asphalt, the ground is steeped in over one hundred years of memories. That commemorative function should be recognized and expressed tangibly. So, the third way a future El Con could honor its roots in El Conquistador Hotel is through a rededication ceremony involving the water tower. As a tangible link to the memory of El Conquistador Hotel, the El Con Water Tower provides a foundation upon which the future El Con can be built.

Community Focused

For El Con to recapture its former magic, focus must be redirected to the one thing that made the mall special: community. Today, El Con Center functions like a giant convenience store. Lots of people come to shop, but nobody lingers. Once you have what you came for, there's nothing to stick around for. This mall used to be a place where people could spend half a day walking around. Now the only practical way to navigate the center is by car. The big-box stores are spread out and don't connect, like commercial islands in a sea of asphalt. The El Con Mall I experienced wasn't perfect, but it was always a popular gathering place. That's no longer the case, and it's a significant loss because while there is no shortage of shopping centers in Tucson, community gathering places like the El Con of old are hard to come by.

If the owners of El Con determine in the future that community will again be the focus, how might they go about building that into the next design? The answer to that lies just across the street from the former mall in the Colonia Solana subdivision. In addition to housing the El Con Water Tower, Colonia Solana boasts a second claim to fame: the subdivision was planned by Stephen Child, an accomplished landscape architect who apprenticed under Fredrick Law Olmstead. Together, Fredrick Law Olmstead and Calvert Vaux designed Central Park in New York City.

Colonia Solana, Tucson (Copyright Arizona Daily Star)

Child's Colonia Solana master plan blended streets and housing with the natural environment in a way that felt organic. After studying how water flowed through the land, Child developed a plan that improved the health of the natural arroyos, contributing to a thriving desert ecosystem that balanced the needs of the environment with those of the residents. In contrast to the geometric pattern of El Encanto Estates, Colonia Solana features a flowing, curvilinear layout that accentuates its nature-centric design.

In the 1920s, Tucson was an up-and-coming city with great potential. This, in addition to outstanding winter weather, attracted many influential people, one being Stephen Child. At the time, Child was a nationally recognized landscape architect. He lived in San Francisco but often visited Tucson in the winter months. While he was in town, Child gave lectures and met with local constituencies to discuss matters related to planning, city beautification, and landmark preservation. On March 16, 1928, Tucson Realty and Trust company hosted a dinner dance at the Tucson Golf and Country Club to reveal a new subdivision. The announcement in the newspaper read, "Secrecy has surrounded the nature of this announcement, but it was stated that it involved a novel subdivision, different from any subdivision ever made available to Tucsonans." [425] Steven Child was the lone person scheduled to speak at the event.

Roughly 125 guests attended the event. Edward Van Der Vries, president of Tucson Realty and Trust, began by introducing Colonia Solana. Special attention was directed to the subdivision's natural features. After all, Child designed Colonia Solana so that the desert landscape would play the starring role. Among its "special advantages" were paved streets, artistically laid out trees, an abundant water supply, rough-rock curbing, numerous small parks planted with natural desert plants, and curved streets that followed the land's natural topography. [426] After his introduction, Van Der Vries turned it over to Stephen Child to explain the fundamental principles underlying the subdivision plan.

Colonia Solana is approaching its one hundredth birthday. Thanks to Stephen Child's brilliant design, it remains as unique today as it was then—a place the State Historic Preservation Office refers to as "the hidden jewel of Arizona." [427] The genius of Colonia Solana lies in the interplay between manmade (i.e., homes and roads) and natural elements.

There's a contemplative element to the subdivision's master plan. Rather than asserting his will, Child studied the land and designed the neighborhood in a way that worked with rather than against the environment. When Colonia Solana was introduced in 1928, it was in what was considered Tucson's countryside, east of downtown. Thanks to Child's innovative plan, the neighborhood still retains that feeling. As described in a 2013 *Star* article,

> Colonia Solana sits on 158 acres of desert landscape at the southeast corner of East Broadway and South Country Club Road. Nearly all of the 110 homes sit on an acre of land, tucked away behind creosote, prickly pear, mesquite and towering eucalyptus. While seated at one of Tucson's busiest intersections, the neighborhood seems bathed in seclusion, with narrow, winding roads and a glorious sense of quiet. [428]

Stephen Child's masterful plan is what sets Colonia Solana apart from other neighborhoods. No other neighborhood in midtown Tucson devoted such care and attention to the natural landscape. Entering Colonia Solana gives the impression that you've left the city. It's like stepping back in time, when this area of town was considered the "boondocks." Just ask Stanley Feldman, a resident of Colonia Solana since the 1940s. "I grew up here when it was way out in the country," he said. "The neighborhood still has much of the same feeling. Here we are in the middle of town, but you can sit in the backyard and feel like you are in the country." [429] This is the magic of Colonia Solana, the secret ingredient that makes the subdivision a highly prized place to live.

During his career, Child designed parks and communities all over the country, but primarily in the western United States. Regardless of the project, Child's work bears a discernible signature. His designs were based on the existing topography of the land. [430] Colonia Solana is often cited as a prime example of Child's work. In a 1928 article for *Landscape Architecture*, Child outlined his intentions for Colonia Solana's design. The cheapest way to develop the property would have been to turn it into a gridiron of straight roads and rectangular plots. The problem with that approach was that it wouldn't be interesting. Child's solution was to take his design cues from the existing topography. [431] In her thesis *Stephen Child: Visionary Landscape Architect*, Mary Blain Korff describes the legacy of Child's design choice: "As a visionary landscape architect, Stephen Child was able to discern, appreciate, and enhance the genius loci of the many different locales in which he worked. Colonia Solana neighborhood in Tucson stands as a concrete example of a true 'design with nature.'" [432]

To achieve meaningful outcomes that stand the test of time, you need a well thought out vision. For El Con to make a comeback, a new vision for the former mall is needed. The right vision for El Con can be fashioned by returning to its original inspiration—Victor Gruen, the "Father of Malls." Quite often, Gruen is characterized as a maligned figure. Southdale Shopping Center, the world's first enclosed mall, opened in 1956. After that, Gruen's enclosed mall concept spread like a wildfire, sucking the life out of downtown areas. Gruen was blamed for the "soulless" nature of shopping malls and their negative impact on small businesses and the environment. Mall critics also point to the "Gruen Effect" in a seeming indictment of

Gruen's motives. The Gruen Effect maintains "that shoppers will be so bedazzled by a store's surroundings that they will be drawn—unconsciously, continually—to shop." [433] To create this effect, Gruen built malls to manipulate the retail environment in a manner that would overload shoppers' senses.

Nothing could be further from the truth. Want to know why Gruen invented malls? Consider this observation by *Star Tribune* writer Barbara Flanagan, who interviewed Gruen the day before Southdale's grand opening. Flanagan began her article with this statement: "If architect Victor Gruen has a mission in life—and he won't admit to it—it's to save cities." [434] By the 1950s, urban sprawl had become a major problem in America. The combination of rising populations and automobile usage made city centers increasingly difficult to navigate. As a result, people left downtown areas and fled to the suburbs. But life in the suburbs had its own challenges. Gruen argued many suburbanites were there involuntarily because living downtown was no longer possible. The result, according to Gruen, was a predictable dilemma:

> People like to garden and have room for their children to play, but they also like to live near the theaters and museums and schools. So the pattern emerges. Families move to the sprawling suburbs where the women are bored to death and there is no social life because they are too far removed from the center of things. They lose the values of an urban civilization. [435]

Gruen regarded the mall as an antidote to increasing urban sprawl. Since suburbanites could no longer access the city center, Gruen would bring it to them in the form of a mall. Having grown up amidst the cultural riches of Vienna, Gruen's concept of the ideal city clashed with the city experiences he had in America. Gruen felt American cities were soulless and sought to "Europeanize" them with malls. He did this by making the mall a desirable space where people congregated for more than just shopping. In other words, Gruen designed Southdale Shopping Center to function as an unofficial town square. Barbara Flanagan quoted Gruen as saying, "I hope it [Southdale] becomes the crystallizing force for this sprawling suburban area. There will be places here for meetings and concerts and galleries of paintings to look at and rooms where classes can be held and places to eat. This is the town square that has been lost since the coming of the automobile." [436]

Gruen believed malls would give suburbanites the town square experience they craved without the need to go into the city. "So cities must have more than one center of life," Gruen reasoned. "Such a center will never offer all the things that downtown offers. But it will serve to link the people of the area. They will rediscover the pleasure of walking again and watching others pass by as they sit in the sidewalk cafes." [437]

Social by nature, humans have always prized social gathering places. The marketplace has served as a communal space since ancient times. From the agoras of ancient Greece to bazaars of Turkey, marketplaces have been magnets for commerce, social interaction, and civic engagement. The marketplace plays a crucial role in fostering cultural identity and a sense of belonging, both of which are crucial to bind people to their communities. The American town square can be traced back to its roots in medieval Europe. European squares were typically located at the city center, featuring a large open area surrounded by buildings on all sides.

For much of the twentieth century, a city's downtown area served as the town square. When Americans abandoned urban areas and moved to the suburbs in the 1950s, shopping malls emerged as the new town square. Those fortunate enough to live someplace with a real town square know how important it is to the community. For those without, chances are the local mall filled that role at some point. This was the case for me growing up in Tucson. From opening day in 1960 through its twilight years in the 1990s, El Con was Tucson's unofficial town square. El Con's tagline in the 1980s was "El Con: The place to be." The slogan wasn't just catchy; it was true. El Con was *the* place where Tucsonans came to shop, socialize, and be part of the action.

When Stephen Child determined how to make the subdivision more than just a "dead, flat piece of land," he focused his attention first on the topography. After completing a site analysis, Child identified what he called one fairly important arroyo or "wash" and two other lesser washes. [438] The common practice among developers at the time was to fill in the washes, but Child decided to make them the focal point of his design. Child turned the main arroyo into the "keynote of the Parkway." [439] This included "a strip half a mile long and 150 feet wide, which is to become one of the most important and distinctive features of the subdivision—Arroyo Chico Parque." [440] The two lesser arroyos "became curving roads, which intersected with the main arroyo maintaining the natural drainage pattern." [441]

By making the arroyos a focal point, Child gave Colonia Solana a foundation to build its identity around. Everything in the subdivision is designed around these washes, giving rise to the informal, free-flowing pattern for which the neighborhood is famous. "At the heart of the neighborhood is Arroyo Chico," Gabrielle Fimbres reports in the *Star*. Fimbres interviewed longtime Colonia Solana resident William DuPont, who notes that the neighborhood is designed around the arroyos. "The streets are based on how the water runs to the arroyo," DuPont says. "You might be heading east and all of the sudden you are heading north. [Developer Stephen Child] wanted a design that kept the essence of the desert vegetation and the natural beauty intact. That is what set Colonia Solana apart from any neighborhood in the state." [442]

A new, community-focused El Con must find the equivalent of an Arroyo Chico to build its identity around. Perhaps El Con should look to Victor Gruen for inspiration. What elements did Gruen incorporate into his mall designs that recreated the European town square experience in suburban America? The answer can be traced back to Gruen's incubation period in New York. When Gruen came to the United States in 1938, he found work as a draftsman in New York City. Gruen's revolutionary storefront designs on Broadway and 5th Avenue earned him instant notoriety. New York was an incubator for some of the main elements that influenced Gruen's conception of shopping malls. What fired Gruen's imagination most were the shops on Broadway and Central Park. In his book, *Mall Maker*, author M. Jeffrey Hardwick highlights the prominent role these two places played in Gruen's inspiration for malls:

Skyscrapers, bridges, and highways did not attract Gruen. He felt instead the pull of two very different New York attractions-the flashing lights of the Great White Way [Broadway] and the bucolic calm of Central Park. Built for nearly opposite reasons, Broadway's brashness and the park's peacefulness shared one important aspect: they were loved and used by the public.. . . In his later retail projects [i.e., malls], Gruen would try to unite these two seemingly contradictory experiences. [443]

Bethesda Terrace is a plaza overlooking the Lake and Ramble areas of Central Park. The star attraction of the plaza is Bethesda Fountain, among the most iconic landmarks in Central Park. The fountain measures twenty-six feet high by ninety-six feet wide. Standing atop a pedestal at the fountain's center is the "Angel of the Waters statue, supported by four cherubs representing health, purity, peace, and temperance. The angel holds a lily in its left hand, representing purity. The state commissioned sculptor Emma Stebbins to create the statue as a monument to New York's Croton Aqueduct, which opened in 1842.

When Central Park was created in 1858, its co-designers, Frederick Law Olmstead and Calvert Vaux, deemed the opening of the Croton Aqueduct as the most significant moment in New York's history. As noted on the website, "Today we may take our water for granted, but late 19th century Manhattanites understood that without the Old Croton Aqueduct, New York would never become the great city it hoped to be." [444] The opening of the Croton Aqueduct marked the birth of the modern New York City metropolis. Stebbins unveiled the Angel of the Waters statue in 1873 (see image next page).

Bethesda Fountain-Angel of the Waters statue (Photo by the author)

When Olmstead and Vaux designed Central Park, Bethesda Terrace and the Fountain were the only formal features included in the original blueprint, suggesting they were meant to be the focal point of the park. Over time, Bethesda Fountain has become a focal point not only for Central Park but also for the entire city. Sara Cedar Miller, historian for the Central Park Conservancy, describes

Bethesda Fountain as the "social and spiritual center of Central Park" and "one of the great gathering places of New York." [445] Fountains in general have an uncanny ability to draw people in. Bethesda Fountain is spectacular, but when you surround it with the stunning architecture of the terrace, along with breathtaking views of the Lake and Ramble, the result is a popular spot New Yorkers flock to year-round.

Given Gruen's affection for Central Park, it's not a stretch to imagine that Bethesda Fountain influenced his vision for shopping malls. The fountain is a prime example of the aesthetic elements Gruen included in his malls to create a town square atmosphere. Other elements include benches, natural lighting, art pieces, plazas, entertainment, and eating areas. Collectively, these elements combined to create a pleasant shopping environment where people were incentivized to linger. People enjoy being surrounded by beauty, and fountains offer a unique kind of beauty that draws people to a space. Gruen knew this when he designed the world's first enclosed mall, so Southdale Center had a beautiful fountain.

Few can deny the convenience of big-box stores. They offer so many items at affordable prices along with a user-friendly element. Walk into any Target, for example, and you're able to navigate the store with ease. Replicated layouts are a key element of Target's store design philosophy. Target introduced its "racetrack" layout in 1975, which has been used to good effect ever since. The racetrack layout calls for one main aisle that circles the store, with additional aisles bisecting the middle and the perimeter. This open floor plan provides broad sightlines and makes navigating the store easier. "Logical layouts, uncluttered aisles and the clean look of our stores allow our guests to easily find what they're looking for," says Tina Schiel, executive vice president of stores for Target. "It makes shopping a pleasant and consistent experience in any store." [446]

Retail design being the science it is, nothing about modern store layouts is unintentional. Target's wide aisles, bright lighting, and racetrack layout increase the odds that consumers will shop longer and spend more than they intend. Unlike shopping malls and the downtown areas they replaced, big-box stores are designed for one thing only—selling products. As Lisa Scharoun states in *America at the Malls*, "Big box stores . . . do not function as a meeting place or town center in the way a traditional enclosed shopping center once did." [447] Despite their logical layouts, effective lighting, and pleasant appearances, big box stores are soulless. As author Siobahn Vivian says, "You can decorate absence however you want—but you're still gonna feel what's missing." For big-box stores, the best lighting, branding, and layout design money can buy doesn't bring people in their community together in a meaningful way.

El Con Fountain was the heart and soul of the mall. It represents the best El Con had to offer. At its prime, El Con functioned as Tucson's unofficial town square. People didn't just go there to shop; they went to El Con to spend time with family, eat, see a movie, have a beer with friends, or take pictures with Santa. Put another way, they went to El Con to enjoy the benefits of a vital community center. El Con Fountain embodied the community-centered spirit of El Con, which made El Con special. If El Con has any hope of reestablishing itself as "the place to be," it must focus on the one thing that earned it that title—the Tucson community. Nothing crystalizes the notion of community better than El Con Fountain.

The pool of Bethesda in Jerusalem was once known for its healing powers. Periodically, the pool's waters bubbled. According to legend, an angel was present in the pool's bubbling waters. It was said that whoever entered Bethesda Pool when the Angel of the Waters was present would be healed of their infirmity. Bethesda Fountain in New York took its name from the pool of Bethesda. The eight-foot-tall statue standing atop the pedestal in the center is the Angel of the Waters from Jerusalem.

For El Con to make a comeback, there needs to be a stirring-of-the-waters event within the community. El Con could resurrect the "Plazas at El Con" redevelopment plan or something like it. This was a great plan, likely inspired by the generosity of Linda Ronstadt and Cele Peterson. In the darkest hour of the big-box controversy, these two women sponsored a forum to discuss the future of El Con. A lot of good ideas came out of that meeting, but the city and El Con's owners chose not to act on them. Not all was lost, though. I believe this forum was the impetus for the Plazas at El Con plan, which El Con's owners announced seven months later. This plan was never implemented, but it showed a lot of promise. In accord with the new urbanism principles discussed at the forum, the Plazas plan would have turned El Con into a pedestrian friendly, mixed-use marketplace that could function as a town square. With the fountain as a focal point, El Con could reestablish itself as a mixed-use lifestyle center—the kind of mall Gruen envisioned from the start.

It may be unlikely that anything will change at El Con Center. While the current center fails completely as a town square, the big-box stores attract hordes of shoppers. It's a shame that this highly prized midtown location, an area rich with history and meaning, is now essentially a shopping pit stop. For many years, El Con Mall was a place to go to experience community. Now that it's gone, I realize the role it played in my own life. For El Con to ever have a chance at regaining its former glory, the fountain must be brought back. Like Arrroyo Chico that flows through Colonia Solana, the fountain must be the focal point of any future plans for El Con. More than anything else, the midtown community needs a town square where people can go to spend time with other people. That can't happen unless the fountain comes back. I'm thankful for all the happy memories over the years at El Con and the lessons I learned. El Con's future is out of my hands, but I hope that someday the mall will experience a stirring of the waters.

El Con Sign with the El Con Tower in the background 2025

(Photo by the author)

AFTERWORD

JCPenney south entrance, 2022 (Photo by the author)

Near the south entrance of the JCPenney building at El Con is a park bench (previous page). This area of El Con Center gets little traffic. It was once part of the east-west corridor that connected Montgomery Ward to Levy's when El Con was enclosed. When the last section of the enclosed mall came down in 2011, the cleared land became available for future development. No new construction has occurred there, and the area remains a no man's land.

The park bench is usually empty, except for the occasional bird perching there. Here is a picture of the bench with the south entrance of JCPenney in the background (see previous page). Note the three rectangles on the wall to the right of the entrance. Now, here is a picture of that entrance taken in 2010 when this area was still enclosed (see below). Note the location of three rectangles to the right of the American flag.

JCPenney south entrance, 2010 (Image courtesy of Jason Damas and Ross Schendel of Labelscar.com)

The picture shows a row of cafe tables between the first pair of lit columns to the right of the wall directory. Compare the JCPenney entrance image from 2022 to the 2010 image, and you'll notice that the cafe tables are in roughly the exact spot where the bench is today. In 2010, I used one of these café tables as a writing workstation. The bench outside JCPenney reminds me of my 2010 fiction-writing project. Sitting there brings back memories of the three months I spent working in a dead mall. So, the bench outside JCPenney is the perfect place to end this story. In this brief afterword, I share my inspiration for writing this book.

Honoring Memories

Demolition of El Conquistador Hotel, 1968

(Places-Tucson-Business-Hotels-Conquistador, F2, 44452, Courtesy of the Arizona Historical Society)

The bench outside JCPenney faces Walmart's back entrance, a building that was built in the footprint of Levy's department store. In this 1968 image (see previous page), the Levy's building is visible in the background while demolition of the hotel proceeds. The area where the hotel appears in the picture is now a parking lot. I'm not the first person to make this observation. In 1982, beloved local columnist Ed Severson wrote an article about moving to Tucson with his parents. During their first month in the Old Pueblo, friends drove the Severson family to the outskirts of town to see the El Conquistador Hotel.

> We drove through the desert and pulled up in front of an oasis. In the middle of all these trees and shrubs stood this big Spanish mansion-looking place, topped by a copper dome. When we got out of the car, our friend said, 'You don't expect to see a place this beautiful in the middle of nowhere.' Today, the exact place where we got out of the car is underneath the asphalt in front of Levy's department store in El Con shopping center. [448]

Severson wrote this article when El Con Mall was in its prime. The idea that Levy's department store, a local institution, or the mall would one day suffer the hotel's fate would have been unthinkable. Yet, just thirty years later, both were gone. Walmart replaced Levy's, and a retail power center replaced the enclosed mall.

Many Tucsonans were outraged when bulldozers razed the hotel in 1968. Resident Rick Secrist, took matters into his own hands. He rented a jackhammer to remove two stone eagles from the hotel's porte cochère, but the police stopped him before he could carry out the plan. Secrist was only a teenager at the time, but he cared enough about preserving the hotel's legacy to risk jail time. Secrist couldn't save the hotel, but twenty years later, he led an effort to get El Encanto Estates placed on the National Register of Historic Places. [449]

The hotel was torn down six years before I was born, so I never had the opportunity to experience it in person. After writing this book, though, I understand why many regard the hotel as a crown jewel of Tucson's architecture. The craftsmanship and attention to detail poured into every element of the property are apparent. Buildings like this don't grow on trees. The hotel was a rare and precious landmark, a symbol of Tucson at its best. It's impossible to capture the hotel's beauty in words, but these images offer a glimpse of what guests experienced during their stay.

Front (south-facing) view of hotel

(Places-Tucson-Business-Hotels-El Conquistador. F1, 6997, Courtesy of the Arizona Historical Society)

Back (north-facing) view of hotel

(BN Places-Tucson-Business-Hotels-El Conquistador, Exterior BN, 203,044,
Courtesy of the Arizona Historical Society)

Reception Room: Hotel Interior

(BN Places-Tucson-Business-Hotels-El Conquistador, Interior BN, 203,050,
Courtesy of the Arizona Historical Society)

Entrance to solarium

(BN Places-Tucson-Business-Hotels-El Conquistador, Interior BN, 203,029,
Courtesy of the Arizona Historical Society)

Detailed view of hotel Porte Cochère with stone eagle statues

(Places-Tucson-Business-Hotels-El Conquistador, F1, 61599, Courtesy of the Arizona Historical Society)

Seeing these photographs, it's easy to understand why Rick Secrist reacted the way he did. The hotel's charm and elegance shine through every image. Having a landmark like this in the community is a privilege, and to see it go would have been devastating. I can't help but wonder why the city or some other entity didn't find a way to save it. And to think something this timeless and magnificent was torn down and replaced with a parking lot? It's unforgivable and an example of short-term thinking at its worst.

Look closely at the partially demolished hotel image below. With the west wing of the hotel gone, an exposed interior wall reveals two identical murals. They appear to be domestic background scenes showing a curio cabinet and potted plants.

Were these murals features of each hotel suite? What was their purpose? Were they painted to engage guests, suggest an ambiance, or tell a story about the hotel's identity? Who can say for sure? This photograph captured a section of the hotel that, under normal circumstances, was obscured from view. If not for this image, these charming details about the hotel would no longer be known. It bothers me to think of how many more delightful curiosities like these were lost when the hotel was destroyed.

Asphalt still covers the area where the hotel once stood. When Ed Severson noted this in 1982, the parking lot belonged to Levy's. Today, it belongs to Walmart. The picture at the beginning of this section is highly ironic. It shows the El Conquistador Hotel in its death throes, flanked by El Con Mall at the height of its power. When the photographer snapped this picture, nobody could have guessed that, three decades later, the mall would be gone, too. Aside from the vacant JCPenney building, nothing of the original mall remains today.

I want to revisit a YouTube comment from the book's introduction. Weighing in on a video about El Con after the transition from mall to power center, the commenter says, "The surrounding big-box stores, such as Walmart & Home Depot, are fine in their own right, but my guess is that 90% of customers will never know what a glorious mall once stood there." He's right. Just like most people who park at the El Con Walmart have no idea about the hotel, many people who shop at El Con Center have no idea that an enclosed mall once stood there. For those of us who experienced all the good that El Con Mall brought to the community, this, like the hotel, feels like an injustice that needs to be remedied.

I'll end with one final El Con Mall story. My wife's grandma, Lucille Kluck, has a son, Rick, who worked at the El Con Levy's in the 1960s. Rick gave Lucille an industrial roll of Christmas wrapping paper from the Levy's gift-wrapping department. Every Christmas, Lucille wrapped a few gifts in this distinctive olive green and red plaid-patterned paper. I liked the paper because it was vintage, and I always commented on how impressive it was that Lucille had so much of it forty-plus years after Rick gave it to her.

Sadly, Lucille passed away in 2024. Roughly a year before her death, Lucille gave me the roll of Levy's wrapping paper. Lucille's daughter, Priscilla, spent several days cleaning out her mother's flat after she died. One day, Priscilla brought me a vintage Levy's gift box that Lucille had held onto. The box was in pristine condition and featured the distinctive southwestern pattern for which Levy's was known. I had forgotten the pattern, so the box took me back to my childhood.

This empty box is a treasure because it offers a direct link to the El Con Mall of my youth. El Con Mall is gone, and from the looks of things, it may never return. Regardless, my intention for writing this book is to give people a sense of how meaningful the mall was to the local community. Hopefully, the stories I shared have allowed you to see El Con Mall and the El Conquistador Hotel in ways that honor their legacies. This book is my gift to everyone who loved El Con Mall and helped to make it special.

Levy's gift box (Photo by the author)

Endnotes

1 P. Weis, "Fleeting moment of Joy," *Tucson Citizen,* June 9, 1976, 7.

2 "Dead Mall," *Wikipedia,* accessed Dec. 17, 2024,
   https://en.wikipedia.org/wiki/Dead_mall.

3 V. Glover, "Are We Done Shopping at the Mall?" *The Carolinian,* Nov. 8, 2022,
   https://carolinianuncg.com/2022/11/08/are-we-done-shopping-at-the-mall/.

4 J. Weinstein, "Dead Malls: Inside one man's mission to document the beauty of
   abandoned shopping centers," *ABC News,* Nov. 23, 2018,
   https://abcnews.go.com/US/dead-malls-inside-mans-mission-document-
   beauty-abandoned/story?id=59230235.

5 M. Galka, "Retail Archaeology: Man documents the downfall of the American
   shopping mall," *FOX 10 Phoenix,* Aug. 9, 2017,
   https://www.fox10phoenix.com/news/retail-archaeology-man-documents-the-
   downfall-of-the-american-shopping-mall.

6 R. Kafes, "Letter to the editor, *Arizona Daily Star,* Jan. 12, 2008, 11.

7 M. Stanley, "Letter to the editor," *Arizona Daily Star,* Jan. 12, 2008, 11.

8 D. Quinn & A. Dalenberg, "Roofed-in part of El Con to be demolished," *Arizona
   Daily Star*, April 3, 2011, 1–5.

9 @tickym, "Comment on El Con Mall: The Dead Mall That Got Away," June 15,
   2024, https://youtu.be/EML0R-mWY-4?feature=shared.

10 @queenaracnia, "Comment on El Con Mall: The Dead Mall That Got Away,"
   Sept. 30, 2017, https://youtu.be/EML0R-mWY-4?feature=shared.

11 @lumberc, "Comment on, El Con Mall: The Dead Mall That Got Away," Sept.
   28, 2017, https://youtu.be/EML0R-mWY-4?feature=shared.

12 @superray21, "Comment on, El Con Mall: The Dead Mall That Got Away," Sept.
   29, 2017, https://youtu.be/EML0R-mWY-4?feature=shared.

13 @jeredblackmoor3295, "Comment on El Con Mall: The Dead Mall That Got
   Away," July 10, 2021, https://youtu.be/EML0R-mWY-4?feature=shared.

14 @DontEverGrowUp, "Comment on El Con Mall: The Dead Mall That Got
   Away," Nov. 11, 2020, https://youtu.be/EML0R-mWY-4?feature=shared.

15 @sounddude177, "Comment on El Con Mall: The Dead Mall That Got Away,"
   December 22, 2019, https://youtu.be/EML0R-mWY-4?feature=shared.

16 @Dana_Scully1, "Comment on El Con Mall: The Dead Mall That Got Away," December 1, 2023, https://youtu.be/EML0R-mWY-4?feature=shared.

17 @benjaminbeebe6555, "Comment on El Con Mall: The Dead Mall That Got Away," October 22, 2020, https://youtu.be/EML0R-mWY-4?feature=shared.

18 T. Stellar, "Internet commerce saves old copper country building," *Arizona Daily Star*, April 7, 2019, 1–9.

19 G. Knott, "Muralist's works tell stories," *Arizona Daily Star*, June 3, 2021, 8.

20 M. Murphy, "Why paint 'why'?" *Arizona Daily Star*, Sept. 27, 2007, 1–2.

21 N. Guest, "Move Bookmans to El Con," *Arizona Daily Star*, December 10, 2006. 2.

22 Karen S., "Review – El Con Mall," *Yelp*, July 6, 2018, https://www.yelp.com/biz/el-con-mall-tucson?osq=el+con+mall.

23 "How spider builds its web?" *Brisbaneinsects.com*, accessed Dec. 28, 2024, https://www.brisbaneinsects.com/brisbane_weavers/SpiderWeb.htm.

24 B. Christman, "Final weekend ticks away for Steinfeld's El Con store," *The Arizona Daily Star*, Aug. 25, 1984, B7.

25 R. Gary, "The end of an era: Herb, Dave and Ted closing 80-year-old shop," *Arizona Daily Star*, Dec. 26, 1990, B6–B6.

26 E. Heltsley, "Park Mall, El Con planning major renovations," *Arizona Daily Star*, Feb. 2, 1998, 1F–4F.

27 S. Hammond, "Dillard's pulling out of El Con," *Arizona Daily Star*, Jan. 6, 2020, 1A–11A.

28 L. Scharoun, *America at The Mall: The Cultural Role of a Retail Utopia* (Jefferson, NC: McFarland & Co., 2012, 120).

29 L. Kaufman and C. Deutsch, "Montgomery Ward to close its doors," *New York Times*, Dec. 29, 2000, 1.

30 S. J. Carrera, "Ailing chain closes," *Miami Herald*, Dec. 29, 2000, 1B–2B.

31 M. Juarez, "Broadway Retailers Ready to Ring up Revitalization, *Arizona Daily Star*, June 23, 2002, 1–14.

32 S. McLean, "Hello, anybody home?" *Tucson Citizen*, Aug. 3, 2007, 1–1.

33 J. Pisani, "JCPenney is closing a Tucson store as part of bankruptcy case," *Tucson Citizen*, June 5, 2020, https://tucson.com/business/j-c-penney-is-closing-a-tucson-store-as-part-of-bankruptcy-case/article_b4df278d-a35c-57c6-9238-de48bbd445f1.html.

34 E. L. Scott, "The El Conquistador Hotel Will Open Tonight In Blaze Of Social Splendor," *Tucson Citizen*, November 28, 1928, 10.

[35] Ibid.

[36] El Conquistador. (1928, December 1). *The Daily National Hotel Reporter*, p. 1. Vol. LVII No. 275

[37] "El Conquistador," *Daily National Hotel Reporter*, December 1, 1928, 1.

[38] "All Tucson will welcome this new store opening, Tomorrow, May 1st," *Arizona Daily Star*, April 30, 1920, 9.

[39] H. Olsen, "Merchants Cooperate for Park and Shop," *Tucson Daily Citizen*, January 24, 1957, 7.

[40] A. Levy, "1957 Year for Decisions," *Tucson Daily Citizen*, January 24, 1957, 13.

[41] Ibid.

[42] L. Scharoun, "Suburbia and the American Dream," in *America at The Mall: The Cultural Role of a Retail Utopia* (New York: McFarland & Co., 2012), 23.

[43] Ibid, 25.

[44] M. J. Hardwick, *Mall Maker: Victor Gruen, Architect of an American Dream* (pp. 9-10). (Harrisburg: University of Pennsylvania Press, 2010), 9–10.

[45] J. A. Wickland, (1956, October 5), "Preview Visitors Call Southdale 'Fabulous,'" *Minneapolis Morning Tribune*, Oct. 5, 1956, 1.

[46] W. Thorkelson, "Shopping Centers Held Boon To Loop," *Minneapolis Star*, Oct. 5, 1956, 17A.

[47] L. Scharoun, "Suburbia and the American Dream," in *America at The Mall: The Cultural Role of a Retail Utopia* (New York: McFarland & Co., 2012), 13.

[48] Ibid.

[49] W. Thorkelson, "Shopping Centers Held Boon To Loop," *Minneapolis Star*, Oct. 5, 1956, 17A.

[50] J. Carson, "Work Starts in Fall On $6 Million Shopping Center," *Tucson Citizen*, June 2, 1958, 1.

[51] C. R. Fulton, "Joe Kivel," *Arizona Daily Star*, February 6, 1983, 5.

[52] Ibid.

[53] C. R. Fulton, "Mall, Downtown's Fates Date To Late '30s," *Arizona Daily Star*, February 7, 1983, 3.

[54] J. Carson, "Work Starts in Fall On $6 Million Shopping Center," *Tucson Citizen*, June 2, 1958, 1.

[55] "Levy's Plans $2 Million El Con Store," *Tucson Daily Citizen*, January 17, 1959, 1.

[56] M. Kuehlthau, "Demolition Of Hotel To Begin Soon," *Tucson Daily Citizen*, June 14, 1968, 29.

[57] C. R. Fulton, "Mall, Downtown's Fates Date To Late '30s. *Arizona Daily Star*, February 7, 1983, 3.

[58] B. Milburn, "Furnishings of old hotel now belong to others," *Tucson Citizen*, June 25, 1968, 9.

[59] "El Con's 10th Birthday Fiesta," *Tucson Citizen*, Sept. 2, 1971, 2.

[60] "Happy Birthday, El Con!", *Arizona Daily Star*, Sept. 1985, 2.

[61] Ibid.

[62] T. Putnam, "Family Traditions and George Washington's Birthday," *Pieces of History*, November 14, 2024, https://prologue.blogs.archives.gov/2017/02/16/family-traditions-and-george-washingtons-birthday/.

[63] "Oriental Imports Shop to Open, *Arizona Daily Star*, May 7, 1964, 5.

[64] Sumiko's ad, *Tucson Citizen*, November 2, 1965.

[65] Ibid.

[66] O. Harrison, "What It's Like To Work Black Friday: Employees Tell All," *Refinery 29*, Nov. 25, 2019, https://www.refinery29.com/en-us/working-black-friday-retail-employee-confessions.

[67] Ibid.

[68] "A Stone's Throw From Sesame Street," *Fort Lauderdale News*, Mach 2, 1973, 16.

[69] Ibid.

[70] "Creegan Draws Crowds," *Post-Star and Times*, March 16, 1974, 14.

[71] "A Stone's Throw From Sesame Street," *Fort Lauderdale News*, Mach 2, 1973, 16.

[72] Wikimedia Foundation, "Hooper's Store," *Wikipedia*, retrieved Dec. 19, 2024, from https://en.wikipedia.org/wiki/Hooper%27s_Store.

[73] H. Hoffower, "Inside the Rise of Pumpkin Spice – The Millennial Obsession That Everyone Loves to Hate," *Business Insider*, Oct. 17, 2021, https://www.businessinsider.com/millennials-starbucks-pumpkin-spice-latte-cultural-icon-2021-10.

[74] "Bakery Tycoon's Secret, Beat Distribution Cost," *Tucson Citizen*, November 1959, 33.

[75] M. F. K. Fisher, *The Art of Eating* (Hoboken, NJ: Wiley Publishing, 2004).

[76] "Concerts Moving to El Con," *Tucson Citizen*, January 1981, 78.

77 L. W. Cheek, "The Malling of Chopin," *Tucson Citizen*, January 14, 1981, 1B.

78 Ibid.

79 Wikimedia Foundation, "Rudolph the Red-nosed Reindeer (TV Special), *Wikipedia,* retrieved Dec. 19, 2024, https://en.wikipedia.org/wiki/Rudolph_the_Red-Nosed_Reindeer_(TV_special)#:~:text=As%20with%20A%20Charlie%20Brown,special%20in%20the%20United%20States.

80 L. Nannini, "Collaborative Effort," *Arizona Daily Star*, December 16, 2001a, 4.

81 C. Bancroft, "Holiday sharing center makes it easy to spread good cheer," *Arizona Daily Star*, November 9, 1988, 1.

82 L. Scharoun, *America at The Mall: The Cultural Role of a Retail Utopia* (Jefferson, NC: McFarland & Co., 2012), 72.

83 "Traffic Jam Ties Up Wards' Debut," *Tucson Daily Citizen*, February 2, 1961.

84 "Ward's Key Tucson Store Marks a First for Arizona," *Arizona Daily Star*, February 1, 1961, sec. Montgomery Ward Special Section.

85 Ibid.

86 Micheline Keating, "TM Theaters Buys 6-Screen El Con Complex," *Tucson Citizen*, September 27, 1978, sec. B.

87 Ibid.

88 J. Tully, "El Con Six opens to full house," *Arizona Daily Star,* August 16, 1979, 2.

89 "El Con 6 Opens Wednesday," *Tucson Citizen*, August 9, 1979, sec. B.

90 "Navigating the World of Film Merchandising and Tie-In Products: A Comprehensive Guide," Factual America, accessed June 6, 2025, https://www.factualamerica.com/filmmaking/navigating-the-world-of-film-merchandising-and-tie-in-products.

91 Dan Huff, "Darth Vader vs. Dangerous Dan," *Tucson Citizen*, June 10, 1980, sec. B.

92 Ibid.

93 Susan Lyons Dean, "Looking for Toys? Prices Vary A Lot," *Tucson Citizen*, December 17, 1981, sec. B.

94 Amanda Onion, Missy Sullivan, Matt Mullen, Christian Zapata, and Cristiana Lombardo, eds. "Video Game History," History.com, February 27, 2025, https://www.history.com/articles/history-of-video-games.

95 RMC – The Cave, "Atari VCS/2600 | The Console that Launched an Industry, posted November 1, 2018, YouTube, 4 min., 6 sec., https://www.youtube.com/watch?v=ELGQZF1xRVE.

[96] Paul T. Henniger, "Television Log," *Tucson Daily Citizen*, March 15, 1977, sec. B.

[97] Marilyn Evans, "Don't Have the Guts to Say It? Let Your T-Shirt Do the Talking," *Tucson Citizen*, July 25, 1979, sec. B.

[98] Ibid.

[99] James T. Egan, "The Mini Page Advice Column," *Tucson Citizen*, June 24, 1983, sec. B.

[100] Ibid.

[101] Associated Press. "Singer Says He Bit Bat; Gets Rabies Shot," *Tucson Citizen*, January 22, 1982, sec. A.

[102] Ibid.

[103] Robin Muellenbach, "Robin's Roost," *The Payson Chronicle*. May 26, 1983.

[104] Cindy Cox. "Gift Ideas for Your Teen," *Lancaster New Era*. December 12, 1983.

[105] Ibid.

[106] Sue Briggs, "What's Hot in 'T-Tops,'" *The Flint Journal*. May 24, 1989, sec. C.

[107] Ibid.

[108] Larry Harnisch, "Millions Scrambling to Unscramble Cube," *Arizona Daily Star*, October 11, 1981, sec. I.

[109] Kathy Estep, "Uno Game Popular with All Ages," *News Herald*, November 27, 1980.

[110] B. Adams, "A place for the gaming community," *Baraboo News Republic*, March 21, 2022, 5.

[111] Admin, "What Is Nylon: Types, Pros & Cons, Uses," ChemixLab, January 14, 2024, https://www.chemixlab.com/explained/what-is-nylon-definition-types-advantages-disadvantages-uses/.

[112] *Collins English Dictionary Online*, "Department store," accessed June 6, 2025, https://www.collinsdictionary.com/dictionary/english/department-store.

[113] L. June, "For Amusement Only: The Life and Death of the American Arcade," *Verge*, Jan. 16, 2013, https://www.theverge.com/2013/1/16/3740422/the-life-and-death-of-the-american-arcade-for-amusement-only.

[114] Edward Stiles, "Life Isn't Quiet in Fair's Arcades: Laughs, Yells and Constant Crashing," *Tucson Citizen*, April 15, 1980, sec. C.

[115] Ellen Goodman, "Pac-Man Claims Another Victim," *Macon News*, May 21, 1982, sec. A.

[116] Ibid.

[117] Charles Bowden, "Evan & Co. Fighting to Keep Our Galaxy Free!", *Tucson Citizen*, October 21, 1981, sec. B.

[118] K. E. Dayhoff, "Remember where you were the day Twinkie the kid died?" *Baltimore Sun*, December 9, 2012, 7.

[119] D. Parry, "Belly Up To Some Wacky Fun," *Palladium-Item*, January 15, 1982, 1–2.

[120] "'Orange Julius capital of the world' here in the Puget Sound area, *News Tribune*, Feb. 17, 1983, 22.

[121] "OJ: success on a secret," *Winston-Salem Journal*, October 6, 1983, 10.

[122] "Willard 'Bill' Hamlin; Created Orange Julius," *Pottsville Republican*, June 6, 1983, 3.

[123] "Orange Julius' fare is popular," *Times-Transcript*, August 20, 1987, 27.

[124] Nancy Yoshihara, "Wear a Swatch on Your Swrist," *Tucson Citizen,* June 25, 1985, sec. B.

[125] Ed Severson, "Swatch Has Young Buyers Taking up Arms to Mark Time," *The Arizona Daily Star,* March 16, 1986.

[126] Ibid.

[127] *Cambridge Dictionary Online,* "Digital Age," accessed May 30, 2025, https://dictionary.cambridge.org/dictionary/english/digital-age.

[128] "Why do we have a fascination with dead malls?", *Reddit.com,* July 26, 2021, https://www.reddit.com/r/deadmalls/comments/os0hsi/why_do_we_have_a_f ascination_with_dead_malls/.

[129] Restorative Environment. (n.d.). Retrieved March 25, 2023, from https://dictionary.apa.org/restorative-environment.

[130] (2018, November 13). What is Kaplan's Attention Restoration Theory (ART)?. Retrieved June 9, 2023, from https://positivepsychology.com/attention-restoration-theory/

[131] C. A. Ackerman, "What is Kaplan's Attention Restoration Theory (ART)?" *Positivepsychology.com,* Nov. 13, 2018, https://positivepsychology.com/attention-restoration-theory/.

[132] Ibid.

[133] Ibid.

[134] B. Corr, "Evoking the Elements of Contemplative Space in Japanese Architecture," *Australian National University,* Oct. 29, 2018, https://core.ac.uk/download/pdf/162631458.pdf.

[135] "Place Attachment & Meaning," *Green Cities: Good Health,* Aug. 16, 2018, https://depts.washington.edu/hhwb/Thm_Place.html.

[136] NeuroLaunch editorial team, "Place Attachment Theory: Exploring Our Emotional Bonds with Environments," *NeuroLaunch.com,* Sept. 12, 2024, https://neurolaunch.com/place-attachment-theory/.

[137] Ibid.

[138] "Ruinenlust," Emotional Granularity, accessed June 18, 2023, https://emotionalgranularity.com/index.php/2019/08/31/ruinenlust/.

[139] Ibid.

[140] "Nostalgia," *Wikipedia,* accessed Jan. 3, 2024, https://en.wikipedia.org/wiki/Nostalgia.

[141] George A. Romero, *Dawn of the Dead,* directed by George A. Romero (1978; Los Angeles: United Film Distribution Company), film.

[142] C. Federico, "Building question: is it Home Depot, or no?" *Asbury Park Press,* March 31, 1996, 2.

[143] Ibid, "Plan to add to Hazlet site denied," *Asbury Park Press,* May 22, 1996b, 1–5.

[144] J. Chen, "Power center: What it means, how it works, types," *Investopedia,* Oct. 30, 2021, https://www.investopedia.com/terms/p/power-center.asp

[145] C. R. Fulton, "El Con's, downtown's fates date to '30s," *Arizona Daily Star,* Feb. 7, 1983, 3.

[146] Ibid.

[147] C. R. Fulton, "Kivel gave ground to open Park Mall," *Arizona Daily Star,* Feb. 9, 1983, 1.

[148] Ibid.

[149] "Mayor, government officials to dedicate park mall center, *Tucson Citizen,* May 2, 1975, 2.

[150] M. Parham, "Diamond's store opening tomorrow," *Arizona Daily Star,* Aug. 4, 1974, 1.

[151] Ibid.

[152] Ibid.

[153] C. R. Fulton, "Developer Kivel's dual interests caused rift with El Con co-owner," *Arizona Daily Star,* Feb. 8, 1983b, 1.

[154] Ibid.

[155] Ibid.

[156] Ibid.

[157] C. R. Fulton, "Developer Kivel's dual interests caused rift with el con co-owner," *Arizona Daily Star*, Feb. 8, 1983b, 1.

[158] C. R. Fulton, "Joe Kivel: associates profile a shy business titan in off-the-rack suits," *Arizona Daily Star*, Feb. 6, 1983a, 1.

[159] E. Heltsley, "Mall to get $100 million neighborhood," *Arizona Daily Star*, Aug. 28, 1981, E1.

[160] W. G. Clemens, "Park Mall's future looking bigger, bright," *Tucson Citizen*, Jan. 27, 1997, 1–6.

[161] M. Prentice, "El Con, Park Mall developer Joe Kivel dies," *Arizona Daily Star*, May 27, 1995, 1.

[162] W. G. Clemens, "Park Mall's future looking bigger, bright," *Tucson Citizen*, Jan. 27, 1997, 1–6.

[163] W. G. Clemens, L. Cohen, J. Higuera, and J. Boice, "Street talk: mall rumors abound," *Tucson Citizen*, Jan. 27, 1997, 2.

[164] W. G. Clemens, "Park Mall's future looking bigger, bright," *Tucson Citizen*, Jan. 27, 1997, 1–6.

[165] J. Boice, and W. G. Clemens, "Park Mall sold to bold investor," *Tucson Citizen*, Oct. 8, 1996, 4.

[166] W. G. Clemens, "Tucson Mall sees no fight in future," *Tucson Citizen*, June 25, 1997b, 10.

[167] Ibid.

[168] Ibid.

[169] E. Heltsley, "2 area malls may be in for big changes," *Arizona Daily Star*, March 10, 1997, 1–2.

[170] Ibid.

[171] Ibid.

[172] W. G. Clemens, "Park Mall's future looking bigger, bright," *Tucson Citizen*, Jan. 27, 1997, 1–6.

[173] Ibid.

[174] W. G. Clemens, "Tucson Mall sees no fight in future," *Tucson Citizen*, June 25, 1997b, 10.

[175] J. Tully, "El Con Six opens to full house," *Arizona Daily Star*, Aug. 16, 1979, 2.

[176] J. J. Higuera and W. G. Clemens, "Ailing El Con may get Walmart," *Tucson Citizen*, Sept. 3, 1997, 1.

[177] Ibid, "El Con Mall may become Tucson's movie star," *Tucson Citizen*, Sept. 4, 1997, 1.

[178] Ibid.

[179] J. J. Higuera, "New El Con megaplex near opening," *Tucson Citizen*, June 22, 1999, 3.

[180] S. Hammond, "El Con 20-plex will add to our movie mania," *Arizona Daily Star*, Jun 27, 1999b, 3.

[181] J. J. Higuera, "New El Con megaplex near opening," *Tucson Citizen*, June 22, 1999, 3.

[182] H. Miller, "Film fans fill seats, feed needy," *Arizona Daily Star*, June 30, 1999, 1–3.

[183] C. Graham, "From love seats to lattes, new El Con theater goes all out," *Tucson Citizen*, July 1, 1999, 1.

[184] C. Graham, "From love seats to lattes, new El Con theater goes all out," *Tucson Citizen*, July 1, 1999, 1.

[185] D. Pittman, "Park Mall ready to expand by 50%," *Tucson Citizen*, April 2, 1998, 1.

[186] S. Hammond, "Park Mall's fresh look," *Arizona Daily Star*, May 16, 1999, 1–2.

[187] D. Pittman, L. Cohen, J. Higuera, and J. Boice, "More of the best," *Tucson Citizen*, Sept. 20, 1999, 2.

[188] Ibid.

[189] Ibid.

[190] V. Phil, "Park Place multiplex opens Friday, with preview Thursday," *Arizona Daily Star*, Aug. 5, 2001, 1.

[191] C. Graham, "Big-city feel," *Tucson Citizen*, Aug. 10, 2001, 1–8.

[192] C. Rene, "Crowd awed by preview at new Park Place theater," *Tucson Citizen*, Aug. 10, 2001, 8.

[193] E. Heltsley, "Park Mall, El Con planning major renovations," *Arizona Daily Star*, Feb. 2, 1998, 1F–4F.

[194] Ibid., "Potent neighbors cast wary eyes on El Con," *Arizona Daily Star*, March 8, 1998, 1–4.

[195] Ibid.

[196] C. Valdez Diaz, "Home Depot to open new store in Marana in '99," *Tucson Citizen*, May 5, 1998, 1.

197 M. R. Graham, "Neighbors fight El Con growth plan," *Tucson Citizen*, Aug. 27, 1998, 1–7.

198 J. Burstein, "Council to consider restricting northern access to El Con Mall," *Arizona Daily Star*, Dec. 8, 1998, 3.

199 S. E. Auslander and J. M. Kiser (eds.), "El Con's second chance," *Arizona Daily Star*, Feb. 25, 1999, A14.

200 N. Peckham, "City votes to close 2 other streets into the mall," *Tucson Citizen*, June 8, 1999, 1–8.

201 Ibid.

202 C. Donal Hatfield, "Council vote on El Con streets is fair compromise," *Tucson Citizen*, June 10, 1999, 6A.

203 N. Peckham, "City votes to close 2 other streets into the mall," *Tucson Citizen*, June 8, 1999, 1–8.

204 N. Peckham, "Area set to fight Wal-Mart," *Tucson Citizen*, June 28, 1999b, 1–2.

205 M. R. Graham, "Neighbors fear El Con changes," *Tucson Citizen*, Feb. 16, 2000a, 1–16.

206 Ibid.

207 K. Bagwell, "El Con neighbors gird for fight over superstores," *Arizona Daily Star*, June 27, 1999b, 1–8.

208 Ibid.

209 J. Amari and J. M. Kiser, "Home Depot," *Arizona Daily Star*, Dec. 31, 1999.

210 R. Beeker, "El Con's wrong retail mix," *Arizona Daily Star*, June 17, 1999, 18.

211 J. Anderson, "Traffic control key if El Con is to be open 24 hours," *Tucson Citizen*, March 2, 1999, 13.

212 K. Bagwell, "El Con neighbors gird for fight over superstores," *Arizona Daily Star*, June 27, 1999b, 1–8.

213 C. Tanz and J. P. Bierny, "City Should Shun "big-Boxes" at El Con," *Tucson Citizen*, Aug. 2, 1999, 5.

214 H. R. News, "To Al Norman, Wal-Mart fight is about way of life," *Columbia Gorge News*, Feb. 7, 2019, https://www.columbiagorgenews.com/archive/to-al-norman-wal-mart-fight-is-about-way-of-life/article_f10d4107-a391-5c24-8898-e4edacd274c7.html

215 Ibid.

216 T. Luna, "No letup for crusader," *Boston Globe*, Oct. 24, 2013, 5–8.

217 Ibid.

[218] Geurin [sic] forms land company. (1928, May 13). Arizona Daily Star, p. 6.

[219] New subdivision offers 11 prizes to tucson people. (1928b, July 8). Arizona Daily Star, p. 6.

[220] Echols to build three homes in Encanto Estates. (1929, January 6). Tucson Citizen, p. 10.

[221] Leighton, D. (2014, September 2). Contest winners got $5 each for el encanto road names. Arizona Daily Star, pp. 2–5.

[222] Mercedes, G. (1988, May 9). El Encanto: neighborhood leader wins fight to save "Beverly Hills" of tucson. Tucson Citizen, pp. 1–4.

[223] Labriola, N. (2023, August 12). El Encanto Estates - simply enchanting. RealTucson.com. https://realtucson.com/2015/05/07/el-encanto-estates/#About%20El%20Encanto%20Estates

[224] E. Heltsley, "Potent neighbors cast wary eyes on El Con," *Arizona Daily Star*, March 8, 1988, 1–4.

[225] Ibid.

[226] Ibid.

[227] T. Turner, "Panel urges historic status for El Encanto," *Arizona Daily Star*, October 28, 1987, 1.

[228] J. R. Wyckoff, "Two elite neighborhoods fight loss of restrictions," *Tucson Citizen*, Feb. 17, 1978, 1.

[229] J. R. Wyckoff, "Two elite neighborhoods fight loss of restrictions," *Tucson Citizen*, Feb. 17, 1978, 1.

[230] D. Block, "El Encanto having growing pains?" *Tucson Citizen*, Feb. 22, 1979, 1–6.

[231] M. Smith, "Elegant homes wary of business corner," *Arizona Daily Star*, March 6, 1978, 6.

[232] M. Kimble, "Residents fighting to save a "little island" on Broadway," *Tucson Citizen*, Nov. 2, 1978, 1–4.

[233] M. Smith, "Lim opposes bank request for rezoning," *Arizona Daily Star*, June 8, 1978b, 2.

[234] D. Block, "El Encanto having growing pains?" *Tucson Citizen*, Feb. 22, 1979, 1–6.

[235] M. E. Quinn, "Lim opposes rezoning request," *Arizona Daily Star*, April 19, 1979, 3.

[236] "Protect Colonia Solana, El Encanto, Council told," *Tucson Citizen*, June 7, 1979, 5.

[237] M. Kimble, "Midtown areas keep out developers," *Tucson Citizen*, Jun 26, 1979, 2.

[238] Ibid.

[239] "Landowner seeks $1.5 million in denial of rezoning for bank," *Arizona Daily Star*, Jan. 10, 1980, 3.

[240] M. Kimble, "A classic battle over classy ground," *Tucson Citizen*, July 13, 1979b, 1–3.

[241] G. Mercedes, "El Encanto: neighborhood leader wins fight to save 'Beverly Hills' of Tucson, *Tucson Citizen*, May 9, 1988, 1–4.

[242] . Kimble, "A classic battle over classy ground," *Tucson Citizen*, July 13, 1979b, 1–3.

[243] K. Bagwell, "Council asks Gutierrez for law to ban superstores," *Arizona Daily Star*, Aug. 3, 1999c, 1–4.

[244] Ibid.

[245] Ibid.

[246] Ibid.

[247] C. Tanz, "Cities have right to define growth," *Tucson Citizen,* Aug. 20, 1999, 19.

[248] E. Portillo, "How Will Battle of Home Depot vs. Tucson End?" *Tucson Citizen,* Sept. 1, 1999, 15.

[249] M. Juarez, "'New urbanization' pioneer to apply community-friendly theme to project," *Arizona Daily Star*, July 19, 2000, 1–13.

[250] S. Carroll, S. "Council limits 'big-box' stores," *Tucson Citizen*, Sept. 28, 1999, 1.

[251] Ibid.

[252] T. Davis, "Citywide big-box vote seems likely," *Arizona Daily Star*, Nov. 9, 1999b, 1–10.

[253] K. Bagwell, "Wal-mart acts to compel a public vote on big-boxes," *Arizona Daily Star*, Oct. 21, 1999e, 1–18.

[254] M. Tobin, "Wal-mart drive may stall ban on big-boxes," *Tucson Citizen*, Nov. 10, 1999c, 1–18.

[255] M. LaFleur, "Judge closes dodge by El Con," *Tucson Citizen*, Dec. 9, 1999, 1–6.

[256] K. Bagwell, "Plans to build 2 big-box stores upheld by city," *Arizona Daily Star*, Dec. 16, 1999f, 1–7.

[257] T. Davis, "City, El Con agree on plan to ease restrictions of big-box ordinance," *Arizona Daily Star*, Jan. 22, 2000, 1–12.

[258] Ibid.

[259] M. Tobin, "Courts to get El Con impasse." *Tucson Citizen*, Jan. 25, 2000, 1–3.

[260] S. Phillips, "Trust hangs on decision," *Tucson Citizen*, Jan. 31, 2000, 7.

[261] R. E. Larson, "Walkout childish, disgraceful," *Tucson Citizen*, Jan. 31, 2000, 7.

[262] A. Kennedy, "Keep men of conscience on council," *Tucson Citizen*, Feb. 1, 2000, 7.

[263] W. Marts, "Inappropriate behavior," *Tucson Citizen*, Jan. 31, 2000, 7.

[264] J. Anderson, "Councilman: mall interested in might, not right," *Tucson Citizen*, Jan. 31, 2000, 7.

[265] J. Burchell, "El Con road closure null, city attorney says," *Arizona Daily Star*, Jan. 28, 2000, 1.

[266] M. Tobin, "Voters may get big-box issue," *Tucson Citizen*, February 1, 2000b, 1.

[267] M. Tobin, "Walkup wants more talks on El Con," *Tucson Citizen*, Feb. 1, 2000c, 4.

[268] Ibid, "Petitions for vote on 'big-boxes' put on hold, *Tucson Citizen*, Nov. 11, 1999, 1–6.

[269] K. Bagwell, "Wal-mart acts to compel a public vote on big-boxes," *Arizona Daily Star*, Oct 21, 1999, 1–18.

[270] M. Tobin, "Walkup wants more talks on El Con," *Tucson Citizen*, Feb. 1, 2000c, 4.

[271] M. Tobin, "Wal-mart appeal may save ballot measure," *Tucson Citizen*, Feb. 3, 2000d, 1–3.

[272] Ibid.

[273] R. E. Walkup, "El Con: a compromise for all Tucsonans," *Arizona Daily Star*, Feb. 6, 2000, 1.

[274] Ibid.

[275] C. Tanz, "El Con plan draws fire," *Arizona Daily Star*, Feb. 8, 2000, 13.

[276] Ibid.

[277] Ibid.

[278] J. Burchell, "Big-box" law is temporarily put on hold," *Arizona Daily Star*, Feb. 9, 2000b, 1–2.

[279] M. Tobin, "Halt El Con plan, people tell mayor," *Tucson Citizen*, Feb. 12, 2000e, 1–5.

[280] Ibid.

281 Ibid.

282 Ibid.

283 M. Tobin, "Forum focus on future of El Con Mall," *Tucson Citizen*, Feb. 10, 2000e, 1–2.

284 M. Tobin, "Halt El Con plan, people tell mayor," *Tucson Citizen*, Feb. 12, 2000e, 1–5.

285 Ibid.

286 M. Tobin, "Halt El Con plan, people tell mayor," *Tucson Citizen*, Feb. 12, 2000e, 1–5.

287 Ibid.

288 Davis, T. (2000b, February 15). El con plan passes 4-3 over neighbors' protest. *Arizona Daily Star*, pp. 1–8.

289 J. Burchell, "Rio Nuevo plan adds El Con, Park malls," *Arizona Daily Star*, July 9, 1999. 1–16.

290 M. Robin, "El Con gets ok to supersize," *Tucson Citizen*, Jan. 9, 2000b, 1–6.

291 T. Davis, "El Con plan passes 4-3 over neighbors' protest," *Arizona Daily Star*, February 15, 2000b, 1–8.

292 Ibid.

293 C. Tscheschlok, "Understanding Tax Incremental Districts (TID) and Tax Incremental Financing (TIF)," EDWC, accessed Dec. 20, 2024, https://www.edwc.org/understanding-tax-incremental-districts/.

294 J. Burchell, "Rio Nuevo plan adds El Con, Park malls," *Arizona Daily Star*, July 9, 1999, 1–16.

295 N. Peckham, "Rio Nuevo panel sought," *Tucson Citizen*, July 31, 1999, 1–6.

296 K. Bagwell, "Council to hear new proposals for Rio Nuevo," *Arizona Daily Star*, Sept. 7, 1999, 1–4.

297 Ibid., "Council asks Gutierrez for law to ban superstores," *Arizona Daily Star*, Aug. 3, 1999c, 1–4.

298 M. Papanikolas, "'Big box' ban: a use or class issue?" *Tucson Citizen*, Aug. 16, 1999, 9.

299 M. Tobin, "Halt El Con plan, people tell mayor," *Tucson Citizen*, Feb. 12, 2000e, 1–5.

300 M. Juarez, "Broadway retailers ready to ring up revitalization," *Arizona Daily Star*, June 23, 2002, 1–14.

301 C. Culbertson, "Downtown plan brilliant," *Tucson Citizen*, July 29, 1999, 5.

302 H. Fischer, "Wal-Mart overruled by court," *Arizona Daily Star*, May 27, 2000, 1–19.

303 Ibid.

304 J. Burchell, "Wal-Mart sues again over 'big-box' law," *Arizona Daily Star*, Oct. 7, 2000c, 1.

305 Ibid.

306 A. Flick, "Wal-Mart's 'big-box' suit dismissed," *Tucson Citizen*, Sept. 24, 2003, 3.

307 Ibid.

308 T. Vitu, "Neighbors: big-box no pox after all, *Tucson Citizen*, June 16, 2001, 1–9.

309 Ibid.

310 Ibid.

311 R. Beeker, "El Con's wrong retail mix," *Arizona Daily Star*, June 17, 1999, 18.

312 M. Mathieu, "Resuscitate heart of Tucson," *Tucson Citizen*, Sept. 29, 2005, 5.

313 N. Greason, "El Con to become the Plazas at El Con," *Tucson Citizen*, Sept. 13, 2000, 1–11.

314 J. Relly, "'De-malling" of El Con," *Arizona Daily Star*, Dec. 13, 2000, 1.

315 N. Greason, "El Con to become the Plazas at El Con," *Tucson Citizen*, Sept. 13, 2000, 1–11.

316 Ibid.

317 Ibid.

318 M. A. Chihak, "Plazas at El Con," *Tucson Citizen*, September 21, 2000, 8A.

319 "EL CON MALL Communique," Issue VII, March 9, 2001, https://web.archive.org/web/20021005202930/http://shopelcon.com/nl_010309.htm.

320 J. Relly, "The 'de-malling' of Park Place," *Arizona Daily Star*, Aug. 5, 2001, 1–6.

321 W. G. Clemens, "Park Mall expands at El Con's expense," *Tucson Citizen*, June 25, 1997b," 1–10.

322 T. Vitu, "Park Place packed," *Tucson Citizen*, Aug. 9, 2001b, 1–6.

323 Ibid.

324 Ibid.

325 Ibid.

326 Ibid., "Wanted: teens," *Tucson Citizen*, Feb. 16, 2001, 1–3.

[327] Ibid., "Mall facelift nearly done," *Tucson Citizen*, July 26, 2001, 1–3.

[328] Ibid.

[329] T. Vitu, "Park Place packed," *Tucson Citizen*, Aug. 9, 2001b, 1–6.

[330] T. Kjos, "Stop-and-go redevelopment leaves troubled mall hurting for tenants," *Arizona*, Dec. 8, 2002, 1–6.

[331] Ibid.

[332] M. Papanikolas, "'Big box' ban: a use or class issue?" *Tucson Citizen*, Aug. 16, 1999, 9.

[333] T. Kjos, "Stop-and-go redevelopment leaves troubled mall hurting for tenants," *Arizona*, Dec. 8, 2002, 1–6.

[334] D. Kreutz, "Many moods of the malls," *Arizona Daily Star*, Sept. 20, 2004, 1–2.

[335] A. T. Denogean, "El Gone Mall," *Tucson Citizen*, September 23, 2005, 1–2.

[336] Ibid.

[337] Ibid.

[338] Ibid.

[339] Ibid.

[340] Ibid.

[341] Ibid.

[342] T. Kjos, "Teetering landmark: El Con Mall," *Arizona Daily Star*, Dec. 8, 2004, 1–6.

[343] Ibid.

[344] Ibid.

[345] M. T. Rosales, "El Con needs Ross-and a whole new identity," *Arizona Daily Star*, May 29, 2006, A14.

[346] Ibid.

[347] Ibid.

[348] Ibid.

[349] S. C. McLean, "Hello, anybody home?" *Tucson Citizen*, Aug. 3, 2007, 1.

[350] Ibid.

[351] Ibid.

[352] Ibid.

[353] Ibid.

[354] M. Kimble, "RealFAST online comments,' *Tucson Citizen*, Aug. 6, 2007, 1.

[355] Ibid.

[356] Ibid.

[357] S. G. Gassen, S. Negri, S., and M. Rosales. M. "Tucson deserves better than dilapidated mall," *Arizona Daily Star*, Jan. 5, 2008, A9.

[358] Ibid.

[359] Ibid.

[360] Ibid.

[361] T. Vitu, "Redefined El Con takes fuzzy shape," *Tucson Citizen*, Feb. 15, 2001b, 1–3.

[362] R. O'Dell, "Wal-Mart asks voters to repeal grocery limits," *Arizona Daily Star*, May 30, 2007a, 1–4.

[363] Ibid., "Wal-Mart petitions rejected," *Arizona Daily Star*, July 6, 2007, 1–4.

[364] Ibid., "Wal-Mart asks voters to repeal grocery limits," *Arizona Daily Star*, May 30, 2007a, 1–4.

[365] E. Sagara, "City rejects Wal-Mart's petition drive," *Tucson Citizen*, July 6, 2007, p. 7.

[366] R. O'Dell, "Wal-Mart petitions rejected," *Arizona Daily Star*, July 6, 2007, 1–4.

[367] Ibid., "Wal-Mart won't sue over big-box law," *Arizona Daily Star*, July 14, 2007, 1–2.

[368] D. Garcia, "An open letter to the citizens of Tucson," *Tucson Citizen*, July 16, 2007, 6.

[369] Ibid.

[370] R. O'Dell, "Wal-Mart petitions rejected," *Arizona Daily Star*, July 6, 2007, 1–4.

[371] Ibid.

[372] B. Poole, "Macy's confirms it will leave El Con Mall," *Tucson Citizen*, Oct. 31, 2007, 1.

[373] Ibid.

[374] C. Smythe, "Macy's departing El Con," *Arizona Daily Star*, Oct. 31, 2007, 1–2.

[375] Ibid., "Reports: Wal-Mart eyes El Con space," *Arizona Daily Star*, May 4, 2008, 1–6.

[376] Ibid.

[377] Ibid.

[378] J. Brodesky, "By going smaller, Wal-Mart avoids city's big-box laws," *Arizona Daily Star*, 2009, Oct. 25, 2009), 1–6.

[379] Ibid.

[380] R. O'Dell, "Council will ask Walmart to reduce hours at El Con," *Arizona Daily Star*, Jan. 20, 2011, 4.

[381] D. Quinn, and A. Dalenberg, "Roofed-in part of El Con to be demolished," *Arizona Daily Star*, April 3, 2011, 1.

[382] C. Tanz, C. Davis, and F. Babb, "El Con neighborhoods still battling Walmart, seeking public hearings," *Arizona Daily Star*, June 30, 2012, 13.

[383] C. Brosseau, "New Walmart at El Con mall ruled Ok," *Arizona Daily Star*, July 10, 2012, 11.

[384] A. Smith, "Walmart's Smiley is back after 10 years and a lawsuit," *CNN*, June 3, 2016, https://money.cnn.com/2016/06/02/news/companies/walmart-smiley/index.html.

[385] D. DaRonco, "Deal could bring Walmart liquor license," *Arizona Daily*, Sept. 11, 2014, 9–10.

[386] J. Brodesky, "Walmart, El Con deal just won't go away," *Arizona Daily Star*, Feb. 20, 2011, 1–2.

[387] D. DaRonco and G. Rico, "El Con sale official at $81.7m," *Arizona Daily Star*, May 20, 2014, 1.

[388] B. Ferdinand, "Review-El Con Mall," *Yelp*, Nov. 9, 2007, https://www.yelp.com/biz/el-con-mall-tucson?osq=el+con+mall.

[389] M. N. "Review-El Con Mall," *Yelp*, May 14, 2017, https://www.yelp.com/biz/el-con-mall-tucson?osq=el+con+mall.

[390] "Hutchinson to present links matter to city: course would be available for general use of public in city," *Arizona Daily Star*, Dec. 18, 1924, 4.

[391] D. Leighton, "The story behind Barnum hill—and golf—at Tucson's Reid Park" *Arizona Daily Star*, Feb. 1, 2021, 1–2.

[392] Ibid.

[393] G. Hall, "Randolph Park plans studied," *Arizona Daily Star*, Oct. 15, 1939b, 6.

[394] D. Leighton, "The story behind Barnum Hill—and golf—at Tucson's Reid Park" *Arizona Daily Star*, Feb. 1, 2021, 1–2.

[395] "City's one and only lake named after creator Reid," *Tucson Citizen*, May 3, 1960, 22.

[396] J. Demers, J. "Reid Park zoo lovers will have more to see after big expansion," *Arizona Daily Star*, Nov. 16, 2020, 1–2.

[397] T. Stellar, "Zoo expansion at Reid Park wrests away a cherished spot," *Arizona Daily Star*, Dec. 13, 2020, 1–5.

[398] M. McKasson, H. McElroy Herrera, and J. Muncz, "Reid Park supporters: zoo expansion should halt for now," *Arizona Daily Star*, Jan. 31, 2021, 12.

[399] D. Leighton, "The story behind Barnum Hill—and golf—at Tucson's Reid Park" *Arizona Daily Star*, Feb. 1, 2021, 1–2

[400] Ibid.

[401] G. Hall, "Randolph Park plans studied," *Arizona Daily Star*, Oct. 15, 1939, 6.

[402] J. C. Martin, "Magnificent city oasis," *Arizona Daily Star*, June 16, 1993, 1–4.

[403] J. Hiner, "A fitting tribute," *Arizona Daily Star*, June 22, 1993, 6.

[404] V. L. Hodge, "Only memories now play host at El Con Hotel," *Arizona Daily Star*, June 21, 1968, 1.

[405] Ibid.

[406] Ibid, "Our compliments to the chief," *Arizona Daily Star*, June 23, 1968, 2.

[407] M. H. Mason, "Hotel should have remained," *Arizona Daily Star*, Jan. 12, 2008, 11.

[408] D. Leighton, "The story behind Barnum Hill—and golf—at Tucson's Reid Park" *Arizona Daily Star*, Feb. 1, 2021, 1–2.

[409] K. Hibbs, "Heat cuts short circus animal walk," *Arizona Daily Star*, June 25, 1975, 1.

[410] "Only a big man can fill the place left by Col. Epes Randolph," *El Paso Herald*, Aug. 24, 1921, 8.

[411] "Colonel Epes Randolph," *Tucson Citizen*, Aug. 24, 1921, 6.

[412] Ibid.

[413] R. Wiley "El Conquistador revisited," *Arizona Daily Star*, Aug. 21, 2011, 1–4.

[414] "Memories of past abound in new model," *Ole! The Tucson Daily Citizen Magazine*, November 30, 1968, 8.

[415] L. Sammeth, "El Conquistador Hotel's arch again greets desert visitors," *Tucson Citizen*, Feb. 21, 1986, 1.

[416] Ibid.

[417] Ibid.

[418] M. Hernandez, "Double-decked history tour," *Arizona Daily Star*, March 14, 1984, 1.

[419] Ibid.

420 M. Stewart, "What's with that?" *Arizona Daily Star*, Jan. 25, 2002, 4.

421 "El Con Tower imperiled again," *Arizona Daily Star*, Oct. 16, 1975, 1.

422 C. Limberis, "Council designates El Con Water Tower as historic landmark, seeks repair funds," *Arizona Daily Star*, Aug. 7, 1991, 2.

423 "Remnant (Bible)," *Wikipedia*, accessed Dec. 29, 2024, https://en.wikipedia.org/wiki/Remnant_(Bible).

424 "Place Attachment & Meaning," *Green Cities: Good Health,* accessed Dec. 29, 2024, https://depts.washington.edu/hhwb/Thm_Place.html.

425 "Stephen Child will speak at realty dinner," *Tucson Citizen*, March 16, 1928, 8.

426 Ibid.

427 G. Fimbres, "Ambience of country life in center of the city," *Arizona Daily Star*, Aug. 11, 2013, 8–9.

428 Ibid.

429 Ibid.

430 "Stephen Child (1866–1936) USHC Architects, Landscape Architects and Planners, accessed Dec. 29, 2024, https://web.mit.edu/ebj/www/ww1/Biography-Child.html.

431 M. B. Korff, "Stephen Child: Visionary Landscape Architect," Thesis, University of Arizona, 1991.

432 Ibid.

433 J. M. Hardwick, *Mall Maker: Victor Gruen, Architect of an American Dream* (Philadelphia: University of Pennsylvania Press, 2010), 2.

434 B. Flanagan, "He brought charm to Southdale," *Star Tribune*, Oct. 7, 1956, 27.

435 Ibid.

436 Ibid.

437 Ibid.

438 M. B. Korff, "Stephen Child: Visionary Landscape Architect," Thesis, University of Arizona, 1991.

439 Ibid.

440 Ibid.

441 Ibid.

442 G. Fimbres, "Ambience of country life in center of the city," *Arizona Daily Star*, Aug. 11, 2013, 8–9.

[443] J. M. Hardwick, *Mall Maker: Victor Gruen, Architect of an American Dream* (Philadelphia: University of Pennsylvania Press, 2010), 16.

[444] "Lesser-Known Tales of the Old Croton Aqueduct: The Angel of the Waters," *Friends of the Old Croton Aqueduct,* accessed Dec. 29, 2024, https://aqueduct.org/lesser-known-tales-old-croton-aqueduct-angel-waters.

[445] Curbed Staff, "Unraveling the History of Central Park's Bethesda Fountain," *Curbed New York,* July 16, 2014, https://ny.curbed.com/2014/7/16/10074022/unraveling-the-history-of-central-parks-bethesda-fountain.

[446] Target Corporate, "Then & Now: Target's Store Design Philosophy," *Target.com,* Jul. 31, 2013, https://corporate.target.com/article/2013/07/target-store-design-philosophy-then-and-now.

[447] L. Scharoun, *America at the Mall: The Cultural Role of a Retail Utopia* (Jefferson, NC: McFarland & Co., 2012), 132.

[448] Severson, Ed. "Tucson's Unique, but Not for Those Reasons You Hear." *Arizona Daily Star.* September 21, 1982.

[449] G. Mercedes, "El Encanto: neighborhood leader wins fight to save 'Beverly Hills' of Tucson, Tucson

Citizen, May 9, 1988, 1–4.

www.ingramcontent.com/pod-product-compliance
Lightning Source LLC
Chambersburg PA
CBHW070906130626
46555CB00001B/17